Effects of Gender Inequality in Resource Ownership and Access on Household Welfare and Food Security in Kenya

T0316413

DEVELOPMENT ECONOMICS AND POLICY

Series edited by Franz Heidhues and Joachim von Braun

Vol. 51

PETER LANG

Frankfurt am Main · Berlin · Bern · Bruxelles · New York · Oxford · Wien

Effects of Gender Inequality in Resource Ownership and Access on Household Welfare and Food Security in Kenya

A Case Study of West Pokot District

Pamela Marinda

PETER LANG

Europäischer Verlag der Wissenschaften

Bibliographic Information published by Die Deutsche Bibliothek
Die Deutsche Bibliothek lists this publication in the Deutsche
Nationalbibliografie; detailed bibliographic data is available in
the internet at <http://dnb.ddb.de>.

Zugl.: Hohenheim, Univ., Diss., 2005

Printed with support of
Katholischer Akademischer Austauschdienst.

D 100
ISSN 0948-1338
ISBN 3-631-55079-0
US-ISBN 0-8204-9878-5

© Peter Lang GmbH
Europäischer Verlag der Wissenschaften
Frankfurt am Main 2006
All rights reserved.

All parts of this publication are protected by copyright. Any
utilisation outside the strict limits of the copyright law, without
the permission of the publisher, is forbidden and liable to
prosecution. This applies in particular to reproductions,
translations, microfilming, and storage and processing in
electronic retrieval systems.

Printed in Germany 1 2 3 4 5　7

www.peterlang.de

For my mother, Brenda Ilusa
and grandmother, Teresa Ilabonga,
who taught me to trust in the rewards that are reaped
through hard work, determination and faith in God.

Preface

Over the past decade, gender studies have become increasingly recognised as central to rural research and to the understanding of rural social and economic relations. Work on gender within a rural context has developed both in terms of scope of research and rigour. While so much is known about the existence of gender discrimination, not so many studies have focused on the social and economic costs associated with gender inequality in resource ownership and access, especially in developing countries. The negative effects of gender inequality in resource ownership and access are manifested in terms of food and nutrition insecurity and its effects. These negative effects affect the health and labour productivity of present and future generations. With the perennial incidences of food insecurity, undernutrition and high prevalence of illness in many sub Saharan Africa countries, there is a need to analyse whether the existing gender inequality in these countries has contributed to the phenomena.

In this volume Pamela Marinda assesses the costs associated with gender inequality in productive resource ownership in Kenya. The analysis dwells on the effects of gender inequality in access and ownership of land, human and financial capital on household welfare and food security. The existence of unequal access to education, land, credit, extension services and uneven division of labour in favour of men, is confirmed by the analysis. In the analysis of food consumption, the study finds unequal distribution of food within the household, with women and children being at a higher risk of micronutrient deficiencies. There is high prevalence of malnutrition among children in the study site, coupled with a high incidence of illness.

The quantitative analysis focuses on a wide range of farm household dynamics ranging from returns to farm and non farm activities, determinants of food security as well as nutrition and health status of children. There are low returns for women in both the farm and non farm activities due to their low level of education. The analysis finds a positive effect of education, access to credit and extension services on agriculture productivity. Education of women is found to have a positive effect on nutrition and health status of children as well as on the number of births per woman. Access to land is found to be important for agriculture productivity and hence household food security. In addition, the study finds a strong correlation between the economic situation and food security situation within households.

The research concludes that, access to land, human capital and finances have an impact on the overall household wellbeing and food and nutrition security. Female headed households were much more constrained in their access to land, education and income, which showed a significant negative impact on their livelihood and food security. To address the overall poverty and especially food and nutrition insecurity problem in the study region, the study recommends that government policies focus on increasing access to education by women, raising household incomes, eradicating women discrimination in land ownership and property inheritance, enhancing nutrition and agricultural extension services and investing in health care facilities, particularly for women.

Prof. Dr. Franz Heidhues   *Prof. Dr. Joachim von Braun*
University of Hohenheim   *International Food Policy*
Stuttgart   *Research Institute (IFPRI),*
                                                          Washington D.C

Acknowledgement

I would like to express my sincere gratitude to a number of people and institutions for their valuable support, encouragement and contribution to this study. First and foremost, I would like to thank my supervisor Prof. Dr. Franz Heidhues who continuously supported this work from its initial stages until its completion. I am grateful to Prof. Dr. Gertrud Buchenrieder for her support and valuable advice during the course of this work. Thanks to Prof. Dr. Jürgen Zeddies and Prof. Dr. Werner Grosskopf for serving on my examination committee.

This research work could not have been possible without financial support from the Catholic Academic Exchange Service (KAAD), who financed my stay in Germany as well as research work in Kenya. I would like to express my thanks to Dr. Thomas Scheidtweiler and Simone Saure from the KAAD - Africa Department, for their encouragement and excellent work. Special thanks go to the Eiselen Foundation – Ulm and the University of Hohenheim - Unibund for financing my research work in Kenya.

I am indebted to men, women and children in West Pokot district who spared time to respond to my questions despite their busy schedules. Thank you for your valuable input without which this research work could not have been possible. Many thanks go to Mr. Ocham, Sr. Peter, Fr. Murumba from Chepareria for their support during my field work. I wish to thank the staff members and students at the department of Rural Development Economics and Policy (Institute 490A) at the University of Hohenheim for their support. Special thanks go to Mrs Contag, Mrs Schempp and Mrs Schumacher for their assistance in all the administrative processes and for providing moral support during my time at the institute. Special thanks go to my colleagues Rainer Schwarzmeier, Sabine Daude, Judith Möllers, Dinh Ngoc Lan, Clemens Breisinger, Beyene Tadesse, Jia Xiangping, Serge, Djoum and Rovier Djeudja for their support. Many thanks go to Anna Canning who edited this work.

My sincere appreciation goes to my friends from the Ecumenical University Community (Ökumenische hochschulgemeinde – Öhg), especially Odilo Metzler, Karin Bassler, Birgit Fuchs, and all my friends in Stuttgart who gave me moral support. Special thanks also go to Anne Richardson, Br. Paul Schure, Staicy Mbinya, Wiltrud Metzler, Anita Lauer, Melecki and Jane Khayesi, Ulrike Piening, Steve Okumu, Rennatus Mdodo, Pia and Thomas Leopold, and Sidney Lulanga for their continued support during my stay in Germany and Kenya.

I express my sincere thanks to my siblings, Violet, Martin, Bernard, Joy-Joan, and Chris, and to my two nephews John-Marvin and Emanuel-Melvin - *Asanteni sana, Mungu awabariki.* Thanks to my mother Brenda Ilusa and Sr. auntie Andisi, for their encouragement and support. To grandpa, Emanuel, and grandma, Teresa, I say, thanks for encouraging me to work hard and trust in God. Finally, my gratitude goes to the almighty God who gave me the wisdom and strength that saw me through my studies. And for the many great things He has in store for me, I say thank you.

Pamela A. Marinda
December, 2005

Table of Contents

List of Tables

List of Figures

Abbreviations

ASAL	Arid and semi-arid lands
ANN	African news network
Cap	Caption
CEDAW	Convention on the Elimination of All Forms of Discrimination against Women
CBS	Central Bureau of Statistics
EMOP	Emergency operation
FAO	Food and Agriculture Organization
GEM	Gender Empowerment index
GoK	Government of Kenya
GNP	Gross National Product
GDI	Gender Development Index
GDP	Gross Domestic Product
GTZ	German Technical Cooperation
HIV	Human immune deficiency syndrome
HDI	Human Development Index
KARI	Kenya Agricultural Research Institute
KFSSG	Kenya food security information steering group
MDG	Millennium Development Goals
NCHS	National Centre for Health Statistics
NPEP	National Poverty Eradication Plan
PRSP	Poverty Reduction Strategy Paper
SD	Standard deviation
SCN	Standing Committee on Nutrition
MTEF	Medium Term Expenditure Framework
NEPAD	New Partnership of African Development
IEA	Institute of Economic Affairs
ITPA	Indian Transfer of Property Act
HH	Household
HoH	Head of household
UNICEF	United Nations Children's Fund
UNDP	United Nations Development Programme
WHO	World Health Organization
WFP	World Food Programme

1 INTRODUCTION

1.1 Background to the Study

Food security is of paramount importance to Kenyan development policy. This is reflected in relevant government food policy documents such as food policy papers (Republic of Kenya, 1981, 1994), five-year development plans and the Poverty Reduction Strategy Paper (PRSP) for the period 2001 - 2004. Sessional paper number 10 of 1965 identifies hunger as one of the enemies of development. The objective of Kenyan food policy is to maintain food self-sufficiency to feed its populace. This objective was the rationale behind the government's pursuit of agricultural policies such as input subsidies, controlled marketing of food commodities and promotion of research and extension particularly for food crops (Nyangito, 2003; Government of Kenya - GoK, 2001; GoK, 2000).

However, food production in the country has continued to decline since the late 1980s. The national food production index, which was over 100 between 1987 and 1992, dropped to 94 in 1993 (Odhiambo and Nyangito 2004; Central Bureau of Statistics - CBS, 2000a). When the production figures are adjusted for population size, it is evident that production has not kept pace with the rapidly growing population (GoK, 2000, CBS, 2000a). The government of Kenya has put various measures in place to achieve food security. They include promotion of food security by maintaining national reserve of maize in physical stock and providing support to the drought contingency funding as well as ensuring that an early warning system is functional in all drought prone districts (GoK, 2000). Other measures include the creation of Kenya's special program for food security (KSPFS) in 2002, and the launching of an Economic Recovery Strategy for Wealth Creation and Employment in June, 2003 (GoK, 2003). Despite these measures, the food security situation in the country has continued to deteriorate.

A number of studies (CBS, 2000b; Manda, et al., 2000; Nyariki, et al., 2002) have dwelt on unearthing the root causes of rural poverty and food insecurity afflicting many rural households in Kenya. The prevailing poverty and food insecurity in Kenya has been blamed on a number of factors such as low agricultural productivity, inadequate access to productive assets (land and capital), inadequate infrastructure, limited well functioning markets, high population pressure on land, inappropriate technologies by farmers, effects of global trade and slow reform process. Despite the empirical evidence on causes of food insecurity and poverty, few studies focus on gender issues in resource allocation and ownership despite the important role played by women in agriculture and maintaining households. Women often play these roles with limited resources, which constrain them to reach their fullest potential (Bouis, 1998; Quisumbing, 2003).

Over the past decade, increasing recognition has been given to the important role equality between women and men for effective and sustainable development. This is recognized in the Millennium Declaration of the United Nations which promises to promote gender equality and empowerment of women as effective ways to combat poverty, hunger and disease, and to stimulate development that is sustainable (UN, 2000). Both women and men are actors, stakeholders and agents of change in their households and communities and contribute to national development. Bringing the perceptions, knowledge, experience, needs and priorities of both women and men to the centre of attention enriches development efforts.

There are many examples of why and how gender equality is critical for sustainable people-centred development, with links to economic development and economic efficiency. Various studies have demonstrated high social returns related to gender equity and increasing resources under women's control. Evidence of higher social returns to investing in women makes gender equity an issue of great interest to policy-makers. For instance, Schutz 2002 argues that regions that have promoted equal education opportunities for men and women have also experienced most economic growth. Such regions include East Asia, South-East Asia and Latin America. Smith et al. (2003) found that women's status had a significant effect on child nutrition status. Other social returns of gender equity are reduction of child mortality and child malnutrition, as well as lowered fertility with increased education.

Studies on agricultural productivity in Africa show that reducing gender inequality could significantly increase agricultural yields. These studies show that giving women farmers the same level of agricultural inputs and education as men farmers could increase farmers' yields by more than 20%, increase their on-farm income and improve household food security (Webb and Weinberger, 2001; FAO, 2002). In some parts of Kenya, where women have had access to agricultural resources and services in their own right, as in parts of the Kenyan highlands, women farmers alone or with only sporadic assistance from immigrant husbands have proved themselves more than capable of increasing farm productivity, efficiency, and profits (Nyariki et al., 2002; Jiggins et al., 1997).

Gender inequality also reduces the productivity of the next generation. This is revealed in the World Bank reports' evidence that increases in women's well-being yield productivity gains in the future (World Bank, 2000). The probability of children being enrolled in school increases with their mother's educational level, and in some circumstances extra income going to mothers has more positive impact on household nutrition, health and education of children than extra income going to fathers (Brown et al, 2001; Webb and Weinberger, 2001; World Bank, 2002). Research on gender inequality in the labour market shows that eliminating gender discrimination in relation to occupation and pay could both increase the income of women, and contribute to national income (Quisumbing, 2003; Fritschel and Mohan, 2001).

Failure to recognize and measure in quantitative terms the unremunerated work of women, which is most often not valued in national accounts, has meant that women's full contribution to social and economic development remains underestimated and undervalued, and a country's real worth unknown. For any country to achieve balanced development there is a need to invest both in women and men and develop and utilize their economic capacity, to ensure effective and sustainable achievement of development goals. This is because macroeconomic policies and institutions that do not take gender perspectives into account impact negatively on women relative to men (UN, 1999; FAO, 2002). Moreover, the perpetuation and exacerbation of gender inequality through these policies and institutions can have a direct negative impact on the achievement of the macroeconomic goals set (UN, 1999).

1.2 The Issues

The Government of Kenya, together with a number of non-governmental organizations (NGOs) in the country has made efforts to promote women's active involvement in all areas of societal development, in addition to ensuring that development is based on the contributions and concerns of both men and women. However, there are still clear gender inequalities in areas where both men and women's roles are visible, for example in health, agriculture and other remunerated work. The constitution of Kenya, which has been in place since independence in 1963, upholds human rights and provides protection of all peoples' human rights, without distinction on the basis of race, colour, sex, language or other status. However, tradition, prejudice, social, economic and political interests have combined to exclude women from prevailing definitions of 'general' human rights and to relegate women to secondary status within human rights considerations. For example, with regard to property rights, the constitution of Kenya allows women to acquire, own and dispose of property. The customary law, on the other hand, forbids women from owning matrimonial property and from inheriting property in the event of the spouse's death or if spouses separate. With land being the most accepted form of security to acquire credit, this then means that Kenyan women's access to credit is restricted.

Second, boys and girls do not have equal education opportunities, especially in marginal areas of the country. This is despite Kenya being praised for spearheading gender equality in education in Sub-Saharan Africa with the enrolment gap between girls and boys narrowing, and the gender parity index[1] (GPI) standing at 0.99 and 0.91 for primary and secondary-level education respectively (UNESCO, 2005). The index does not, however, capture discrepancies in enrolment in different parts of the country. In addition, due to lack of adequate education, women are often left out when it comes to agricultural extension services (Jiggins et al., 1997).

The existing gender inequalities in access to resources have negative impacts both at national and household level. At national level, the impacts include imbalances in economic power-sharing; unequal distribution of unremunerated work between women and men; lack of adequate support for women's entrepreneurship; unequal access to and control over capital and resources such as land and credit; and inequalities in access to labour markets, thus contributing to overall poverty and hindering economic development. At household level, the costs are in terms of high mortality of children, high birth rate and undernutrition, reduced participation in and control over household decision-making, unequal access to production resources, leading to low agricultural productivity and hence worsening household food security.

1.3 Statement of the Research Problem

Food security covers food production, access, distribution and food utilization by individual household members (Heidhues, 2000). At national level, food security entails an adequate supply of food supplies through local production, storage, food imports and food aid. At household level, food security is defined as a state of affairs where all people within the household at all times have access to an adequate diet for an active and healthy life (Braun, 2004; Heidhues, 2000; FAO, 2000).

---

[1] The Gender Parity Index (GPI) is a value used to assess gender differences in various indicators. It is the value of an indicator for girls divided by that for boys. A value of less than one indicates differences in favour of boys, whereas a value near one indicates that parity has been more or less achieved.

Food insecurity is one of the greatest challenges facing Kenya. There has been an increase in Kenya's average poverty level and hence an increase in food insecurity. The number of the absolute poor increased from 10 million in 1994 to 13.4 million in 1997. By the year 2000, the overall poverty situation in Kenya was 56% of the total population estimated at 31 million people (Manda et al., 2000; Geda et al., 2001; CBS, 2000b). The high prevalence of malnutrition (25 to 30%) and a 33% increase in food aid in the late 1990s are additional indicators of food insecurity in the country (GoK, 2001). In June 2004, food shortage was declared a national disaster, with over 3.3 million Kenyans in need of emergency food assistance (GoK and GTZ, 2004). The communities in arid and semi arid lands are particularly vulnerable to food insecurity because of recurring natural disasters of drought, livestock diseases, animal and crop pests, and limited access to appropriate technologies, information, credit and financial services (CBS, 2000a; Kinyua, 2004).

West Pokot district in Rift Valley province is one of the food-insecure zones in rural Kenya. The district lies in the arid and semi arid lands of Kenya. It is among the poorest districts in Rift Valley province with an absolute poverty level of 68.5% and a food poverty level of 69.7% (Institute of Economic Affairs, IEA, 2002). It also has the second lowest monthly average household income (KES 3304) in Rift Valley (IEA, 2002). This region is prone to transitory and chronic food insecurity. The inadequacy in food affects mainly women and children, leading to hunger and malnutrition. According to the Institute of Economic Affairs (2002), West Pokot is one of the of the regions in the country that has high infant malnutrition and almost half the children below five years old are malnourished and 108 out of 1000 children die before they reach the age of one (UNICEF, 2003). These Children are likely to carry the heavy burden of malnutrition throughout their life.

Nutrition is a key component of human development. Malnutrition disempowers individuals by causing or aggravating illness, lowering educational attainment, and diminishing livelihood skills and options. This makes it harder for individuals to grasp new opportunities in a globalizing world, and reduces their resilience to cope with the challenges and shocks it generates. Malnutrition reduces mental capacity; and malnourished children are less likely to enroll in school, or enroll later than other children (SCN, 2000; FAO, 2004). Hunger and malnutrition therefore reduces school performance. If created in childhood, these human capital deficits tend to persist and affect labour capacity throughout an individual's life cycle, diminishing it by sizeable amounts. Productivity in non-market activities such as caring for infants, children and other dependants can also be reduced. The effects of enhanced asset ownership and use tend to interact positively. As a result, the effects of human capital on the productivity of other assets (such as financial, social, natural and physical capital) will be forgone (SCN, 2004). The evidence showing the importance of food and nutrition security for improved educational attainment is ample and convincing. There has been a rise in the percentage of female headed households in Kenya. A World Bank report states that about 30% of all rural households were female headed by 1995 (World Bank, 1996). By 2005, the percentage of female headed households was estimated at 37% (CBS, 2005). The government of Kenya attributes the large number of female headed households to widowhood, divorce or separation, which generally are thought to contribute to lower levels of economic wellbeing and thus making these households more vulnerable to food insecurity (CBS, 2005). With the increasing number of female headed households, laws on property rights have to be reviewed to ensure that women have access to property and other resources for increased agricultural production and food security. As Kenyans await a new constitution in the hope that the government will define and keep under review a national land policy ensuring equitable access to land and associated resources and elimination of gender discrimination in laws, regulations, customs and practices related to land and (Section 78 of the draft Constitution of Kenya, 2005) and other resources (Republic of Kenya, 2005), it is worth estimating the costs incurred due to unequal access to resources by men and women in Kenya.

This study assesses gender-based inequalities regarding access to and control of land, financial and human capital, and how they affect household welfare, and food and nutrition security in West Pokot. The study focuses on resource allocation, access and control at household level, since a household as a unit may serve as a framework of specialization of effort and redistribution of goods. However, it may be a mechanism for limiting access to productive resources and for disproportionately allocating the burdens of work and its returns to its members. In addition, equitable resource allocation at household level is a condition for economic development.

1.4 Research Objectives

The overall research objective for this study is: To assess gender-based differences regarding access and ownership to and control of land, financial and human capital, and how these factors affect the household socio-economic welfare and food security. Specific objectives for the study are to:

1. Assess inter and intra-household allocation of land, human capital and financial capital based on gender.
2. Determine the food security situation in the study region and make comparisons based on the gender of the household head and access to key production resources – land, financial capital and human capital.
3. Analyze technical efficiency in crop production in male and female managed farms.
4. Assess the costs of unequal resource allocation in terms of:
   a. Nutrition status of household members
   b. Agricultural productivity
   c. Returns to non agricultural activities
   d. Fertility rate and child morbidity

1.5 Hypotheses

This study is based on the following hypotheses:

- There are significant differences in agricultural productivity between male and female-headed households as a result of limited access of female-headed households to land, education and financial capital.
- Women's limited access to education and financial capital leads to poor nutritional status of children within households
- There are significant differences in household incomes (both agricultural and non agricultural) by level of education of respondents
- Given the same level of production technology, there should be no significant differences in the levels of maize productivity between male and female farmers. Hence, any significant differences would be attributed to differences in access to production resources.

1.6 Significance of the Study

This study provides gender disaggregated information regarding household resource allocation in a rural Kenyan setting. It gives an insight into the negative effects of gender inequality in resource ownership and access which manifest themselves in terms of food and nutrition insecurity and its effects. The findings of this study are useful for policy-makers, who can use them in designing social and agricultural policies relevant for increasing agricultural productivity and promotion of gender equality in accessing production resources.

The study provides insights into the determinants of nutrition status, and agricultural productivity as well as factors contributing to high morbidity and fertility rates in the study region. Such information is relevant to various stakeholders such as the Ministries of Agriculture, Health and Education, governmental and non-governmental organizations working in the study region and other food-insecure regions in rural Kenya who can use it to analyse the efficiency of their various policies and present programmes. This can be by using the information to evaluate their present programs for modifications and/or changes, and in the planning and implementation of new, relevant and appropriate agriculture and food security-related programs. In terms of research, the study adds to the pool of knowledge on gender issues in resource distribution, agricultural production, and food and nutrition security.

1.7 Conceptual Definition of Terms

Terms that are important for the comprehension of this work are briefly defined below:

Food Security - reliable access to food in sufficient quantity and quality for a healthy and productive life, for all individuals.

Nutrition Security - Food security coupled with a sanitary environment, adequate health services and knowledgeable care to foster good nutritional status through the life cycle and across generations.

Gender - refers to the roles and responsibilities of men and women that are created in our families, our societies and our cultures. The concept of gender also includes the expectations held about the characteristics, aptitudes and likely behaviours of both women and men (femininity and masculinity).

Gender Equality - means that women and men have equal conditions for realizing their full human rights and for contributing to, and benefiting from, economic, social, cultural and political development. Gender equality is therefore the equal valuing by society of the similarities and the differences of men and women, and the roles they play. It is based on women and men being full partners in their home, their community and their society.

Gender Equity is the process of being fair to men and women. To ensure fairness, measures must often be put in place to compensate for the historical and social disadvantages that prevent women and men from operating on a level playing field. Equity is a means. Equality and equitable outcomes are the results.

1.8 Organization of the Thesis

The work is divided into seven Chapters. Chapter 1 gives an introduction to the research work. Chapter 2 discusses the link between gender equality and food and nutrition security. It also addresses the link between gender equality and economic growth. An overview of food and nutrition issues in Kenya is provided in Chapter 3, followed by the theoretical framework, research methodology and data base in Chapter 4. Chapter 5 deals with descriptive analyses of household demographic and socio-economic characteristics, gender differences in access to land, human capital and financial capital. The measurement of the household food security level and nutritional status of household members is presented in this chapter. Econometric analysis of the determinants of household income, as well as determinants of household food and nutrition security are dealt with in Chapter 6. Also in this chapter, the analysis shows the relationship between access to education, child morbidity and fertility rate. In addition, results of the technical efficiency analysis of male and female managed farms are provided in this chapter. In Chapter 7, a summary of the findings, conclusions and policy-oriented recommendations are presented.

2 GENDER EQUALITY, ECONOMIC GROWTH AND FOOD SECURITY

The UN Millennium Development Goals are the world's commitment to making a drastic cut in extreme poverty, hunger and disease by 2015. The first Millennium Development Goal addresses poverty and chronic hunger. Besides being a goal in itself, nutrition is critical for achieving the other Millennium Development Goals. Undernutrition contributes to dysfunctional societies with individuals too weak, too vulnerable to disease, and too lacking in physical energy to carry out the extraordinary tasks of escaping the poverty trap. Malnutrition and hunger lead directly to ill health and poverty. Lack of nutrition means children cannot concentrate adequately in schools, compromising their efforts to achieve universal education (SCN, 2004).

The third Millennium Development Goal focuses on promotion of gender equality and empowerment of women, with particular emphasis on gender equality in education. The chosen target for this goal was to eliminate gender disparities in primary and secondary education by 2005, and in all levels of education by 2015 (UN, 1999). The rationale for this goal is the high intrinsic value of education and thus the importance of gender equity in this critical aspect of well-being (Sen, 1999). In addition, gender equity is seen as a development goal in its own right, as has been recognized in the Convention on the Elimination of All Forms of Discrimination Against Women (CEDAW), signed and ratified by the majority of developing countries (UN, 1999).

This research work is concerned with the impact of gender inequality in access to education, land and financial capital on food and nutrition security. It therefore focuses on the first and third Millennium Development Goals. Reduced gender bias in education furthers the achievement of two other development goals, namely reducing fertility and child mortality.

This chapter is organized as follows; the first section reviews literature that pertains to the possible effect of gender inequality on economic growth, fertility and child mortality. The sections that follow discuss possible reasons why gender inequality in education and access to resources may have negative effects on food and nutrition security within the household. Finally, a Kenyan perspective on the eradication of hunger and poverty and ensuring gender equity is discussed, followed by a brief discussion on measuring gender inequality.

2.1   The Role of Gender in Food and Nutrition Security

The international Food Policy Research Institute's (IFPRI) '2020 Vision' is a world where every person has access to sufficient food to sustain a healthy and productive life, where malnutrition is absent, and where food originates from efficient, effective and low cost food systems that are compatible with sustainable use of resources (Braun, 2004). With regard to food security, women play an important role in maintaining the three pillars of food security – food production, food access and food utilization. Strengthening these pillars through policies that enhance women's abilities and resources contributes to meeting world food needs by the year 2020 (Brown et al., 2001; Andersen et al., 2001). Women farmers contribute to food production through subsistence farming.

Improvements in child nutrition are closely linked to increased social access of women to resources they can use to improve care for children and increase the diversity and quantity of food served to children. Nutrition-related activities have a gender dimension in terms of the norms, roles and responsibilities of men and women. Although the gender roles and responsibilities vary by setting and over time, domestic time demands on women are greater than those on men (Benson, 2004). In rural Africa, women are usually responsible for a considerable portion of household food production, food processing and preparation of food within households. In addition, collection of water and firewood, as well as child care and caring for the sick is the sole responsibility of women. The broad range of activities limits women's abilities to improve their own nutritional status and that of their children.

An analysis of food and nutrition security with a focus on gender is particularly appropriate in assessing how the nutrition security of children and all household members in general can be improved. In maintaining the second pillar of food security, women play an important role in making sure that household members, and especially children, receive the adequate care and an adequate share of the food that is potentially available. To do this, women allocate their time and income to ensure households' food security. Real income is one of the key determinants of household consumption. Some studies demonstrate that it is not just the level of household income, but who earns it that influences household food security. Evidence suggests that men spend a higher proportion of their income on goods for personal consumption, while women are more likely to purchase goods for their children and for general household consumption (Quisumbing, 2003; Briere et al., 2003).

Evidence from Asia, Africa and Latin America confirms the positive impact of female control of income on household food expenditure, caloric intake, and anthropometric indictors (Smith et al., 2003). At similar levels of income, households where women control a larger share of the income are more likely to meet the calorie requirements of the households. Given the positive nutritional outcomes associated with women's incomes, the growing percentage of female-headed households is a cause for concern, since many studies suggest that women are over-represented among the poor. Therefore, improving the level of equity between men and women is good for nutrition security (Oniang'o and Mukudi, 2002). In the absence of such equity, women have poorer nutritional status, have less access to health care and education and face higher food insecurity due to reduced production on their own farms or lower income-earning potential in the labour market.

The third pillar of food security – food utilization – means ensuring that the food consumed contributes to physical and cognitive development. This entails providing care that includes caring for the physical, mental and social needs of growing children and other household members (Heidhues, 2000; Smith et al. 2001; Benson, 2004). Care affects food security in two broad ways: first through feeding practices such as breast-feeding and the preparation of nutritious foods for household members; and second, through health and hygienic practices such as bathing of children and the washing of hands before food preparation. These caring practices are time-intensive, considering the other tasks women have to perform relating to household production and farm production. In some instances, women have turned to processed food and 'street foods' to save time. Development of technology that relieves women's time burdens in agricultural production and household maintenance without sacrificing their ability to earn an independent income is therefore crucial (Brown and Haddad, 1995; Coates et al., 2003).

An analysis of food and nutrition security with a focus on gender is the main focus of this study. Such an analysis sheds some light on any existing gender inequalities as far as resource ownership is concerned and how they affect household welfare as well as its food and nutrition security.

2.2 A Kenyan Perspective on the Elimination of Hunger and Gender Inequality

The Kenyan government endorsed the Millennium Declaration at the Millennium Summit in September 2000. The goals, targets and indicators highlighted at the Summit have given ongoing national frameworks, initiatives and processes a new sense of direction and a time-frame – 2015. While looking at the progress in achieving the Millennium Development Goals, it is important to highlight the strategies the Kenyan government has adopted to improve human development by 2015, and where nutrition can be incorporated as an input, and not just an output. In addressing the problem of unequal access to resources and its impact on food and nutrition security, this study dwells on two Millennium Development Goals (MDGs): Goal 1, eradication of poverty and hunger; and Goals 2 and 3, achieving universal primary education and promotion of gender equality and the empowerment of women (UN, 2000; GoK, 2004a).

The Government has various poverty reduction policies and programmes that have been designed with the participation of the poor and other stakeholders. At the micro level, these include the National Poverty Eradication Plan (NPEP), the Poverty Reduction Strategy Paper (PRSP), and the Medium-Term Expenditure Framework (MTEF). With these approaches the Government hopes to reverse the current poverty situation (Keino, 2004).

2.2.1 Elimination of Poverty and Hunger

The National Poverty Eradication Plan (NPEP) lists its main objectives as: the reduction of poverty in both rural and urban areas by 50% by 2015; reduction of gender and geographic disparities, and a healthier, better educated and more productive population (Republic of Kenya, 20001). The report on *Perspectives of the poor on Anti-poverty Policies* further reiterates that women and children in general suffer more from intra-household elements of poverty than men.

Through the NPEP and the PRSP, the government has put in place an Economic Recovery Strategy for Wealth and Empowerment Creation (2003 – 2007) to revive the ailing economy and create jobs. Some of the objectives the government aims at achieving include: reducing the poverty level by at least 5% from its current level of 56.8%; achieving a high GDP growth rate estimated at 1.1 % in 2002 to 7% in 2006; containing the annual inflation rate at below 5% and increasing domestic savings to enable higher levels of investment for sustainable development (Keino, 2004; GoK, 2004a).

In combating hunger, the government has designated the national food policy and food security policy as its top priority, since no meaningful development in economic, social or cultural spheres is possible without it. According to the Millennium Development Goals Report for Kenya, 2002, and a report by the Demographic Health Survey (KDHS) CBS, 2003), malnutrition and child mortality still remain high in Kenya. The increase in child mortality and the increase in protein-energy malnutrition in children under five are clear indicators of a drop in the quality of life. Despite this trend, it is projected that there will be a decrease in the prevalence of malnutrition due to efforts in place to improve food security. Investment in agriculture, livestock and fishing has been identified as the way forward towards economic recovery and provision of food, both in productive and marginal lands. The government also aims at eliminating vitamin A deficiency in children under the age of five by 2005 through the production and consumption of nutritious locally produced foods (CBS, 2000a, CBS, 2000b; GoK and UN, 2002).

Good governance and democracy are key to economic growth. The MDGs Report for Kenya indicates that the current government has demonstrated renewed commitment to reducing the high levels of poverty and hunger through the existing initiatives mentioned above and the Economic Recovery Strategy for Wealth and Employment Creation for 2003-2007, as well as its commitment to the principles of the New Partnership for Africa's Development (NEPAD), which is linked to national planning, poverty reduction and economic recovery GoK and UN, 2002).

2.2.2 Achieving Universal Primary Education

To achieve the goal of universal education, the government has in place a policy of free primary education. This is aimed at reversing the trends of low enrolment and high dropout rates. The government's policy of free primary education will contribute substantially towards attaining the second MDG of universal primary education by year 2015. The current and recent unsatisfactory performance of the primary school system is often linked to Kenya's previous cost-sharing policy and differential geographic access to educational facilities, staffing problems and mismanagement of education resources. The major challenges facing the universal primary education initiative include: financing the infrastructure and human resource expansion; regional disparities in access, whereby low enrolment in some areas is closely related to the nomadic lifestyle of its local population; high wastage rates, repetition and dropout rates, and low transition exacerbated by poverty and the HIV/AIDS pandemic; reducing child labour, which has been identified as one of the factors explaining declining enrolment rates in primary school in Kenya (GoK and UN, 2002).

In an effort to close the educational achievement gaps between regions and economic classes, the government has invested in four key programmes. These include the children's bill, which provides the framework for enforcing universal primary education in the country and became an Act of Parliament in 2002; the school feeding programme that targets arid and semi-arid lands; the textbook fund; and the bursary fund to enable the poor to further their education (GoK and UN, 2002).

2.2.3 Promotion of Gender Equality and Empowerment of Women

The third MDG promotes gender equality and empowerment of women. The goal targets the elimination of gender disparity in primary and secondary education preferably by 2005, and at all levels of education no later than 2015. Kenya's MDGs progress report indicates that although the female-to-male ratio in primary and secondary school is almost equal, there is a major gap in enrolment in tertiary institutions. There are a host of factors at the household level that account for low progression of women to tertiary education. Factors such as premarital pregnancies and early marriage may be among the determinants of this trend.

To promote gender equality, there is a national gender development policy that has been approved by the government, but has not yet been implemented. Other than attaining education, women need to take up leadership positions to influence decisions affecting household accessibility to basic needs such as water, food and shelter. This is also supported by the New Partnership for Africa's Development (NEPAD), which emphasizes women's participation in macroeconomic debates as well as women taking up political positions (GoK, 2004a; Keino, 2004). Kenya continues to perform dismally in terms of participation of women in politics. There has been an increase in the number of women members of parliament from five in 1990 to 18 in 2002/2003 (8% of total parliamentary membership). In terms of leadership positions, only seven women serve as government ministers compared to 44 positions held by men (GoK, 2004a).

The involvement of women in non-agricultural wage employment is low. This is linked to poor performance by females at the end of their secondary schooling. The annual economic survey data on wage employment reveal that about 24.3% of women were employed in the civil service by 2002, with the majority concentrated in the lower-level job groups, while a few occupied decision-making positions in the civil service (GoK, 2003). According to the MDG progress report, the government is committed to mainstreaming gender issues in its legislation, policies and programmes. It is also signatory to international conventions and treaties on women's rights and empowerment. Moreover, as a signatory to the Convention on the Elimination of all Forms of Discrimination Against Women, the government is obliged to provide equal opportunities to men and women. The Children's Act passed by parliament in 2002 provides a framework for equal opportunities for girls and boys. The government has also approved the National Gender and Development Policy (GoK and UN, 2002). While gender concerns are most easily recognizable at the household level, they are also important within the policy-making arena. Women's participation in democratic decision-making bodies is encouraged. If decision-making is left to men alone, the political priorities that emerge may pay little attention to women's problems or to improving food and nutrition security.

Despite the progress made by Kenya in combating hunger, illiteracy and gender inequality, much more has to be done before Kenya will be able to break out of its poverty trap. Despite high enrolment in primary schools, underprivileged regions of the country still have a big gender disparity in literacy levels. The most affected are the arid and semi-arid parts of the country. The government therefore needs to focus attention on these regions to achieve uniform improvements in literacy levels across the country. There is also a need for the government to concentrate on other services that are crucial for improving livelihoods, such as water and sanitation, as well as direct nutrition interventions.

2.3   Linkages between Gender Equality and Economic Growth

Section 2.3 discusses the link between gender equality, economic growth, fertility and child mortality.

2.3.1 Gender Bias in Education and Economic Growth

Many developing countries exhibit considerable gender inequality in education, employment and health outcomes. In sub-Saharan Africa, there are large discrepancies in education between men and women. Due to low levels of education, employment opportunities differ greatly by gender, with women being employed in low-paying jobs (Klasen, 2004; Abagi et al. 2000). Gender inequality may have adverse effects on a number of valuable developmental goals. For example, gender inequality in education and access to resources may prevent reduction of child mortality, of fertility, and hinder expansion of education for the next generation. Gender bias in education may generate problems for development policy-makers, as it compromises progress in other important development goals. Secondly, gender inequality reduces economic growth, while economic growth furthers well-being as measured through indicators such as longevity, literacy, and reduced poverty. Thus, policies that further economic growth should be of great interest to policy-makers in sub-Saharan Africa (UNICEF, 2004; Klasen, 2004 and Abagi et al., 2000).

Lower gender inequality in education means greater female education at each level of male education, therefore, reduced gender inequality should promote higher-quality education and thus promote economic growth. Higher human capital associated with reduced gender bias in education can increase economic growth directly by increasing the productivity of workers (Klasen, 1999). Empirical evidence shows the relationship between gender inequality in education and economic growth. In various studies, gender inequality in education has a negative impact on economic growth. In many models, emphasis is placed on the importance of human capital accumulation for economic growth (Appleton et al., 1999; Klasen, 2004).

Reduced gender bias in education can have an indirect effect by increasing the rate of return to physical investment, which in return raises investment rates, and increased investment has positive effect on economic growth. Similarly, reduced gender bias in education has indirect externality effects via demographic effects (Klasen, 2004). Four mechanisms are believed to be at the centre of this demographic impact on economic growth. First, reduced fertility lowers the dependency burden, thereby increasing the supply of savings in an economy. Second a large number of people entering the workforce as a result of high population growth will boost investment demand. If this higher demand is met by increased domestic savings or capital inflows, these two factors will allow investments to expand, which will boost growth (Klasen, 1999; Bloom and William, 1998). Third, a lowering of fertility rates will increase the share of the working age population in the total population. If all the growth in the labour force is absorbed in increased employment, then the per capita economic growth will increase even if wages and productivity remain the same. This is because many workers have to share their wages with fewer dependants, thereby boosting average per capita incomes (Klasen, 1999). This is a temporary effect since, after a few decades, the growth in the working age population will fall while the number of the elderly will rise, thereby leading to an increasing dependency burden. This effect is believed to have contributed to the high growth rates in East and South-East Asia (Bloom and William, 1998).

The study by Hill and King (1995) examines the impact of gender differences on education in an empirical growth context. In their study, they try to account for growth in GDP by relating the levels of GDP to gender inequality in education. They find that a low female-male enrolment ratio is associated with a lower level of GDP per capita, over and above the impact of levels of female education on GDP per capita. In another study on education and economic growth, Dollar and Gatti (1999) find that female secondary education achievement (measured as the share of the adult population that have achieved some secondary education) is positively associated with growth, while male secondary achievement is negatively associated with growth. In the full sample, both effects are insignificant, but it turns out that in countries with low female education, furthering female education does not promote economic growth, while in countries with higher education levels, promoting female education has a sizeable and significant positive impact on economic growth (Klasen, 1999).

In a study by Lagerloef (1999) as cited by Klasen (2004), the impact of gender inequality in education on fertility and economic growth is examined. Lagerloef (1999) argues that initial gender inequality in education can lead to a self-perpetuating equilibrium of continuous gender inequality in education, with the consequence of high fertility leading to high population growth rates. Here, the impact of high fertility operates mainly via human capital investment for the next generation; hence, high population leads to low economic growth through low investment in human capital. Thus gender inequality would generate a poverty trap. Poverty is a major threat to food security, both of the family and of particular individuals within the family. And a combination of poverty and gender inequality is an even greater threat. Lower levels of education coupled with inadequate access to other resources can severely limit the earning potential for women.

2.3.2 Gender Bias in Education, Fertility and Child Mortality

Apart from studies linking gender inequality to economic growth, there are a large number of studies that link gender inequality in education to fertility and child mortality. These include, for example, studies by Murthi et al. 1995, Summers 1994, and Hill and King 1995. In Summers (1995), females in Africa with more than seven years of education have, on average, two fewer children than women with no education. Hill and King (1995) find a similar effect of female schooling on fertility. The two studies find that lower gender inequality in enrolment has an additional negative effect on the fertility rate. Countries with a female-male ratio enrolment ratio of less than 0.42 have, on average, 0.5 more children than countries where the enrolment ratio is larger than 0.42, in addition to the direct impact of female enrolment on fertility. Studies by Murthi et al. (1995) and Summers (1994) found similar linkages. Thus, reduced gender bias in education furthers two important development goals, namely reduced fertility and child mortality, which are quite apart from its impact on economic growth (Sen, 1999).

There exists a direct positive externality effect of women's education. Female education is believed to promote the quantity and quality of education of their children through the support and general environment educated mothers can provide to their children (Smith et al., 2001; Klasen, 1999). Similarly, at household level, reduced gender inequality in education generates positive external effects. For example, it is likely that equally educated siblings are likely to strengthen each other's educational success through direct support inspired by educational activities. In addition, couples with similar education levels may promote each other's life-long learning. Reduced gender bias in education increases access to employment for women, which may enhance economic growth. Greater education of women also increases their health knowledge, which in turn improves the health of their children (World Bank, 2001), as well as increasing their bargaining power (Smith et al., 2003). In turn, increased bargaining power increases women's say over household resources, which often leads to greater allocations to child health and nutrition. The evidence is irrefutable that education for girls/women improves girls' own lives now and in the future. Better-educated women marry later and have fewer unwanted pregnancies. In addition, their earning power may lower the number of children parents want as income earners. Moreover, educated females reduce the infant mortality rate through better child-care practices. Studies have shown that educating boys does not have noticeable effects on fertility rates (Annan, 2000; Fritschel and Mohan, 2001).

Studies in Latin America and Southeast Asia have shown that increased income going to mothers has an impact on child survival as compared to income going to fathers. With higher levels of education, women can obtain employment in the non-agricultural sector and hence increase their income-earning possibilities (Quisumbing, 2003).

2.4   Gender Bias in Education and Asset Ownership

African women play an important role as producers of food, managers of natural resources, income earners and caretakers of the household's food and nutrition security. Women in sub-Saharan Africa account for 70 - 80% of household food production. Despite their contribution, customary and legal institutions in many African countries discriminate against women in terms of basic human rights. With regard to access to land, education and public resources, women in many sub-Saharan Africa countries are disadvantaged. Worldwide, the gender gap has closed faster in education than in asset ownership, but for sub-Saharan Africa, both gaps are closing more slowly than they are in the rest of the world. Asset ownership is potentially more important in Africa than it is in the rest of the world, due to the important role women play in Africa for food and nutrition security (Alderman et al., 1995; Quisumbing, 1995; Alderman et al., 2003).

In addition to reducing employment opportunities for women and reducing their bargaining power, gender inequality in education contributes to gender bias in access to technology, which may hamper the ability of women to increase their agricultural productivity, domestic or entrepreneurial activities and thus reduces economic growth (World Bank, 2001). Various studies have shown that women farmers in Africa suffer from lack of access to modern technology and inputs, which lowers their productivity. In addition, limited agricultural extension services in many sub-Saharan Africa countries are often made available to educated farmers. Thus, many female farmers are excluded from receiving extension services due to their low level of education. In addition, education and skills development aimed at agricultural production are usually focused on men, and research to generate appropriate technology is usually not guided by the needs of women, even though they are responsible for a very large share of the production for which the technologies are being developed (Alderman et al, 2003; otieno, 2001; Heidhues, 1994).

Much of female labour, particularly housework and many subsistence activities, goes unrecorded in the system of national accounts. With regard to time allocation, women's time burdens are often too large. In addition to household and farm production activities, they are the ones responsible for child care and care of sick and older members of the household. Greater access to employment outside the home will lead to a substitution of unrecorded female labour by labour in the formal economy, thus making women's labour visible and, as a result, increase the measured economic output.

Various studies in sub-Saharan Africa show that differences in agricultural productivity between men and women disappear when women are given access to the same production resources, technology, and information (Otieno, 2001; Pannin and Bümmer, 2001; Jiggins et al., 1997). Failure to make available resources, technology, knowledge and access to decision-making costs developing countries dearly in terms of forgone economic growth and forgone improvements in the well-being of the disadvantaged groups in their populations, including women (Heidhues, 2000; Andersen and Pandya-Lorch, 1998; SCN, 1998).

Although women are responsible for a large share of food and agricultural production and processing, they seldom receive extension services, technical assistance, credit, or input subsidies. They frequently do not have access to financial or capital markets, and in most cases they are barred from obtaining legal rights to land. The weakness of women's land rights results in an inability to use land as collateral to obtain access to credit (Njehia, 1994; Heidhues, 1995; Heidhues and Buchenrieder, 2004). Some studies which demonstrate that plots of land controlled by women have lower yields than those controlled by men may contribute to the idea that women lack the farming expertise (Alderman et al., 1995). Other studies (Pannin and Brümmer, 2001, Jiggins et al., 1997) however, show that the lower yields are usually the result of lower use of labour and fertilizer per acre rather than managerial and technical efficiency. Unequal rights and obligations within the household, as well as limited time and financial resources, pose a greater constraint to women. Given equal access to resources and human capital, women farmers can achieve equal or even, as some studies show, significantly higher yields than men (Quisumbing et al., 2003; Guerny, 1996).

2.5   Measures of Gender Equality

In this section, the most frequently used measures of gender equality are described. They include: the gender development index and the gender empowerment index

2.5.1 Gender Development Index

Gender bias in development has often been interpreted as a failure to include women in development projects. Recognition of the gender gap led to the establishment of the Gender-related Development Index (GDI) in 1995. Gender-related development index (GDI) value is a composite index that measures average achievement in the three basic dimensions captured in the human development index—a long and healthy life, knowledge and a decent standard of living—adjusted to account for inequalities between men and women UNDP, 2003). The GDI combines gender-related measures of life expectancy, adult literacy, enrolment in primary, secondary and tertiary education, and estimates of earned income to arrive at a country-by-country evaluation of the gender gap in achievement. The GDI adjusts the human development index downward, based on the belief that gender inequality reduces the overall level of well-being in a country. The extent of this downward adjustment is determined by gender gaps in the earned income component (Klasen, 1999). Countries with the lowest GDI are very poor African countries which are currently or have recently been affected by civil war, with many women and children being forced to become refugees.

Although there are clear links between the level of economic development and the gender-related index, due to the level of the income measure, poorer countries with gender equality in education rank higher on the GDI than on the HDI. In Kenya, there have been slight changes in the GDI since 1995. Table 2.1 shows the GDI values for Kenya since 1995. Although there seems to be a big improvement in the GDI between 1995 and 1997, the methodologies used in calculating the GDI coefficients for the two years are different; hence, the two years may not be comparable. Between 1998 and 2000 there was a slight improvement in the GDI (Kiriti and Tisdell, 2003; GoK, 2004a).

Table 2.1: Kenya's Gender-related Development Index (1995 – 2000)

Year	GDI
1995	0.459[*]
1997	0.517
1998	0.508
1999	0.511
2000	0.512

Source: UNDP - Human Development Reports for 2001, 2002, 2003
Note: * Not comparable with other GDI values

There are some shortcomings associated with using the GDI as a measure of gender equality. These include difficulties in measuring changes over time in the GDI due to differences in the methods of calculation used; the possibility of gross inequality between females and males to increase and for the GDI to remain constant, other things being equal; and the fact that the GDI may conceal significant inequalities since its components are aggregate measures (Kiriti and Tisdell, 2003).

2.5.2 Gender Empowerment Measure

Another gender index used to measure gender equity is the so called gender empowerment measure (GEM). GEM is a composite index that measures gender inequality in three basic dimensions of empowerment: economic participation and decision-making, political participation and decision-making and power over economic resources (UNDP, 20001). The GEM assesses the extent of gender equity in economic and political power. For this, the index uses variables constructed to measure the relative empowerment of women and men in political and economic spheres of activity. It thus tries to measure gender equity in participation in governmental and managerial decision-making, professional roles, and economic activities generally (UNDP, 2001).

Gender equity in access to economic and political opportunities is of intrinsic importance as it determines the status of women in society. A society that neglects the economic and political potential of women is likely to perform worse than a society using its talents regardless of gender (Klasen, 1999).

The United Nations Development Program (UNDP) does not have a GEM value for Kenya due to unavailability of data. However, there has been a huge improvement in the number of women representatives in parliament since the introduction of the multi-party system in 1992. In 1992, there were no women elected to parliament. In 1997, women occupied six (3.6%) out of the 202 seats in parliament and 17 seats (8.1%) in 2002. There are also an insignificant number of women professionals and technical workers, and very few female administrators and managers (GoK, 2004a).

Using the GEM as a gender equality measure has been criticized for a number of reasons. The criticisms include: its focus on income but not the users of income; the fact that the GEM does not capture the economic and political power held by women and their roles in the development process; the GEM does not allow for inter-country comparison due to the flexibility in the earnings gap and the weighting and averaging procedures; the GEM focuses too much on representation at national level and in the formal sectors of the economy, hence neglecting other sectors of the economy. A country may have a high level of female participation in parliament and hence a high GEM ranking, but this does not necessarily reflect the actual political power of women. The GEM neglects many important aspects of women's economic and political roles that exist outside of national politics and the formal economy, as in the case of many developing countries (Kiriti and Tisdell, 2003), where many women work in the informal and agricultural sector. In most developing countries, for example Kenya, where poverty levels are high, most women's interest is focused on basic survival and they may not be interested in being members of parliament or local authorities.

2.5.3 Data, Measurement and Specification

Measuring gender inequality is not easy due to the lack of country-specific disaggregated data by gender. The scarcity of gender-disaggregated information on land rights and access to other resources has made it impossible at national level to examine whether, on balance, women's access to two major income-earning resources – land and human capital – has deteriorated or improved through time. Although there has been considerable progress in collecting gender-disaggregated data on education and employment, there is inadequate information on gender inequality as regards access to productive resources, land and technology. There are limited consistent data on employment by gender and labour force participation by gender. Cross-country comparisons are difficult to make since definitions of participation vary from one country to another, particularly when referring to women (Klasen, 1999).

Second, a great deal of gender inequality relates to intra-household resource allocation, for which there is very little reliable information. In cases where the outcome effects of gender inequality are documented, it is often difficult to get information on the intra-household decision-making process. Many women's activities are not accounted for in the system of national accounts (SNA). These activities include household and farm production activities. According to UNDP (1995: 89), about 66% of female activities in developing countries are unrecorded in the SNA, in comparison to about 24% of male activities. Thus, linking gender inequality to economic growth may suffer from the shortcomings described above and would therefore underestimate the impact of gender inequality on economic growth.

This study provides gender-disaggregated data on resource ownership in Pokot, Kenya, and thus gives an overview of how resources are distributed at household level. In addition, data collected for this study made it possible to assess the impact of resource ownership on food and nutrition security based on the gender of the household head. Moreover, the costs of gender inequality in accessing education are estimated for both farm and non-farm income for male and female respondents. Thus, the study contributes valuable information as far as research on gender in Kenya is concerned.

3 AN OVERVIEW OF KENYA: RESOURCES AND FOOD SECURITY SITUATION

Chapter 3 gives an overview of Kenya. It starts with a description of Kenya and its resources and socio-economic indicators. The main resources which are the focus of the study i.e. human capital, financial capital and land are then discussed. This is followed by a discussion on Kenya' food and nutrition security situation. Finally, a discussion on some of the food security and agricultural related policies in Kenya are presented.

3.1 An Introduction to Kenya

Kenya is located on the east coast of Africa and is divided into two almost equal parts by the equator. The country is transected from north to south by the Great Rift Valley. The neighbouring countries of Kenya are: Ethiopia to the north, Sudan to the northwest, Somalia to the east, Tanzania to the south, and Uganda to the west. Lake Victoria and the Indian Ocean lie to the west and east of Kenya respectively.

Kenya comprises an area of 582,650 square kilometres. Of this, 13,400 km^2 are covered by water bodies and 569,250 km^2 are land. About 80% of Kenya is arid and semi-arid, and only 11.4% (6.6 million hectares) of the land is potentially arable. About 2.0 million ha of land is potentially good, while 2.0 million ha and 2.0 million ha are of moderate and low potential respectively (FAO, 2003). Approximately 670 km2 of land are currently under irrigation. The country has varied climatic conditions that can be divided into four broad zones: arid, semi-arid, humid and semi-humid. The region north of the equator is hot and receives comparatively little rain. The southern region falls into three meteorological zones: the coast is humid, with an average annual temperature ranging from about 24°C (76°F) in June and July to about 28°C (82°F) in February, March, and April; the highlands are relatively temperate, and the Lake Victoria region is tropical. The rainy seasons occur from October to December and April to June. The terrain is composed of low plains rising towards the central highlands, bisected by the Great Rift Valley, and fertile plateaus in the west. The lowest point is the Indian Ocean, which is 0 m above sea level, and the highest point is Mt. Kenya, which is 5,199 m above sea level (Central Intelligence Agency- CIA, 2004;).

The agricultural sector is the economic mainstay of the country, providing the country with both substantial export earnings and a basis for industrial and commercial growth (Odhiambo et al., 2004; Kimenyi, 2002). At independence in 1963, agriculture accounted for 80% to 90% of rural employment and approximately 80% of the foreign exchange earnings (Republic of Kenya, 1981; Nyangito, 2003). More than forty years later, despite considerable expansion in the industrial and manufacturing sectors, the agricultural sector still remains the single most important sector in the Kenyan economy, providing 80% of the working population with a livelihood and accounting for over 70% of Kenya's foreign exchange earnings (CBS, 1998, CBS, 2000; Nyangito, 2003). Agriculture accounts for about 20% of GDP and 18% of employment in agriculture and agro-industries. The service and industrial sectors accounts for 62% and 19% of GDP respectively (CBS, 2000b).

The main food crops are maize, rice and wheat. Other food crops grown on a low scale include sorghum, millet, pulses, root and tubers. The main export crops are tea, coffee and horticultural crops, while sugar, cotton and pyrethrum are the main industrial crops. Other export crops include wattle back and cashew nuts. Poultry farming and animal husbandry is practiced in Kenya with cattle, small ruminants and camels forming the herds (Nyangito and Nzuma, 2004; Odhiambo et al., 2004). The rapid decline of pulses production (since 1993) and also of maize, sorghum and millets, more recently, is of serious concern. Total annual on-farm production of food crops has lagged behind consumption, resulting in food deficits, and thereby preventing the achievement of Kenya's aspiration of food security. This poor performance is due to, not only biophysical constraints (diseases, pests and drought), but also to socio-economic/policy bottlenecks such as input to output economic ratios, inadequate infrastructure, marketing, price levels and stability (Odhiambo et al., 2004; Kenya Agricultural Research Institute –KARI, 2005).

In comparison with its neighbours, Kenya is the most industrialized country in East Africa. The main manufacturing industries include cloth, paper, cement and sugar industries. The industrial sector, which accounts for around 13 per cent of GDP, is dominated by food-processing industries, most of which are located in the urban centres (Odhiambo, et al., 2003). There is also a vibrant timber industry. However, this is now threatened owing to the degradation of the forests. The natural resources that are available in Kenya and have a direct impact on food security include forests, water, and wildlife. The tourism sector is also an important source of income for Kenya. Other natural resources available in Kenya are limestone, gold, soda ash and fluorspar (CBS, 1998).

3.2   Socio-economic Indicators

Since independence, one of the major objectives of the Kenyan government has been to achieve rapid economic growth. The country achieved high economic growth rates of 6.6% per annum in the period 1964 - 1973. However, this performance declined in the second decade with a growth rate of 5.2% during 1974 – 1979 period. There was a further decline to 2.5% during the 1990 – 1995 period. This decline continued with the economy recording a negative growth of -0.3% in the year 2000 (UNDP, 2002a; Nyangito and Nzuma, 2003). The gross national product (GNP) per capita in 2002 was USD 360 (Institute of Economic Affairs, IEA, 2002). By the year 2000, Kenya was estimated to have a population of slightly more than 31.6 million and a population growth rate of 2.7%.

The Welfare Monitoring Survey II indicates that Kenya's population structure comprises a very high proportion of young people: 41% of the population is between the age of zero and 14, 6% are between 15 and 64 years and 2.8% are over 65 years old (CBS, 2000a and CBS, 2000b). About 85.5% of the adult population can read and write (CBS, 2000b; C.I.A, 2004). There is a big disparity between the rural and urban households with regard to accessibility to health and education facilities (GoK and GTZ, 2001). The Poverty Reduction Strategy Paper (PRSP) for the period 2000 – 2003 and the 2001 Human Development Report for Kenya identify landlessness, lack of education, high prevalence of illness, low productivity, inequitable access to land and capital and widespread unemployment, particularly among young people, as the main development problems facing the country (Republic of Kenya, 2000; UNDP, 2002). Vulnerability to poverty, especially among women and people living in the arid and semi-arid regions of the country is a developmental challenge the country faces (World Bank, 2000; UNDP, 2002a and b).

In 2000, Kenya ranked 137 out of 174 countries in the HDI[2]. The HDI declined in 2002 and the country was ranked at position 148 out of the 174 countries. This indicates a decline in living standards, life expectancy and decreased access to education (UNDP, 2003). The Human Development Report 2001 for Kenya produced by UNDP indicates declining economic performance, socio-economic disparities and a decreasing human development index, which

---

[2] HDI is a composite index which measures average achievement in three basic dimensions of human development: health, which is measured in terms of life expectancy; education (knowledge), which is measured in terms of the gross enrolment ratio of adult literacy; and economic growth, which is measured in terms of the standard of living of the people.

have resulted in human development challenges for the country (UNDP, 2001).
Table 3.1 shows the HDI trends for Kenya from 1975 to 2002.

Table 3.1: Kenya's Human Development Index (1975 – 2002)

Year	HDI
1975	0.443
1980	0.489
1985	0.512
1990	0.533
1995	0.523
2000	0.513
2002	0.488

Source: UNDP (2002a) and UNDP (2003)

From the figures in Table 3.1, the HDI for Kenya improved between 1975
and 1990. This was due to the strong economic growth the country experienced
after independence up to the early 1990s. In the mid 1990s, both the HDI and
GDP started to decline. This was due to the decline in government expenditure
on health and education, and an increase in unemployment as a result of the
implementation of structural adjustment programmes (SAPs). Due to cost
sharing and job cuts, many poor people were unable to obtain access to social
facilities such as education and health care, thus leading to a drop in the standard
of living for many and hence an increase in general poverty within the country
(UNDP, 2001; CBS, 2000a).

In 1996 Kenya's economic growth stagnated, and hence failed to keep up
with the rate of population growth. In 1997, the IMF suspended Kenya's
Enhanced Structural Adjustment Program (ESAP) due to the government's
failure to maintain reforms and curb corruption (Nyangito, 2003; Odhiambo et
al., 2004). A severe drought from 1999 to 2000 compounded Kenya's problems,
causing water and energy rationing and reducing agricultural output. The IMF,
which had resumed loans in 2000 to help Kenya through the drought, again
halted lending in 2001 when the government failed to institute several anti-
corruption measures (Nyangito, 2000). Despite the return of strong rains in
2001, weak commodity prices, endemic corruption, and low investment limited
Kenya's economic growth to 1%. Growth fell below 1% in 2002 because of
erratic rains, low investor confidence, meagre donor support, and political
infighting up to the elections in December 2002 (Nyangito and Nzuma, 2004).

With a drop in the quality of life in Kenya in the last ten years, the government has to increase its efforts to provide people with an environment that enables them to access resources and opportunities in order to live quality lives. These efforts involve combating poverty and unemployment by increasing access to productive resources, education, health, housing and sanitation; and addressing different types of inequalities existing between regions within the country (UNDP, 2002). There is general agreement that substantial donor support and rooting out corruption are essential to making Kenya realize its profound economic potential (Nyangito and Nzuma, 2004; Kimenyi, 2002).

3.3   Household Production Resources

Rural farm households are endowed with a stock of resources that may be termed the household resource base. These resources are allocated to a range of activities that are required to maintain the household's level of subsistence consumption and possibly to generate a surplus. The household resource endowments include land and other natural resources such as water and forests, labour time, financial and human capital. In the sections that follow, the focus is on the resources of interest for this study, in other words, land, human capital and financial capital.

3.3.1 Land

The most important natural resource in Kenya is land, which is predominantly used for agriculture. The land is classified into three categories: high-potential, medium-potential and low-potential, based mainly on rainfall received. The high and medium-potential areas, which comprise of 20% of the total land, are the areas suitable for arable rain-fed agriculture. These areas are suitable for crop and dairy farming, each occupying 31% and 30%, respectively (Odhiambo et al., 2004). The low-potential lands, commonly referred to as arid and semi-arid lands (ASALs) are dominated by nomadic pastoralism, which utilizes about 50 per cent of the land in these areas. Ranching and other livestock-keeping activities occupy about 31% of the area and the rest is used for agriculture including irrigated agriculture.

About 75% of the population in Kenya live in rural areas and are involved in subsistence farming. Smallholder farmers who hold less than 1.2 ha of land dominate agricultural production in Kenya (Odhiambo et. al., 2004). The country depends heavily on rain-fed agriculture to produce most of its food.

Land Laws and Land Rights in Kenya

Land is both a social and economic asset. As an economic asset, land works either as a financial tool or a production tool. Land as a production tool is essential in the production of agricultural goods. At the same time, land can be held as a hedge against inflation (Nyangito, 2003). In so far as land is a factor of production and a store of value, it also has a great social and political significance. Access, ownership and use of land in society depend on the legal structures governing land access and use. In Kenya, there is an elaborate system of formal and informal regulations that govern access and use of land. These regulations range from unwritten taboos, customs and traditions to the constitution. This section describes the various land laws and regulations that impact on land use and therefore agricultural development in Kenya.

Evolution of Land Laws in Kenya

The evolution of both formal and informal land laws in Kenya can be traced back to three important phases in the history of Kenya: the pre-colonial period, the colonial period and the post-colonial period. Before colonialism, communities governed land through community (informal) rules, also known as customary laws. Under this system, no individual owned the land. Instead, land belonged to the whole community, with individuals having the right to use it in a manner acceptable to the community. The land tenure system varied from community to community depending on cultural values, geography, climatic and socio-economic conditions. Community leaders acted as judges and had the power to control land use (Odhiambo and Nyangito, 2002).

In the colonial period, the colonialists enacted various laws to govern the manner in which land was to be owned and managed. The introduction of English property law immediately replaced the customary law in the areas they had occupied. This law marked the beginning of individualization of land ownership in Kenya, and community governance of land (customary law), lacked legal mandate (Wanjala, 2000; Odhiambo and Nyangito, 2002). To consolidate the settlers' grip on the land, the colonial government institutionalized the Transfer of Property Act of India (ITPA), a law that governed property transfers, leases, mortgages, covenants etc. In addition, to ensure the security of tenure of the settling proprietors, the Registration of Titles Ordinance (now Cap 281 in Kenyan law) was enacted in 1920. The effect of registration under this law was to declare the title of the registered proprietor of land conclusive and indefeasible (Wanjala, 2000; Wanjala, 1990). These institutions are still in place today.

In 1953, 'African reserves' and 'white highlands' were established. Indigenous people occupying the Central Rift Valley – located in Kenya's high-potential areas – were consequently moved to some 14 land units called 'Native reserves' administered by the Native Land Trust Board. The prime agricultural land was set aside for white settlers and was governed by English property law. This resulted in widespread landlessness among the natives, deterioration of land quality due to fragmentation, overstocking and soil erosion, and the disintegration of social and cultural institutions in the reserves. Due to mounting pressure on land in the reserves, and in the belief that the deterioration of life in the reserves was due to overpopulation, bad land use and a defective tenure system, the authorities saw the need to reform the whole land tenure arrangement (Swynnerton, 1953 as cited in Odhiambo and Nyangito, 2002). The Swynnerton Plan of 1953 was instituted to guide intensified agricultural development in the reserves by encouraging individualization of tenure and to provide security of tenure through irrevocable title. The authorities assumed that the natives would be encouraged to invest their labour and profits in the development of their farms and enable them to offer it as security for credit to develop their farms (Wanjala, 1990).

The land reform programme in the reserves had three main stages: adjudication, consolidation and registration. Adjudication involved ascertaining individual or group rights amounting to ownership over land within an area. The second step of consolidation involved merging the fragments into single economic units, while registration entailed the entry of establishment rights into the land register and the issuing of a title deed. Although the new tenure laws defined the rights of an individual proprietor, traditional rights of access and inheritance continued to determine the farmers' freedom of disposition. Public and private credit agencies were reluctant to extend credit to small-scale farmers except under the most exhaustive scrutiny (Mutoro, 1997; Odhiambo and Nyangito, 2002, Kimenyi, 2002).

At independence in 1963, the government enacted the Registered Land Act (cap 300), which was to govern land formerly under customary law. This law, which was an embodiment of the English law, was intended to encourage individualization of tenure as outlined in the Swynnerton plan. After five years of independence, the Land Adjudication Act was amended to cater for group rights, particularly of pastoral and nomadic areas where individualization had little success. Group rights were to be registered under the Land (Group Representatives) Act (Cap 287). The intention of this Act was to maintain the status quo in the semi-arid areas where the way of life was pastoral and nomadic (Wanjala, 2000). The other significant post-independence legislation was the Magistrates' Jurisdiction (Amendment) Act of 1981, which vested in councils of elders the powers to hear and determine cases revolving around beneficial ownership of land, the division and determination of boundaries of land, claims to occupy or work on land, and trespass claims (Wanjala, 2000).

Another significant development in post-independence land policy was the establishment of settlement schemes to resettle the landless. The government of Kenya, with the assistance of the British government, purchased land and settled Africans who had been displaced during colonial incursion. An additional measure by the government to address the issue of landlessness was to encourage people to pool resources together and purchase land collectively. This method failed, however, since it failed to meet its original objective of settling the landless, but instead benefited only a few rich and middle class individuals and land-buying companies and cooperatives (Republic of Kenya, 1981). Land ownership in Kenya currently falls under three property regimes. These are: the Indian Transfer of Property Act (1882); the Registered Land Act (Cap 300); and the customary law system (Wanjala, 2000; Wanjala, 1990).

The Indian Transfer of Property Act (ITPA) is an embodiment of English law extended to Kenya from India as early as 1887. The colonialists used this Act to govern land in the 'white highlands'. The Act embodies the freehold estate and, despite its old common law content, this law still governs large tracts of land in Kenya today, significantly in the agricultural high-potential areas of Kenya.

The Registered Land Act is a derivative of English law and applies mainly to land that was formerly part of the 'native reserves'. The present version of the Act was enacted in 1963 and derives from the neoclassical thinking that conferring private property rights to land on individuals would contribute to and enhance proper resource management (Wanjala, 1990).

The third legal property regime governing land use in Kenya is the informal law or customary law. This regime is multifaceted and diverse. It varies by region, ethnicity and even by clan. It is based on the socio-cultural values and institutions of the local communities utilizing the land resource.

Although all the land ownership systems discussed above exist in Kenya today, the Registered Land Act (Cap 300) is the primary legal instrument that governs land. Land previously held under the ITPA and the customary law systems is being converted to registered land. In the arid and semi-arid regions, where people's lives remain largely nomadic, registration has been embodied in the Land (Group Representatives) Act. This act does not form a new tenure arrangement. This act provides an innovative legislative framework within which certain groups of people can relate to land without fundamental alterations in their customary land arrangement (Odhiambo and Nyangito, 2002). Land policies and legislation in Kenya have therefore given rise to three land tenure systems: private tenure, customary tenure and public tenure. Private tenure includes all land held on freehold or leasehold by individuals, companies, cooperative societies, religious organizations, public bodies and legal bodies. The customary land tenure system was mainly found in areas that have not been transformed through consolidation and registration. The customary tenure system is designated as Trust Land (land in special settlement areas or reserves). The public tenure arrangement designates the government as the private landowner. It includes open waters, national parks, forests and alienated government land.

It is important to note here that most of the laws governing land ownership in Kenya are either outdated or have some weaknesses (Odhiambo and Nyangito, 2002). For example, the Registered Land Act does not make fixed surveys mandatory, and has been a constant source of boundary disputes and conflicts. It is hoped that with the constitution review process that is now in progress, land laws will be revised, amended or repealed altogether.

Land and Women's Inheritance Rights in Kenya

In Kenya, like in most (patrilineal) African countries, the usufruct right to land prevails and customary land use practices often determine access to land in terms of use rights or ownership (FAO, 2004). Traditionally, women's access to land in Kenya was and still is very tenuous, since it depends on the good will of the male members of their families. A woman's access to land thus had to be through the husband if she was married, the father is she was unmarried, and the father was still alive, the brothers if she was unmarried or divorced, and the son if she was widowed. Women usually lose the rights to land following the death of their spouse, especially if they have no male children.

Today, however, many changes have taken place in the area of women's rights to inherit, although gender differences still exist. Even in areas where customary law is the operative law, some elements of the statutory provisions apply. For example in parts of Murang'a, women may inherit land only as a trustee on behalf of their children. They cannot dispose of their property, and they lose the right to hold it on remarriage (Kameri-Mbote, 2002). Notable changes in gender roles, which include women assuming the role of breadwinner, being less dependent on men, women acquiring wealth independently of inheritance – i.e. through purchase – have contributed to the rapidly changing way of thinking on inheritance of property (land included) by women (Oniang'o and Kimakoti, 1999).

3.3.2 Financial Capital

Capital formation is vital for economic growth, which in turn is of prime importance for food security. Efficient financial markets are crucial for capital formation (Schrieder and Heidhues, 1994; Schrieder, 1996). The two sources of capital are foreign and domestic funds. In most low-income countries, internally mobilized funds account for 90% and more of overall investment funding. Thus, at national level, internal resource mobilization (savings and deposits) is vital for economic development and subsequent improvement in food security (Schrieder, 1996; Heidhues, 1995). At household level, credit and savings often serve as substitute insurance for the poor and are often used to provide basic necessities when household incomes decline temporarily (Heidhues and Schrieder, 1996; Zeller and Sharma, 2001).

Access to credit, savings, and insurance services could improve transitory and chronic food insecurity in three ways. First, credit or savings can provide capital for financing inputs, labour, and equipment for income generation. Second, access to credit and liquid financial savings services enables households to adopt more effective precautionary savings strategies. In addition, insurance services can reduce the cost of bearing risks, thereby enhancing households' capacity to invest in more risky but also more profitable technology and enterprises. Third, financial services could more efficiently stabilize consumption of food and other essential goods during lean times (Heidhues and Schrieder, 1994; Heidhues, 1995; Sharma, 2001).

Households experiencing or anticipating food shortages may deal with the problem in a number of ways: they may diversify their crops and off-farm income sources, sell assets, seek to increase their savings, or borrow from relatives, moneylenders, or formal markets. The poorer the household, the more severe the consequences of a food shortage can be, as their assets and borrowing options become depleted, these households may slip into chronic food insecurity (Zeller and Sharma, 2001; Zeller et al., 1997).

In Kenya, both the formal and informal institutions play an important role in providing credit. Microfinance institutions have been identified as the most appropriate avenues for mobilizing and channelling investment funds to micro-enterprises. Kenya has over fifty institutions that practise microfinancing. Of these, only ten practise pure microfinancing, whereas the rest are involved in microfinance as part of their more general social welfare activities (GoK, 2003). Informal institutions are in form of rotating savings and credit associations, individual money lenders, and rotating labour clubs. These associations are found in both rural and urban areas and provide emergency financial assistance to members. Groups often take up collections in the event of illness or death, and they may also visit the member's home to provide extra labour. Many groups also undertake an income-generating project, which might include agriculture, fish farming, beekeeping, or handicrafts. Many women, especially poor women, recognize the need to be members of these groups, since through these groups they can participate in community projects by contributing to community fundraising events at local schools, clinics, or churches, in addition to economic security for members, which translates into a high propensity to save.

In Kenya, the Association of Microfinance Institutions (AMFI) is the umbrella organization under which microfinance institutions are registered. AMFI was legally registered in March 1999. It comprises 11 large MFIs that together serve over 97,000 clients. Its members include institutions of different sizes and legal structures, such as NGOs, cooperatives and village banks. AMFI's mission is to develop a microfinance industry and an institutional framework that serves poor and low-income people in Kenya. Its long-term objectives are: to ensure that the microfinance legislation is passed by parliament; and to increase membership in the network among MFIs. AMFI funding comes primarily from grants and membership fees (Faulu Kenya, 2005). The Kenya Rural Enterprise Programme (K-REP Bank), Faulu Kenya and Yehu are examples of microfinance institutions that are enabling the poor to succeed through small business loans. Their common goal is to provide increased access to financial services for low-income people in Kenya, who are disenfranchised from mainstream commercial banking and financial services sectors, and to encourage and facilitate micro and small entrepreneurs to meet their self-determined development goals and dreams for the future for themselves and their families. These institutions aim to have a major impact on expanding the economic assets, participation and empowerment of low-income people, especially women, as entrepreneurs and economic agents. They do this by opening their access to finance, knowledge and markets.

There exist many other financial institutions and programmes that offer, among other things, finance to the poor. These rural finance institutions have demonstrated the potential for raising productivity and income for the poor. In addition, group savings and lending schemes seem promising for reaching the interior parts of rural areas, thus keeping the financial intermediaries' costs low. It should, however, be noted that not many rural women seek credit facilities with formal financing institutions, since they lack collateral and are considered to be high-risk customers. For this reason, many women obtain emergency loans as well as long-term loans from informal microfinancing institutions.

3.3.3 Human Capital

Section 3.3.3 discusses human capital in Kenya. Human capital is one of the focuses of the study. In this section, the education and health system will be discussed, followed by a discussion of division of labour.

3.3.3.1 Education

Education plays a key role in human development by helping to enhance people's capabilities to effectively improve their well-being and participation in the development process of a nation. In the colonial period, there were great disparities in educational opportunities, not only between the races but also between the different regions in Kenya. During that time, the education system stressed technical and vocational education for Africans. The main objective of this education system was to enhance Africans suitability as labourers and craftsmen on the settlers' farms (GoK, 2001).

Since independence in 1963, there has been a rapid expansion of education in Kenya. Student enrolments in primary and secondary schools increased from 0.9 and 0.03 million in 1963 to 5.5 and 0.6 million in 1995 respectively (Appleton et al., 1999). At primary level, the expansion was partly due to free primary education introduced in 1974. At the secondary level, much of the expansion was due to the establishment of community self-help (*Harambee*[3]) schools which educated around half the secondary school students in the 1970s. Empirical evidence shows rapid expansion of education in Kenya since independence, as well as an increase in labour supply in urban labour markets due to high rural-urban migration. Studies by Appletonet al., (1996), and Manda et al., (2002) estimate the private returns to education in the manufacturing sector in Kenya. These studies report a fall in the rate of returns to schooling for primary and secondary education and give a high rate of returns to university education over time. The studies also report a change in the level[4] of education of new entrants in the labour market over time. A rapid expansion in university education is reported to have taken place in the late 1980s and early 1990s with the establishment of four more universities (Appleton et al., 1999).

Since independence, the system of education in Kenya has been restructured significantly. In 1966, the Kenyan education system was changed from eight years of primary to seven years. Secondary education comprised six years: four years lower and two years of upper secondary education. University education was supposed to take three years. This system was altered again in 1985 with the introduction of 8-4-4 system, meaning eight years of primary, four years of secondary and four years of university education. The new system (8-4-4) was intended to meet the increasing demands of the economy for technically and professionally qualified personnel. Today, more than 6 million Kenyans are enrolled in various educational institutions and adult literacy rates are estimated at about 60 per cent for men and 40 per cent for women (Appleton et al., 1999; Manda et al., 2002).

Education plays an important role in the economic growth of a country since it is a measure of a country's human capital accumulation. Various studies on returns to education in sub-Saharan Africa reveal that returns to education in

---

[3] Harambee means pooling together for a common cause. People meet at an agreed place and date to make their contributions in cash or kind. As a landmark for Kenya's self-help movement, Harambee has been pivotal in community financing for education since independence.

[4] New entrants to wage employment in the manufacturing sector were expected to have secondary education in 1995, compared to new entrants to the same sector in 1985 and 1978 that had primary-level education.

Africa are high (Psacharopoulous, 1994; Appleton 1999). However, Pritchett (1996) argues that there is no correlation in sub-Saharan Africa between economic growth post-1960 and educational expansion, even after controlling for accumulation of physical capital. Kenya, like the subcontinent as a whole, has experienced educational expansion and poor economic performance (Appleton, 1999; Manda et al.,2002). At present, Kenya's educational achievements are above average for the subcontinent (an illiteracy rate of 22% in 1995 compared to 44% in the subcontinent as a whole), while its income is below average (in 1997 its GDP per capita was US$1,110 compared to US$1,470 in the subcontinent (Appleton et al., 1999)).

Although returns to secondary education were very high in the 1970s in Kenya, they fell drastically in the 1980s and the 1990s. Returns to primary and tertiary education have remained high in the three decades. Similar studies also show that an increase in female education benefits both men and women, while male education benefits males more than it does females (Appleton, 1999; Manda et al., 2002). These studies suggest that constraining the average education for females through poor female access to education may in fact reduce male productivity and earnings. Therefore, equal educational opportunities for both girls and boys should be encouraged.

Stressing the importance of education of women in sub-Saharan Africa, Smith and Haddad (2001) describe education of women as a powerful tool against malnutrition, since it leads to increased knowledge and skills which enable women to earn higher incomes, and thus enhance household food security, improving health and nutrition. In addition, education improves the day-to-day care women give to their children. Women's education improves their relative status in society and hence gives them the ability to influence how resources are allocated.

Between the periods 1980 and 2000 the adult literacy rates for both male and female went up (see Figure 3.1). Despite the improvement in the adult literacy rates, there are still regional differences in school enrolment for boys and girls, with more emphasis being given to education of boys in some regions of the country. This has contributed to underdevelopment in regions where fewer women have formal education, since fewer women are represented at higher levels of policy-making who would have otherwise lobbied for development projects in their regions for the benefit of all people in those regions.

Figure 3.1: Adult Literacy Rates in Kenya between 1980 and 2000

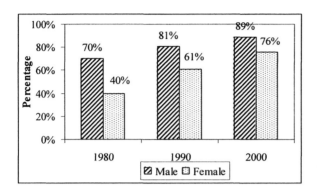

Source: UNDP (2004)

Despite the impressive gains, the Kenyan educational system faces problems of high dropout and repetition rates, in recent years (Bedi, et al., 2002). In January 2003 the government of Kenya expanded the public primary school system by making it free to all children. The effect of this proclamation has been overcrowding of the primary school classrooms. An estimated 5-6% of Kenyan primary school pupils drop out annually and repetition rates are estimated to be around 15-16%. UNESCO (2005) pointed out that, the net primary school enrolment ratio from 1992 to 2002 for boys and girls in Kenya is 68 and 69 (respectively); the net primary school attendance between 1992 and 2002 was 71% for boys and 73% for girls. However, the amount of primary school entrants that reached grade 5 during this period is 88% and the gross secondary school enrolment ratio is 32 for boys and 29 for girls (UNESCO, 2005; Bedi, et al., 2002). One other shortcoming of the school system in Kenya is the high cost of secondary and tertiary or post secondary education. Many talented young people are not able to go on with secondary or tertiary training because of the high cost they have to bear. This phenomenon has contributed to the high rate of unemployment with its many side effects.

In West Pokot district, formal education started with the construction of a primary school in Kachelibe in 1928, but it was only after 1979 that primary education started spreading to other parts of the district (GoK, 1985). The situation has relatively improved in the past years, with 254 primary schools and 18 secondary schools are now in the district (GoK, 2002). The total primary school enrolment rates (in percent); are 64 for boys and 57 for girls, and that for secondary schools (in percent) are; 13 for boys and 11 for girls, with an average of 3 years of secondary school attendance. The estimated adult literacy rate in the district is 53.5 percent for men and 35.5 percent for women (GoK, 2002). There is only one youth polytechnic institution in this district.

According to Schutz T.P (2002), educating women is a key method for boosting agricultural productivity in SSA. Simulations using data from women in Kenya suggested that, yields could increase by 25 percent if all women attended primary school (Smith, et al., 2003).

3.3.3.2   Division of Labour

Rural labour relations have long been observed to be socially embedded. Role-sharing and working conditions are not static, but are continually being redefined in the wake of processes of social change. As a result of a progressive disintegration in existing family structures, changes are also taking place at the level of the gender division of labour, often at the expense of women. The tendency is for women, in addition to their traditional household tasks – such as the time-consuming and strenuous fetching of water and firewood – to be more and more involved in the sort of work for which men were formerly responsible (FAO, 2001; Harris -White, 2000).

How work is divided and organized by gender within the family is closely related to the size of the family and to the availability of labour, as well as the amount of work needing to be done in women's own separate fields. In West and East Africa for example, the disintegration of the extended family and the transition to the nuclear family has often resulted in a shortage of work capacity within the family, so that the woman's help in all aspects of field work is needed more. If the women have fields of their own, the men as a rule expect them to cultivate them alone or with the help of their children, although helping in the men's fields generally takes priority over their own. The changes in family structure are accompanied by reduced willingness and capacity on the part of the men to act supportively (GTZ, 2004; Oniang'o and Kimokoti, 1999).

The division of labour between men and women in crop production varies considerably from region to region and community to community. Gender ideologies assign responsibility for domestic production and socially productive work to women, thus constraining women to price-unresponsive work. At the same time, work burdens for women are heavier than those of men. Some studies explain gender segmentation with reference to concepts of light and heavy work (Harris-White, 2000). But much of the work regarded as light and therefore female (such as transplanting rice, weeding, sowing, post-harvest activities) is in fact arduous, intensive and skilled, while work regarded as heavy (such as carrying water), may be performed with great energy economy (Harris-White, 2000).

Despite their often complementary roles in agriculture, studies (e.g. Quisumbing, 2001; Oniang'o and Makudi, 2002) have shown that in almost all societies, women tend to work longer hours than men. The difference in workloads is particularly marked for rural women, the world's principal food producers. In addition to food production activities, women have the responsibility of preparing and processing the food while fulfilling their fundamental role of nurturing and caring for children and tending to elderly members of the household. According to Quisumbing et al., (2004) and GoK and GTZ (2004) women in sub-Saharan Africa work 10 to 30 per cent longer than men, with the latter averaging 7 to 8 hours. A study conducted in rural Kenya indicates that women generally worked 13-16 hours a day, compared to about 6 hours for the men (Mutoro, 1997).

In Kenya, small farm operations in many parts of the country are not only land but also labour-intensive. Apart from the availability of inputs, efficient allocation of labour is essential for successful farm management and agricultural production. Labour is an important cost item on farms and therefore proper allocation of family labour is important (Mutoro, 1995). In older days, when family labour was insufficient, various ways of attracting labour from outside were used. Among the Luhya for example, labour was provided through the group method known as *Obulala* or *Lisango*. This group labour was organized at three levels, similar to the organization among the Kikuyu. The first level was *ngwatio* and usually consisted of three to ten women who would move and work as a group from day to day, from plot to plot, until the work of all the participants had been done. The second was the *wira*, in which a man or woman requested a number of participants (up to eight) on a specific day to complete a specific task, such as weeding, clearing land and digging. It was obligatory under *wira*, but not *ngwatio*, for the host to provide food and/or beer. The third form was ndunguta, in which a man without a family, land or livestock would be taken into a household to herd his host's cattle, sheep or goats (Mutoro, 1997). Women without a family were taken in by some families for domestic and agricultural work. Although traditional forms of labour still exist with modifications, today most of the labour drawn from outside the household is paid for (Mutoro, 1997).

Labour shortage is a constraint in many small-scale farming areas in Kenya, despite high population densities in rural areas. This can be explained partly by the seasonal variations in labour demand that point to the conflict between the estate and the smallholder, by the migration of males away from the family holdings, by lack of capital and low remittances, which may make it difficult to attract labour out of the household.

3.3.4 Access to Extension Services

The inadequate provision of relevant, reliable and comprehensive information support to all stakeholders in agricultural production has been identified as a major constraint, which has contributed to the decline in agricultural development in SSA (Kiplang'at, 2003). There is therefore a need to develop an effective and efficient agricultural knowledge and information system, which provides relevant information at all levels and to all actors in the agricultural production cycle. According to Munyua (2002), information needs of rural communities are embedded in the hierarchy of their activities and for rural communities to fulfill their respective roles, they require information on input supply, new technologies, early warning systems (droughts, pests and diseases), credit, market prices and their competitors. Therefore, there is need to connect research and extension networks with rural communities in order to provide access to much-needed knowledge, technology and services, in an effort to bridge the information gap.

However, agricultural extension in Sub-Sahara African countries is still largely the responsibility of the governments through the Ministries of Agriculture and the National Agricultural Extension divisions in various countries. This leads to a continuation of the traditional "trickle down" flow of information from research to extension and from extension to farmers. Therefore, there is need for a farmer-centred management approach in dissemination of agricultural information and the need for integration of researchers, extension workers, educators, input suppliers and farmers in the agricultural innovation process (Kiplang'at (2003).

In Kenya, although the private sector provides some extension services, the Ministry of Agriculture through the National Agricultural Extension division, is still largely responsible for extension services (Kiplang'at, 2003). As a result, in 2001, the government of Kenya came up with a National Agricultural

Extension Policy (NAEP). This policy was prepared to guide and harmonize management and delivery of extension services in the country, and accommodate the impending changes. The policy was designed for the use of the Ministry of Agriculture staff, private sector extension providers, non-governmental organizations (NGOs), community-based organizations (CBOs) and development partners supporting agricultural extension in the country (Kiplang'at, 2003).

Jiggins, et al. (1997) found out that there is a bias against women, in accessing extension services in Kenya. They stated in their findings that, even the criteria laid by the World Bank for the selection of contact farmers do not favour women. In practice, extension services in Kenya often add other criteria such as; minimum landholding size, literacy and the ability to purchase inputs. Village chiefs and other formal authorities, who are typically men, and field extension agents, who are almost always men, usually make the selection, thus introducing other potential bias against women.

3.4 Food and Nutrition Security in Kenya

Access to adequate food is recognized as one of the basic human rights that is important in improving the nutritional status of people. People go hungry not necessarily because there is a decline in food availability but because they lose the ability to acquire food, either through their own production, purchase, exchanging labour or other legitimately held food assets (Sen, 1981). The FAO's latest estimates show that 842 million people were undernourished in the period 1999-2001. This figure includes 10 million in the industrialized countries, 34 million in countries in transition and 798 million in developing countries. Out of the 789 million undernourished people in developing countries, 198 million are found in sub-Saharan Africa (FAO, 2003). This implies that countries in sub-Saharan Africa are faced with the challenge of reducing the number of hungry people and ensuring food security for their populace, as well as dealing with other challenges such as the fight against HIV/AIDS.

Food security is defined as access by all people at all times to food required for health. At national level, food security entails adequate supply of food through local production, storage, food imports and food aid. At household level, food security is defined as that state of affairs where all people within the household have, at all times, access to an adequate diet for an active and healthy life (Heidhues, 2000; Frankenberger and Maxwell, 1992). Increasing attention is paid to household-level food distribution since it is the social unit where most people access food. A household becomes food-insecure when all the potential sources or even most important sources of food are strained or even threatened (Heidhues, 2000). Members of households who go without sufficient quantities of food to maintain good health are forced to reduce activity levels. They may become less productive and lose resistance to diseases.

The government of Kenya recognizes the paramount importance of ensuring food security for its people through national food policy. Despite this, food production in the country has continued to decline since the late 1980s. The national food production index, which was over 100 between 1987 and 1992, dropped to 94 in 1993. When the production figures are adjusted for population size, it is evident that production has not kept pace with the rapidly growing population (GoK and UNICEF, 1998). Food deficits have continued to be experienced in Kenya, with the most recent worst food shortages being felt in the years 2000 and 2003/2004, which saw an increased influx of food aid into the country. With the gap between the food needs and domestic production widening, it is expected that the food security situation will continue to deteriorate if remedial measures are not taken. According to the FAO report (2003), Kenya is one of the countries where undernourished cases increased in the period 1999-2001. This can be attributed to the drought, which saw many people go hungry, and also due to the increase in HIV/AIDS cases that has rendered many affected people less productive.

One of the fundamental issues in Kenya is local food production. The main foods are maize, wheat, rice, milk, starchy tubers and roots. The production of these foods depends on the rainfall patterns and they are therefore vulnerable to weather variations. According to the economic surveys of 1995, 1996, and 1997, the agricultural sector has performed poorly since 1989. The production of the main staple – maize – continued on a downward trend over the period. Although there was a general recovery in 1994/1995, the situation reversed in 1995/1996 due to erratic rains (GoK and UNICEF, 1998); there were slight increase in yields in 1999, but this trend reversed again in the year 2000 as a result of late and insufficient rains which affected the yields negatively, in addition to deterioration of pastures and water supplies for livestock (FAO, 2001). This implies that a decline in production of maize is a sign of food insecurity in Kenya. Lack of promotion of traditional drought-resistant crops has contributed to the aggravation of the situation, especially in arid and semi-arid areas of the country.

As a result of declining production and increased demand for food, the average national per capita calorie supply also declined in the last decade.

Estimates show that the per capita supply, which rose from 2040 to 2070 calories between 1982 and 1986, reversed and maintained a downward trend from 1987. The national figures are, however, skewed towards lower values, implying that the majority of Kenyans have values lower than the population median estimates (GoK, and UNICEF, 1998).

Declines in food production need not result in declines in food security, as long as the country achieves an expansion of non-food production, which generates the revenue needed to compensate for deficits. A country can supplement its own production by importing certain foods. Food aid, though controversial, has been another source of food security, although it has created dependency, especially in arid and semi-arid regions of the country (FAO, 2003).

3.4.1 Household-Level Food Security

The Welfare Monitoring Survey (WMS I) data shows that about 51% of the rural and 38% of the urban population in Kenya is unable to access the minimum requirement of food and essential non-food commodities (GoK and GTZ, 2001). According to WMS I and WMS II, the food poverty line for rural areas was estimated at KES 927 per adult for rural areas, while the line for urban areas was drawn at KES 1,254. The mean non-food expenditure for rural areas was estimated at KES 312 per adult equivalent, and that of urban areas at KES 1,394. These households were classified as absolutely poor and were defined as those that could not meet their minimum calorie requirement of 2,250 calories per adult (as stipulated by FAO/WHO recommended daily allowances) even if they spent all their income on food (CBS, 2000b, CBS, 2001).

Households that did not produce their own food were found to be more vulnerable to food insecurity compared to those that had their own production of main food staples. On average, 54% of households spent their total budget on food, with 27 per cent of the food budget in rural areas being spent on maize grain and maize flour. In general, the order of importance in the allocation of food budget among the rural poor was maize followed by vegetables, beans, milk, meat, sugar, roots, oils and fats (CBS, 2001).

Although household expenditure on food is linked directly to the preferences of those controlling the income within the household, purchase of food may also depend on household earnings and market prices. With the liberalization of food marketing in the country, transportation of cereals from surplus to deficit areas has succeeded to some extent in ensuring minimal price differentials between seasons. However, the trend towards export production has exposed poor households to increased risk of food insecurity (Nyangito, 2004).

Household food poverty data shows variations between geographical areas with the Coast, Western, Eastern and North Eastern Provinces being classified as absolutely poor. Central Province stands out as the only province in the country with lowest prevalence of absolute food poverty (30 per cent). There are also disparities between rural and urban areas in terms of food security, with a higher percentage of adults experiencing absolute food poverty in rural Kenya compared to urban areas (CBS, 2000a; CBS, 2000b).

High poverty rates tend to go hand in hand with food insecurity. The Welfare Monitoring Survey identified the food-insecure groups as concentrated among female-headed households, especially in rural areas, urban poor, poor pastoralists, the poor in drought-prone areas and households that are resource-poor but live in high-potential areas (GoK, 2001).

3.4.2 Nutritional Situation of Women and Children in Kenya

Severe malnutrition occurs as a primary disorder in children, adolescents and adults in conditions of extreme privation and famine. It also occurs in situations of dependency, for example, in the elderly, those with mental illnesses and emotional problems, and in prisoners. Malnutrition in adolescents and adults is commonly associated with other illnesses, such as chronic infections, intestinal malabsorption, alcohol and drug dependence, liver diseases, endocrine and autoimmune diseases, cancer and AIDS (WHO, 1999). Malnutrition and poor nutritional status among children are common problems in many rural and suburban slum areas in Kenya. The declining supply of calories in Kenya, as mentioned earlier, means that food insecurity is on the rise in the country. National nutritional data on chronic malnutrition among children under five confirms the severity of the problem (GoK, 2000; UNICEF, 1998). According to UNICEF, in the period 1995 and 2003, the percentage of children under five who suffered from underweight, wasting and stunting (moderate and severe) was 20%, 6 % and 31% respectively. In the same time period, the percentage of children who suffered from severe underweight was 6%. The trends in child malnutrition show a decrease in prevalence of the three malnutrition indicators between the 1980s, 1990s and 2000. The decrease in malnutrition can be attributed to improved health care facilities, sanitation and literacy levels of women (UNICEF, 2004).

It should, however, be noted that nutritional well-being is an outcome of several underlying factors at household-level: availability of food, adequate care for mothers and children and a proper health environment, and a decline in one factor may adversely affect the nutrition status of an individual. The underlying factors are influenced by basic determinants: the potential resources available to a country or community, as well as political and social factors that affect their utilization (Haddad and Smith, 2002).

UNICEF (1998) outlines the causes of child malnutrition as immediate (most proximate), underlying and basic (most distant) as can be seen from Figure 3.2. The two immediate causes are inadequate dietary intake and disease. The underlying causes of malnutrition, which manifest themselves at the household level, are food insecurity, inadequate maternal and childcare practices, poor health environments and services. Finally the basic causes of child malnutrition manifest themselves at societal level. They include environmental, technological and human resources (UNICEF, 1998; Smith et al., 2003,).

The tragedy of childhood malnutrition is rooted in part in the discrimination and disempowerment so many women endure. Intra-household gender inequality is manifested in the abilities of men and women to make choices, and also reflected in inequality regarding control over resources. What endangers women endangers children too. According to The State of the World's Children 1998 report (UNICEF, 1998), a full commitment to the rights of women is one of the best ways of protecting children's well-being and nutritional development. Women's status with regard to access to resources can be seen as an underlying as well as a basic cause of malnutrition, since women play an important role in maintaining household food security.

The basic causes – political, economic, social, environmental, cultural and religious factors – play a major role in causing malnutrition. Social trends in consumption of particular varieties of foods can result in the 'wrong' foods being eaten, often in excess. Poor eating habits and food preferences may lead to malnutrition through the habitual consumption of certain foods to the exclusion of others, or of large quantities of non-nutritious foods. Environmental factors such as natural disasters - typhoons, tornadoes, earthquakes, floods and droughts can cripple massive fertile areas, meaning that food cannot be produced. In such a situation, the affected areas will have inadequate amounts of food. Cultural and religious factors can cause malnutrition. Cultural and religious laws force their members to abstain from certain foods. This may lead to a deficient intake of nutrients by people abiding by these laws, thereby causing malnutrition among them. Unequal distribution of resources in a country can contribute to poverty in certain areas of the country, and hence cause food insecurity among the poor due to low purchasing power of food and other commodities. Unequal distribution of food in a country often causes stockpiles in one area and deficits in another (UNICEF, 1998).

Figure 3.2: Causes of Child Malnutrition

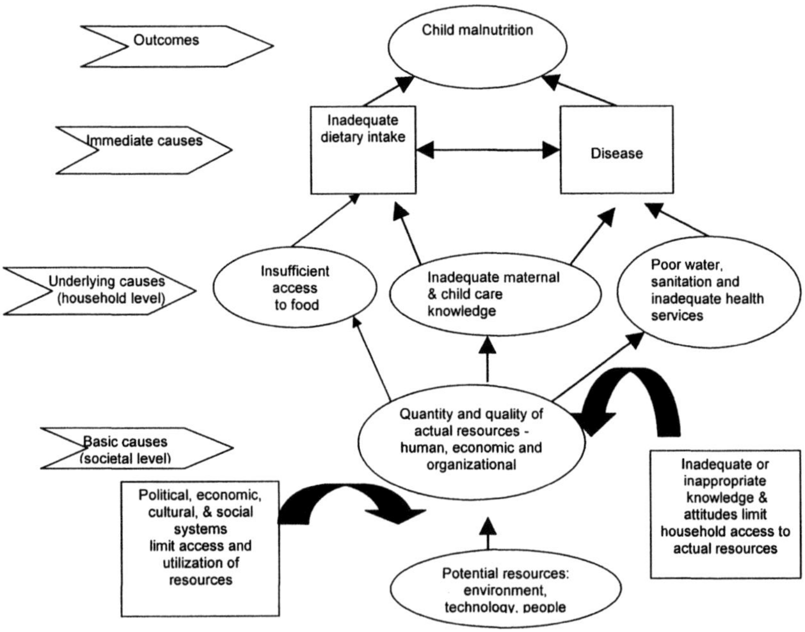

Source: Adapted from UNICEF (1998)

Maternal nutrition is important in determining the nutrition of her children. In some communities, the basis of malnutrition starts before birth, with mothers of low body mass index (BMI) on average giving birth to babies of low birth weight. The nutritional status of women during and before pregnancy is therefore important. The amount of weight gain required by a woman during pregnancy is set out by WHO (1995). In Africa alone, a study carried out by WHO (1995) indicated that there are about 20 to 40% malnourished women, depending upon whether there was a catastrophe, war, famine or drought. The nutrition status of mothers affects the nutrition of the next generation and the vicious cycle of malnutrition may carry on its effects over many generations, as can be seen in Figure 3.3. Underweight mothers are likely to give birth to underweight children. They may be unable to produce enough milk, in addition to being unable to give quality care to the children. In turn, low birth weight children have reduced immunity to diseases, impaired mental ability and are not able to grow normally. In turn the children become stunted and unhealthy, leading to reduced labour productivity and lower educational attainment. These characteristics impair the productivity of future adults.

Figure 3.3: Impact of hunger and malnutrition throughout the life cycle

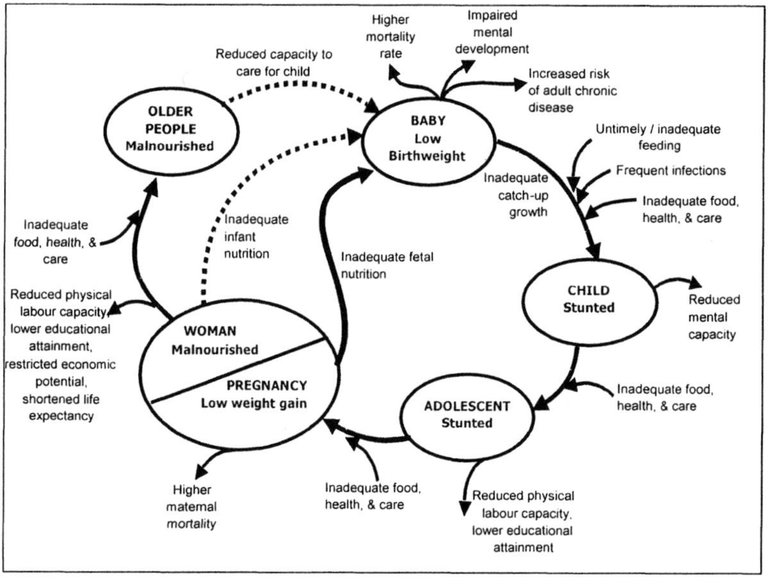

Source: FAO (2004); Benson (2004)

3.4.2.1   Measuring Nutritional Status in Children

The indicators for measuring nutritional status include assessing body characteristics such as: weight and height, dietary intake, illness and death, laboratory reports of body products and economic status. The most commonly used indicators utilized in Kenyan nutritional surveys for the under-five population are based on measurement of height and weight. They are presented as indices of height for age (stunting), weight for height (wasting), weight for age (underweight).

The height for age index measures the degree of stunting (the failure to grow adequately in height in relation to age). This index is a cumulative growth deficit associated with chronic inadequate food intake, ill health, incorrect feeding practices and low socio-economic status. Children falling below the cut-off point of minus two standard deviation (-2SD) from the median of the reference population[5] are classified as stunted. The weight for height index measures the degree of wasting. It is the failure to gain weight adequately in relation to height that reflects recent or acute under nutrition. Wasting results from a recent inadequate food intake and/or recent acute illness. It is also associated with seasonal morbidity and food availability. Children who are below two standard deviations ((-2SD) from the median of the NCHS reference are regarded as wasted. The weight for age index measures the degree of underweight. The value for age index is composed of height for age and weight for height indices. Children whose weight for height index falls below minus two standard deviations (-2SD) are classified as underweight (Frankenberger and Maxwell, 1992; WHO, 1999).

A child's health depends on the well-being of the mother, her knowledge and level of awareness, personal hygiene, the feeding practices she adopts and, above all the care she gives to the dependent child. The child's well-being is also influenced by relatives and others in the community through their knowledge, practices and attitudes. Among children, nutritional status is a sensitive indicator of their health and well-being, and malnutrition in children below the age of five years leads to poor physical and mental development. In addition, it increases the risk of death due to the resultant weak immunity against infection (UNICEF, 1998; Benson, 2004).

Mild, moderate and chronic forms of malnutrition are widespread in Kenya, indicating the failure to attain the nutritional right of children. Children's right to

---

[5] The reference population used is the international reference population defined by the U.S. national centre for health statistics (NCHS). Since there are no comparable Kenyan/African standards developed so far, the NCHS is applied for nutritional status assessment of children.

freedom from malnutrition and quality care seems to be violated in most parts of the country (UNICEF, 1998). This is evident in feeding trends across the country by age, which indicate that children below two years are mainly fed on porridge that in most cases is very watery and of low nutrient density. According to a study conducted in 2000 by WMS II, the prevalence of malnutrition in Kenya differs across regions, with Coast, Eastern and Western Provinces reporting higher numbers of malnutrition cases, at 41.9%, 40.7 % and 40.6% respectively (CBS, 2001).

3.4.2.2 Measuring Nutritional Status in Adults

In adults, body mass index (BMI), which is a ratio of weight in kilograms divided by height in metres squared, is the main indicator used to assess their nutritional status. BMI correlates with body fat. The relation between fatness and BMI differs with gender and age. For example, women are likely to have a higher percentage of body fat than men for the same BMI. On average, older people may have more body fat than younger adults with the same BMI. Adults with a BMI of between 18.5 and 25 are considered to be normal. All those who fall between 17.0 and 18.49 suffer from mild malnutrition. All those who fall between 16.0 and 16.99 have moderate chronic energy deficiency (CED)/mild malnutrition, while those with fewer than 16.0 have severe CED/severe malnutrition (UNICEF, 1998; WHO, 1999). Weight alone may be used as an indicator of overall health and nutritional status, and women who weigh less than 40 kg are at risk of giving birth to underweight babies and having other delivery-related complications (UNICEF, 1998). In addition, underweight among women may be an indication of general poverty and difficulty in securing food at the household level. On the other hand, over-nutrition among Kenyan women increases with age and older women are more likely to be overweight than younger women. Socio-economic status, nutritional status of women and province of residence are important determinants of over-nutrition among Kenyan women (GoK and UNICEF, 1998).

Height is a measure of past nutritional status and women whose height falls below 150 cm are at a higher risk of delivery complications. Geographical diversity also exists both in prevalence and causes, with high malnutrition concentrated in the arid and semi-arid districts such as Garissa, Samburu and West Pokot. This is mainly associated with the poor marketing outlets, low food production as a result of harsh climatic conditions and poor access to basic services including health (CBS, 2001).

3.5   Agricultural Sector-Related Policy Reforms

Agriculture plays a vital role in the lives of people in Kenya. It constituted over 30% of GDP in 1999, which far exceeded the GDP share of the manufacturing sector (17%). Agriculture is the main source of income, as it employs more than 70% of the population, especially in the rural areas. The main feature of Kenya's agriculture is domination of small scale farmers who account for 75% of total agricultural production and 70% of marketed agricultural output. On average, small scale farmers produce over 70% of maize, 65% of coffee, 50% of tea, 80% of milk, 85% of fish and 70% of beef and related products (FAO, 2001). Production is carried out on small holdings averaging 2-3 hectares mainly for both dairy and beef subsistence and commercial purposes. Large scale farming is practiced in Kenya on farms averaging 50hactares and above and accounts for 30% of marketed agricultural production, covering mainly tea, coffee, horticulture, maize and wheat as well as livestock for commercial purposes (Kinyua, 2004).

Like all other sectors of the economy, the agricultural sector experienced the policy reforms of the 1980s. In the pre-reform period, which was characterized by government controls, production and marketing for most commodities from smallholders was organized under cooperative societies whose main function was procurement of production inputs and marketing of outputs. In addition to the cooperatives, state-run farmers' organizations were also set up to support and market major commodities (Nyangito, 2003). They included; Kenya Tea Development Authority (KTDA) for tea, Kenya Cooperative Creameries (KCC) for milk, National Cereals and Produce Board (NCPB) for cereals, National Irrigation Board (NIB) for irrigated crops and the Horticultural Crops Development Authority (HCDA) for horticultural crops. In addition, there were state boards that regulated the production and marketing of all important commodities. These included the Sisal Board of Kenya, the Tea Board of Kenya, Pyrethrum Board of Kenya, the Kenya Meat Commission, the Cotton Board of Kenya, Kenya Sugar Authority, and the Coffee Board of Kenya (Odhiambo and Nyangito, 2003).

Most of the farmer-owned cooperatives and state-owned boards did not seem to achieve their objectives. For example, the NCPB's objective was to ensure price stabilization and food security in cereals. However, due to high operational costs and managerial problems of the boards, there were inefficiencies in delivery of services to farmers and delayed unreliable payments. This resulted in prices in surplus maize-producing areas falling, while in deficit areas, prices rose above the expected (Nyangito and Nzuma, 2004).

Policy reforms in agriculture in the 1980s focused on removing the government monopoly over the marketing of agricultural commodities, and lifting associated price controls on the importing, pricing, and distribution of farm inputs. In the early periods there was reported to be official resistance to this process, but reforms started to be implemented with greater commitment in 1993 (Odhiambo and Nyangito 2003). According to Nyangito (2003), the agricultural policy reforms that have been implemented have been less successful in stimulating growth in the agricultural sector since complementary policy components and sequencing are often missing in the reform measures. For example, there is no institutional framework for the efficient operation of markets and no system of rights and obligations to knit society together and respond to citizens' needs. Private entrepreneurs lack the managerial skills, financial capacity and physical infrastructure to take over the cooperatives and boards, hence leading to poor response in the agricultural sector to policy reforms. Despite these shortcomings, the reforms have helped to bring about macroeconomic changes.

There has been a declining trend in the efficiency and effectiveness of the Ministry of Agriculture extension services, due to declining budgetary allocations to the sector, lack of clear objectives, failure to identify the role of beneficiaries and poorly defined organizational and institutional structures. This has resulted in a lack of increase in productivity in agriculture due to weaknesses in technology development and transfer by the Kenya Agricultural Research Institute (Otieno, 2001; Nyangito, 2003).

As regards input policy reform, the government has liberalized input markets such as chemical, fertilizers, artificial insemination services and agro-chemicals. This policy reform is faced with a number of problems, which include: quality assurance, high price of inputs making it only possible for a few farmers (mainly large-scale) to afford them, underdeveloped input supply channels and lack of extension services, which have failed to create awareness among most farmers about the right fertilizers, methods of application, application rates and benefits from using certain inputs (Odhiambo, et al., 2004; Nyangito and Nzuma, 2004; Nyangito, 2003).

Agricultural credits provided at subsidized rates through the Agricultural Finance Corporation (AFC) were stopped after market liberalization, and now the lending rates of the AFC have remained lower in comparison to other commercial banks and are more stable. Since the liberalization of interest rates, small-scale farmers have not been able to access credit and the bulk of the credit goes to large-scale farmers. With this trend, small-scale farmers and female farmers are at a distinct disadvantage, since they have neither the land certificate nor evidence of a regular, non-farming source of income that are required to obtain a loan (Mutoro, 1997; Nyangito and Nzuma 2003).

Kenya has faithfully complied with its basic commitments on agriculture in the belief that it will benefit from free trade. The results of implementation, however, have been disappointing. The reform process has neither helped the sector nor improved food security. The annual average growth of Kenyan agricultural value added fell from 3.3% during the 1980s to 1.4% in the 1990s without compensation in terms of growth in the industrial or services sectors. An increase in imported foodstuffs displaced rural farmers from the domestic market. Without an alternative source of income, farmers have found difficulties in purchasing imported foodstuffs, however cheap they may be, hence exacerbating poverty, food insecurity and malnutrition in Kenya (CBS, 2001b; Nyangito, 2003).

3.6   Measures to Achieve Food Security

There has been an increase in Kenya's average poverty level and hence an increase in food insecurity. The number of the absolute poor increased from 10 million in 1994 to 13.4 million in 1997. By the year 2000, the overall poverty situation in Kenya was 56% of the total population estimated at 30 million people. The causes of poverty and food insecurity in Kenya include low agricultural productivity, inadequate access to productive assets (land and capital), inadequate infrastructure, limited well functioning markets, high population pressure on land, inappropriate technologies by farmers, effects of global trade and slow reform process (Kinyua, 2004). The communities in arid and semi arid lands are particularly vulnerable to food insecurity because of recurring natural disasters of drought, livestock diseases, animal and crop pests, and limited access to appropriate technologies, information, credit and financial services (Kinyua, 2004).

The government of Kenya has put various measures in place to achieve food security. The measures include the creation of Kenya's special program for food security (KSPFS) in 2002, and the launching of an Economic Recovery Strategy for Wealth Creation and Employment in June, 2003 (GoK, 2003; Kinyua, 2004). In developing the KSPFS, the poverty reduction strategy paper and the Kenya rural development strategy were used as building blocks. The

KSPFS describes measure to alleviate poverty in the country and the food security program focuses on the more than 15 million absolute poor households living in rural areas as farmers, pastoralists and fisher-folk. The KSPFS is working towards the food security needs by encouraging and supporting community based organizations in their efforts to improve agricultural productivity and other income generating activities. The KSPFS approach is empowering farmers through access to information, new technologies, credit and access to agricultural extension services. Through this program, farmer tours are organized so that farmers can benefit from successful farmers in other parts of the country. By 2004, the program had spread to 40 districts out of the 70 districts in the country. Despite benefiting farmers much faster than extension provision alone, the program faces challenges of lack of adequate resources for capacity building (for both farmers and extension workers) and credit and grants to farmer groups (Kinyua, 2004).

The Economic Recovery Strategy for wealth generation and employment was launched in order to halt and reverse further economic degeneration and poverty. In order to attain the goals stated in the Economic Recovery Strategy, the Ministry of Agriculture, livestock and Fisheries developed the strategy for Rehabilitation of Agriculture 2004 – 2014 that defines ways and means of economic recovery through improved agricultural growth. The strategy recognizes the need to mobilize resources to stimulate agricultural growth and need for coordinated resource utilization. The key player in implementing this strategy is the private sector with the government playing a facilitative role (GoK, 2003).

In order to assess the food situation in the country, the government in collaboration with the World Food Program and other partners to develop the Kenya food security information steering group (KFSSG). The scope of this system includes the early warning and comprehensive food security status monitoring and assessment. The KFSSG include representatives from over 50 different organizations (GoK departments, UN agencies, donors and NGOs). Membership to KFSSG is restricted to organizations which have demonstrated a clear commitment to collaborative approach and which possess technical, policy or administrative capability in the area of food security and drought management. The KFSSG has various sector working subgroups. The subgroups include food aid, health and nutrition, water and sanitation, agriculture and livestock, and education subgroup (Wheeler, 2003). With strong support from the WFP and the GoK, the KFSSG has been successful in its operations leading to extension of its coordiantaion to food aid targeting, logistics and distributions at all levels in areas covered by WFP emergency operations (EMOP). By 2001,

22 districts in the country (about 86% of the land area in Kenya) was covered by the emergency operations and KFSSG. The government of Kenya provides a large portion of the maize for food distribution by the WFP emergency operation. In 2001, the government of Kenya implemented the Community Based Targeting Distribution System (CBTD) to make food aid distribution more effective (Wheeler, 2003).

The major traded food crops in Kenya are maize, wheat and rice, while the non-traded food crops comprise sorghum and millet, pulses (beans and peas) and roots and tubers (cassava, sweet potatoes, Irish potatoes and yams). Maize is the staple food in Kenya and food consumption patterns reveal an increasing consumption of this cereal in comparison to other cereals like rice and wheat (FAO, 2002). However, over the years maize output has not been steady. For example, in the 2004 production season, maize yields dropped by 25% below normal, resulting to a national deficit. As a result, maize prices were 50 – 70% higher on average in most markets in arid and semi arid districts (KARI, 2005; Odhiambo, et al., 2004).Before liberalization, the National Cereals and Produce Board (NCPB) held a monopoly to market all cereals and to import whenever there were deficits or export whenever there were surpluses. It also safeguarded against food insecurity by maintaining strategic reserves of foodstuffs, particularly maize, which would be released to the market at times of grain shortages. With liberalization, however, the NCPB's monopoly on trade in food commodities has been dismantled and the board is involved in the market as a buyer and seller of last resort on a commercial basis, although it still maintains the function of keeping food reserves for the nation (Odhiambo, et al., 2004).

4 THEORY, MODELS AND RESEARCH METHODS

There are a number of theoretical models that try to explain the theory of intra-household resource allocation. In some models, the household is posited to act as a single decision-maker (the 'unitary' model) and such models are silent on the issue of intra-household distribution. The unitary approach is sometimes referred to as the 'common preferences' model, the 'altruism' model or the 'benevolent dictator' model. The unitary model assumes that the household has a single set of preferences and on this basis combines time and goods purchased for its well-being or consumption. It also assumes that there is a household head who has the final say as regards how goods and time should be utilized within the household (Haddad et al., 1997; Thomas, 1997). This model explains differences in well-being or consumption within the household. Nonetheless, some recent studies (notably, Thomas, 1997; Pena and Bouis, 1997) disagree with it, especially when it comes to decision-making in low-income households in developing and developed countries. Under conditions of greater poverty, pooling is even less common. In some cases, spouses are often kept ignorant of the amount the other earns (Quisumbing, et al., 2004).

The alternative to the unitary model is the bargaining model, which is broadly referred to as the 'collective' model. This model focuses on the individuality of household members and assumes that allocations result in Pareto-efficient outcomes, where it would not be possible to increase the welfare of one individual without reducing that of another (Haddad et al., 1997). The collective model of the household does not assume that spouses share the same preferences and is especially relevant for this study. In the collective model, it is assumed that husbands and wives maintain 'separate purses' and do not pool their resources. In this study, we test the unitary model versus the collective model by examining whether household welfare and food security at the study site are sensitive to differences in the distribution of income and human capital between men and women. This is examined in the context of the impact of paternal and maternal incomes, and schooling on the nutrition status of children, as well as making comparisons in household welfare and food security in male and female headed households.

In this chapter, the conceptual framework is presented. This is followed by a description of the analytical framework, survey design and methods used for data collection.

4.1   Conceptual Framework

In order to understand the interaction between the farm and household, a combination of the farming systems and nutrition approach are used in the conceptual framework. This is done in order to elaborate the relationships between the various components linking resource allocation, farm activities and nutrition.

The idea that the household represents a locus of economic activity dates back at least to Chaynov's study of Russian peasants, first published in 1926, although the economics of the farm and household as independent systems but with interactions between them was fully brought into the mainstream by Gary Becker in the mid-1960s (Ruthenberg, 1980; Haddad et al., 1997; Becker, 1996). The farm and household are closely linked with regard to operations and objectives. The most important is the provision of food for the household, together with goods for personal consumption like raw materials. Other important aims of the farm are safeguarding the future by the accumulation of capital in the form of animals or plantations and increasing the social status of the household by the accumulation of wealth or by special technical, social and economic achievements. The household, on the other hand, is a distinct labour-supplying unit to the farm, and the amounts and kinds of labour provided vary with the family cycle (Ruthenberg, 1980; Heidhues, 1989). For farmers to rationally organize their systems, given their objectives, they require knowledge, capital, and labour.

All land used wholly or partly for agricultural purposes, including grazing land other than communal land, is considered as belonging to a farm unit. The boundaries of the farm unit with its economic environment are defined by the purchase or procurement of inputs and sales of inputs and the sale or disposal of outputs. The farm receives labour from the household and the labour market. It purchases production inputs from the markets for investments. It supplies outputs to the farm household and the markets, and the household may supply capital to the farm and/or to the other capital market.

The farming systems approach, which looks at the farm household in the wider context of its environment, is used in the analysis. Ruthenberg (1980) defines a farming system as a unit with several activities that are closely related to each other by the common use of farm's labour, land, capital, by risk distribution and by the joint use of the farmer's management capacity. Wattenbach and Friedrich (2001 as cited by Luibrand, 2002) go further to expand on the definition of a farming system as 'a natural resource management unit operated by a farm household, and includes the entire range of economic activities of the family members (on-farm, off-farm agricultural as well as off-farm non-agricultural activities) to ensure their physical survival and their social and economic well-being'.

Ruthenberg (1980) and Doppler (1994) consider the concept of the farming system important for understanding the interaction between farm and household as open systems with constraints and potentials, and having complex interactions with external components that are important for the survival of the system. The internal factors related to a farming system concern resource endowment – family labour, capital generated internally by household members, know-how. The boundaries between the farm unit and its environment are defined by the purchase or procurement of inputs and the sale or disposal of outputs. The farm receives labour from the household and the labour market. It purchases production inputs and obtains capital from the markets for investments. It supplies output to the household and the markets, and the household may supply capital to the farm and/or to the capital market. Within the household, women and men have different roles to play as far as farm, off-farm and household production activities are concerned. Access and control over resource is also determined at the household level, and how resources are distributed between men and women may affect the overall productivity of the farm, off farm as well as household production activities. Figure 4.1 and Figure 4.2 show the linkages and interrelationships between various internal and external factors related to the farming system.

The external factors affecting a farming system include labour market, extension services, ecological and socio-cultural environment, and financial market. The natural conditions (climate, soil, diseases) constrain the ecological environment. The state of knowledge of household members and information about agricultural techniques (innovations) determines the possible physical production functions of the various farm activities. The farmer's choice of the ecologically feasible activities and possible techniques depends on the institutional environment (land tenure, farm size, labour laws, credit and extension services). The input combination, output mix, and input intensity in any activity on the farm depend on the economic environment, which influences the system through the prices of inputs and outputs. The farm household's demand for food, fibre, fuel and other needs that the farm can meet depends on the culture and the socio-political state of the society concerned (Ruthenberg, 1980; Heidhues, 1989). The structure of a farm system at any time thus depends on the technical, economic, social, cultural and political influences that impinge on the farmer, his household members, and his hired workers.

Figure 4.1: Internal relationships within the family-farm unit

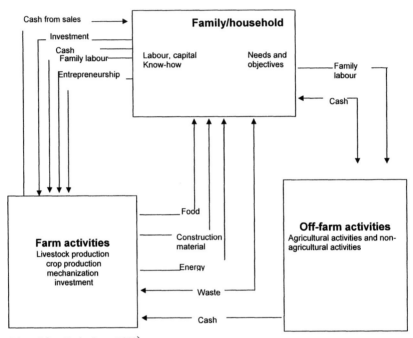

Adapted from Ruthenberg (1980)

Figure 4.2: External relationships to the farming systems

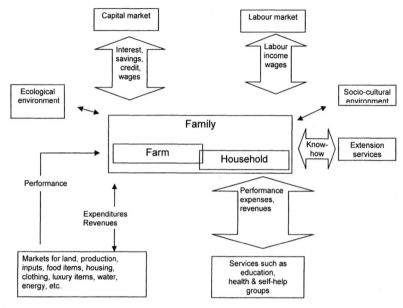

Source: Doppler (1994)

The unit of analysis in this study is the farm household, and the analysis involves various features of farm productivity. Household incomes are calculated to determine the level of farm income of the households under investigation. Household financial capital analysis also includes external capital from borrowing (loans/credit), income received as gifts or remittances. Calculation of the net family income is carried out by deducting variable costs from farm revenues. This represents the economic performance of the farm/the gross margin.

Farm revenues consist of revenues from crop cultivation and livestock, and the revenue from renting out draught animals and land. Farm expenses consist of the variable costs for inputs, hired labour, rent for land and work animals, and expenditures on maintenance and repair of equipment. Further analysis focuses on labour input by men and women, access to means of production in male and female-headed households, participation in decision-making and control over the outcome of the productive process. In Kenya, a patriarchal family system is practiced. In male-headed households, both men and women provide the labour, but men control the decision-making over production activities. In female-headed households, decision-making is carried out by the women or, in some instances, an older male member of the family. Access to adequate food, either from the farm or the market, nutrition knowledge and income are known to have an impact on the food consumption behaviour of household members, thus affecting their nutrition status. In this study, we focus on the basic and underlying causes of malnutrition that manifest themselves at household level.

Link between Agriculture, Nutrition and Household Resource Allocation

Agriculture and nutrition are linked in a number of ways. They are linked, for example, through changes in and access to income, food prices and variability, labour allocation, particularly of care-givers, expenditure on energy and nutrients, nutrient composition of food and effects of the health and sanitation environment at the household and community levels, which may increase or reduce morbidity due to exposure to diseases, contaminants and chemicals. The choice of agricultural technology may have an impact on the community health and sanitation environment. When agricultural products are sold in the market place, the income earned may be used to purchase goods and services that contribute to nutritional changes. Similarly, when those products are consumed directly by members of the producing household, their dietary intake is affected. Morbidity is an important determinant of appetite and how well nutrients are absorbed by the body. Morbidity is affected by the health and sanitation conditions within the household, and environment.

The household has a fixed amount of time and capital that it must decide to allocate among various income-generating activities, given exogenous prices for consumer goods and production inputs and outputs. Depending on how resources are allocated to on-farm and off-farm production activities, a certain amount of income is generated that can be spent on various consumption items. An increase in household income may lead to higher food expenditures and the extra expenditure on food at household level may mean increased nutrients for individual household members, depending on the food distribution within the household. Allocation of resources within the household also depends on who has the control of various resources. A gender-sensitive approach to access and control of resources within the household strengthens the links between agriculture and nutrition. This approach is the main focus of this study. Figure 4.3 shows the link between household resource allocation, agriculture and nutrition in a conceptual framework of the study.

Figure 4.3: Conceptual Framework

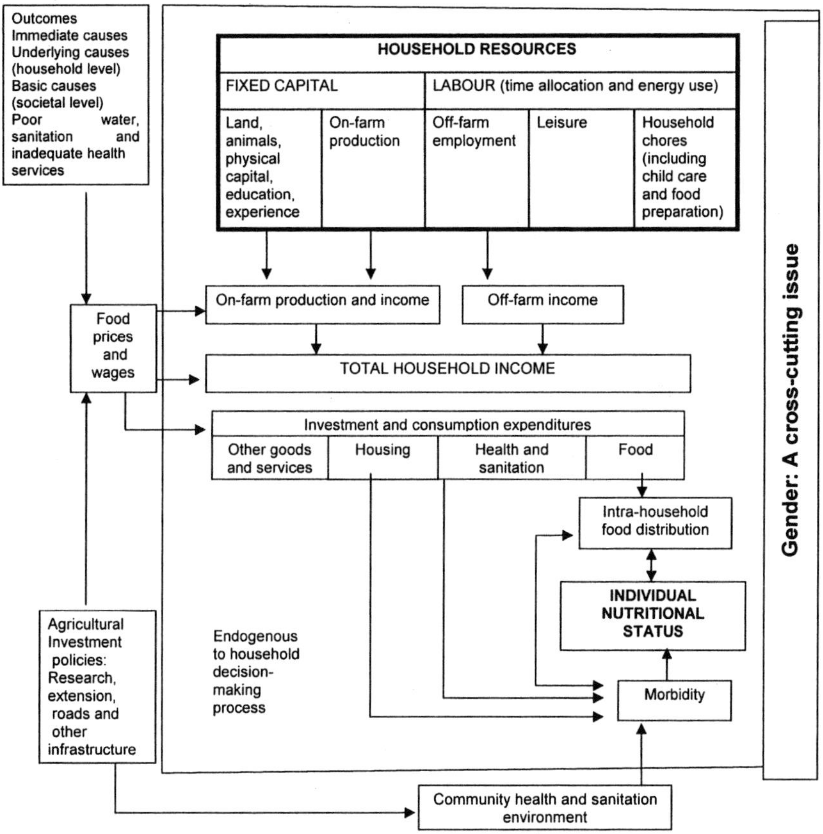

Outcomes Immediate causes Underlying causes (household level) Basic causes (societal level) Poor water, sanitation and inadequate health services	**HOUSEHOLD RESOURCES**				
	FIXED CAPITAL		LABOUR (time allocation and energy use)		
	Land, animals, physical capital, education, experience	On-farm production	Off-farm employment	Leisure	Household chores (including child care and food preparation)

On-farm production and income   →   Off-farm income

Food prices and wages

TOTAL HOUSEHOLD INCOME

Investment and consumption expenditures

Other goods and services	Housing	Health and sanitation	Food

Intra-household food distribution

INDIVIDUAL NUTRITIONAL STATUS

Agricultural Investment policies: Research, extension, roads and other infrastructure

Endogenous to household decision-making process

Morbidity

Gender: A cross-cutting issue

Community health and sanitation environment

4.2   Analytical Framework

In this section the different methods used in the analysis are presented. The analysis focuses on resource use on the farm and off-farm activities, as well as effect of the resources on household socio-economic welfare and food security as depicted in the conceptual framework in section 4.1 of this study.

4.2.1 Land as a Production Resource

Land is one of the main production resources in Kenya, as discussed in Chapter 3. Using data on access to and control over land by male and female members of the household, and on crop and livestock production activities, the analysis examined the following: gender differences in land holdings and use; labour use by gender in crop and animal production; farm revenue and farm expenditure; and comparison of gross income per hectare of land. To ascertain the determinants of crop productivity, a multiple regression was undertaken. Technical efficiency analysis was carried out to determine any existing production inefficiencies in farms managed by female and male farmers and factors contributing to the inefficiencies.

4.2.1.1 Multiple Regression Model

The question in this section is whether there are any systematic differences in crop productivity between female-headed households (FHH) and male-headed households (MHH). Differences in crop productivity between the two household groups may be caused by two different reasons. First, they might be caused by gender differences in resource endowment. Secondly, they may be caused by access to technology by gender, or by the way female and male farmers use different techniques to transform their inputs into output.

The main productive resources in a farming system, as mentioned in the conceptual framework, are land, human capital (education, labour) and financial capital (income, access to credit). The specific model is estimated as follows:

$$lnY = \alpha + \beta_g D_g + \beta_r D_r + \beta_e D_e + \beta_c D_c \sum \beta_1 lnx_1 + \beta_2 lnx_2 + \beta_3 lnx_3 + \beta_4 lnx_4 + \beta_5 lnx_5 + u$$

$$(4.1)$$

where

ln is the natural logarithm

β and α are coefficients to be estimated,

Y is the dependent variable – total yield of crop (maize)

x_1 is area of land cultivated

x_2 is labour input

x_3 is education measured in terms of years of schooling

x_4 is household non farm income

X_5 is age of household head

D_g is a dummy variable for gender of household head
D_r is the dummy variable for region
D_c access to credit dummy (1= access to credit, 0, otherwise
D_e access to extension services dummy (1=access to extension services, 0= otherwise
u is the error term to capture random variations

The variables included in the model are further defined as follows: for the regression analysis for farm productivity, land productivity is the dependant variable and is defined as the total value per hectare cultivated of all crops grown in the 2002/2003 cropping season, and output from livestock. For the regression analysis for determinants of maize production, the yields of maize was used as the dependent variable. In this study, the flow of financial capital from both farm and off-farm activities was considered as it affects farmers' possibilities to acquire inputs. Off-farm activities in the study area include trading with livestock, vegetables and fruits, charcoal and other commodities, and monthly remittances received as salaries for those in formal jobs. Financial capital is expected to have an effect on production since it can be used to purchase farm inputs and pay for technology used on the farm.

The human capital variables included in the model are education, time (measured in terms of labour input) and age. Education of the household head is measured in total years of schooling. The aim of including this variable is to see the impact of the household head's education on productivity, since education enables one to process information relating to use of inputs and different farm technologies and may also improve the allocative efficiency of resources within the household (Panin and Brünner, 2000). Labour input is a measure of total adult person-hours during the cropping season, and is a sum of family labour and hired labour. Hired labour composed of male and female adults, therefore the total number of labourers hired, was added to that of household labour. Labour provided by children is equivalent to 0.3 labour provided by an adult man (Fadani, 1999). The total availability of household labour in person equivalent is calculated as follows:

$$PE = M + W + 0.3 * C$$

with PE = total available household person equivalent
M = total number of adult men living permanently in the household
W = total number of adult women living in the household
C = total number of children living in the household

The age of the household head is used as a proxy to measure farming experience. Although there is an assumption that older farmers have more experience than younger farmers and hence can influence productivity positively, it is also possible that age can influence productivity negatively, since older farmers may be lacking quality education.

The gender dummy variable is used with the assumption that crop output for male and female heads of households are different by α_0 therefore a statistical test for difference in yield between MHH and FHH due to difference in resource endowment and use establishes whether α_0 is statistically different from zero on the basis of a t - test.

Tests were done to determine whether variables $x_{1\ldots5}$ are correlated. These included looking at the variance inflation factor (VIF) or tolerance of variables (Wooldridge, 2002a). If the variables are collinear, the VIF value would be high and so these variables would not be included in the regression. Another way that was used to establish whether variables are correlated is by looking at the pair-wise relationships between variables. If r values are greater than 0.80, the variables are strongly interrelated and therefore should not be included in the regression analysis.

4.2.1.2 Technical Efficiency

The main objective of this section is to analyse determinants of inefficiency for farms managed by male and female farmers. The level of technical efficiency of a particular firm is characterized by the relationship between observed production and some ideal or potential production (Greene, 1993). The measurement of firm-specific technical efficiency is based upon deviations of observed output from the best production or efficient production frontier. If a firm's actual production lies on the frontier, it is perfectly efficient. If it lies below the frontier then it is technically inefficient, with the ratio of the actual to potential production defining the level of efficiency of the individual firm (Harrero and Pascoe, 2002).

There are three main approaches used to measure technical efficiency and these are categorized according to their three distinctive techniques: parametric and non-parametric methods, and productivity indices, based on growth accounting and index theory analysis principles (Coelli et al., 1995). Stochastic Frontier Analysis (SFA) and data envelopment analysis (DEA) are the most commonly used methods. Both methods estimate the efficient frontier and calculate the firm's technical efficiency relative to it. Stochastic approaches incorporate a measure of random error, and require that a functional form be specified for the frontier production function. Here, the output of the firm is a function of a set of inputs, inefficiency and random error. An often-quoted disadvantage of this technique, however, is that it imposes an explicit functional form and distribution assumption on the data. The data envelopment analysis (DEA) approach uses a linear programming technique to construct a piece-wise frontier that encompasses the observations of all firms. The frontier shows the best performance observed among the firms and is considered as the efficient frontier. An advantage of the DEA method is that multiple inputs and outputs can be considered simultaneously, an inputs and outputs can be quantified using different units of measurements. DEA does not impose any assumptions about the functional form, and hence it is less prone to mis-specification. Furthermore, DEA is a non-parametric approach, so it does not take into account random error. Hence, it is not subsequently subject to the problems of assuming an underlying distribution about the error term. However, the statistical estimates of DEA may be biased if the production process is largely characterized by stochastic elements (Harrero and Pascoe, 2002).

Internal and external factors affect the production efficiency of a farm. Internal factors that determine production efficiency include a farmer's education level, age and experience. These individual characteristics are important since they influence a farmer's ability to use and manage the available resources. External factors that affect production include the physical (soil and weather conditions) and institutional environment that affects farmers' incentives for production. Institutional environment includes access to markets, financial institutions for agricultural credit and access to agricultural extension services. Other determinants include various farm characteristics such as use of hired and rented factors, human capital characteristics, size of farm, and input use. Efficiency variations between farms can be explained by the farm location and environmental characteristics. Farm location is important since farms may operate under different climatic or altitude conditions, and have different soil quality (Morrison, 2000). Physical infrastructure can also differ regionally. The effect of the farmer's age on efficiency is considered as a proxy for farming experience, and many studies have shown a positive relationship between technical efficiency and farming experience, while others have shown negative effects.

Using Stochastic Frontier Analysis (SFA)

The Cobb-Douglas stochastic frontier model is used in this study to estimate production frontiers of male and female farmers. The use of this approach is justified, since the sample size is big enough and therefore the problem of normality of data does not arise. The SFA is used instead of the DEA, since SFA takes into consideration the random term representing noise in the data, making the estimates more reliable. The SFA has the advantage that it takes care of inefficiency effects. This supports the rational assumption that not all units included in the analysis produce under the same technological conditions (Coelli et al., 1998; Kumbhaker and Lovell, 2000).

SFA analysis can be estimated using maximum likelihood estimation (MLE), corrected original least square (COLS) and two-step Newton-Ralph procedures. Although the three procedures produce consistent estimates, the MLE has been widely used to estimate frontier functions since it is asymptotically more efficient than the COLS estimator. Olson, Schmidt and Waldman (1980) indicate that both the COLS and the MLE estimators have no significant differences in terms of the efficiencies. Coelli (1995), however, found that the MLE estimator outperforms the COLS estimator when the contribution of the inefficiency error to the total error term is large.

In agriculture where farms produce under different conditions, technical efficiency analysis is of interest since technical efficiency scores can be used to characterize the status of performance among different individual farms. In many developing countries, many farmers produce at low levels of efficiency (Battesse and Coelli, 1988). Given the difference in efficiency among farms, the issue is why some producers can achieve high efficiency while others are technically inefficient. Variations in technical efficiency may arise from managerial skills and farm characteristics, as already discussed above.

To measure efficiency, the actual attained value of the farm is compared with a value that is possible to attain at the frontier. Variables that are determinants for efficiency/inefficiency can be determined and recommendations as to how to maximize efficiency can be made (Coelli, 1995).

Figure 4.4: Individual farm observation of technical efficiency

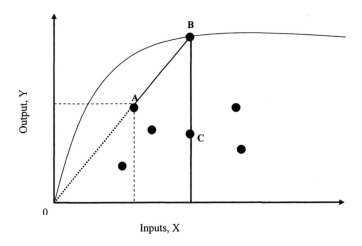

Farms that operate at the frontier production function are classified as being 100% efficient. Farmers who do not produce on the frontier have efficiency rating of less than 100% or an efficiency index of less than one.

Figure 4.4 shows an output-oriented production possibility frontier for a given set of inputs. If the inputs employed by a farm were used efficiently, the output of the firm, producing at point A, can be expanded radially to point B. Hence, the output-oriented measure of technical efficiency (TE0 (y,x) can be given by OA/OB. This is only equivalent to the input-oriented measure of technical efficiency under conditions of constant returns to scale. While point B is technically efficient, in the sense that it lies on the production frontier, farms that produce at points A and C are technically inefficient. Less output is achieved at point A and point C than is achieved at point B, but the same amount of inputs is used in both cases (Kumbhaker and Lovell, 2000).

The Cobb-Douglas model can be specified as follows:

$$lnY_1 = \beta_0 + \sum_{j=1}^{k} \beta_j lnx_{ji} + V_i - u_i \qquad (4.2)$$

where
ln is the natural logarithm
y_i is the observed output quantity of the i-th farm;
β_0 is the production function;
β_j is a vector of parameters to be estimated;
V_i is an error term, independent and identically distributed;
x_{ji} are inputs
U_i is a non-negative random term, accounting for inefficiency, truncated to zero to ensure non-negativeness.

The important component of the stochastic frontier production model is the decomposition of the error term ε into two independent components. The error term is composed of two elements: the traditional error term v_i and the non-random variable u_i which is associated with technical inefficiency (Lovell et al., 1977).

$$ε = v_i - u_i$$

The component v_i is assumed to be normal distributed with zero mean. The component u_i is a one-sided component and is non-positive for the production functions and is derived from a normal distribution. This component is independent of v_i. The component u_i of the disturbance represents the shortfall in actual output from its maximum possible value given by the stochastic frontier. U_i is equal to zero for any production unit whose output lies on the frontier and u_i is greater than zero for any output lying below the frontier.

4.2.2 Human Capital

In this study, the analysis concentrates on gender differences in schooling and economic returns to education by gender in a rural setting. It is argued that there are direct and indirect economic costs as well as social costs of gender discrimination in access to education. The direct financial costs can be measured in terms of the opportunity cost of forgone wage earnings and forgone benefits to the government in terms of unpaid taxes, when an individual does not attain a certain level of education (Manda et al., 2002). The non-monetary benefits of education, such as improved nutrition status and health of children, reduced birth rates among females, and improved sanitation are difficult to quantify in economic terms. Nevertheless, the correlation between education and the nutrition status of family members is discussed in the section on food and nutrition security of this study. In this section, we estimate private returns to education in monetary terms and therefore do not capture possible non-monetary benefits of education. Correlations between education, child morbidity and fertility rate are discussed separately in this work

4.2.2.1 Returns to schooling

Education of household members is an important factor in a farming system, since individuals' level of education has an influence on their decision-making power regarding household's resource allocation and efficiency of resource use, thus affecting productivity on the farm, off-farm activities and within the household. In addition, educated individuals are assumed to be more innovative. In order to estimate returns to schooling, earnings in the agricultural sector and in non-farm jobs are used. Non-farm employment is defined as salaried employment, which includes employment in public/government or private sector and any informal self-employment such as carpentry, running a shop, sewing and driving. Data collected at household level on employment status, household size, household incomes and data on individual characteristics (education, age, work experience) are useful in the estimation.

A worker's specific human capital is approximated by level of education and years of experience. A worker's experience is defined as age minus six years[6] and the number of years of schooling. Some individuals spent more years at one level of education due to failing examinations/repeating classes, so the number of years spent in school does not have an impact on their wages. At the same time, their productivity may not be enhanced with each year spent in school. For this reason, levels of education completed are considered. The levels of education are used in the analysis as dummies and are described below. Mincer (1974 as cited by Manda et al., 2002) indicates that experience and on-job training are particularly important in determining the wage. Individual

---

[6] The average age for a child to start primary school education in Kenya is 6.

experience is therefore included in the equation. Other variables used in the analysis are defined as follows:

Variable	Definition
Dependent variable	Yearly wages
Primary education dummy	1 if a person joined but did not complete primary education, 0 otherwise
Secondary education dummy	1 if the person joined but did not complete secondary education, 0 otherwise
College education dummy	1 if a person completed college education, 0 otherwise
University education dummy	1 if a person has university education, 0 otherwise
Potential experience[7]	Number of years the person has been working
Potential experience squared	Square of the number of years a person has been working
Kapenguria	1 if a person lives in Kapenguria, 0 otherwise
Male	1 if a person is male, 0 otherwise

4.2.2.2   Estimation of Wage Earnings Function

Mincer's theory of investment in human capital examines the relationship between schooling and earnings. In estimating the determinants of earnings, the equation by Mincer (1974) and Heckman (1979) are adapted as follows:

---

[7] Due to the quadratic nature of experience, experience squared is included in the equation. There may be an increase in wages with increasing experience up to a certain age. After this, there is no increase in wages with an increasing number of years of experience.

$$W_i = \alpha + \sum \beta_1 S_{ik} + \beta_2 A_i + \beta_2 A_i^2 + \beta_3 Z_i + \beta_4 G_i + u_i \qquad (4.3)$$

Where: the dependant variable W_i is the yearly earnings for worker i; $i=$ 1.....N individuals; S_k is a dummy variable for being educated at least up to level k; A represents experience variables; Z = a dummy variable for region; G = dummy variable for gender of individual; α, $\beta_{1....5}$ are parameters to be estimated and u is an error term. It is assumed that non-farm incomes are affected solely by individuals' characteristics because these are the attributes that are relevant in the labour market. Equation (4.3) gives us an estimate of the rate of return to schooling for individuals in wage employment and self employment (non-farm employment).

In order to estimate the rate of returns to schooling for self-employment in agricultural (farm) activities, it is presumed that the individuals' decision to work in the farm sector is affected not only by individual characteristics but also by the characteristics of other household members. Thus, the number of working members in the household aged 15 to 65, regardless of the type of job and household size is included. A vector H, containing the household characteristics is introduced. It is expected that the returns to schooling for those in farm employment and non-farm activities will differ due to personal and household characteristics (average education of household members, age, and dependency ratio).

$$W_i = \alpha + \sum \beta_1 S_{ik} + \beta_2 A_i + \beta_3 A_i^2 + \beta_4 Z_i + \beta_5 G_i + \beta_6 H_i + u_i \qquad (4.4)$$

Equations (4.3) and (4.4) give estimates of the rate of return to schooling in different sectors in a rural economy: non-farm employment, and on-farm employment. From economic theory it is known that in rural areas markets might be missing or imperfect (Heidhues, 1995), and hence returns to schooling and other personal characteristics cannot be expected to reflect the individuals' real productivity (Appleton et al., 1999).

Like other conventional studies that measure the private rate of return to schooling, the estimates measure the benefits of education in the form of higher wages relative to the combined opportunity and direct costs of acquiring education. Private rates of return to education include private benefits and costs, and the social rate of return to education includes the direct costs of education to the government as well as benefits in terms of higher taxes.

The estimated equations (4.3 and 4.4) do not take care of the fact that there exists a correlation between education and unobservables such as school quality, pre-existing worker ability, health and family background, which may bias estimates of β. This study cannot fully address the biases caused by unobservable variables, since measures of these variables (e.g. family background, school quality) were not included in the data base. Second, wage benefits used in the equation do not capture non-monetary benefits of education. Although individuals may have more years of schooling, the non-monetary impact of schooling of these individuals is not accounted for; they therefore have a lower rate of return to education than in reality.

The decision to work or not to work by some individuals in the sample regardless of their education level may bias the regression results. For example, women may choose not to work for different reasons. It is likely that these women may report low wages or no wages at all. Thus, it is likely that wages of the individuals in the population who choose not to participate in non-farm employment despite their high level of education would be underestimated. To solve this problem, the two-stage Heckman selection model was used. The Heckman selection model helps to avoid the sample bias caused by a large number of non-participants in non-farm employment despite having higher levels of education that would allow them to be employed by the government or other non/farm employers the formal sector. The Heckman selection model is a two-step estimation model. In the first stage of estimation, a probit function is estimated in which the dependent variable is the probability that the individual participates in non-farm employment (Batzlen, 2000; Bierens, 2002; Quisumbing et al., 2004). The dependent variable takes the value of 1 if the individual is a participant in non-farm activities, and 0 if not. The independent variables in the probit estimation include the individual characteristics. This regression is used to estimate the inverse Mills' ratio (estimated expected error), which is then used as an explanatory variable in the second regression.

$$\lambda = \frac{\phi(X)}{1 - \Phi(X)}$$

where λ denotes the inverse Mills' ratio, and ϕ and Φ, respectively, are the density and distribution functions for a standard normal variable (Heckman, 1979 as cited by Smit, 2001). In the second stage, the inverse Mills' ratio (IMR) is included in the initial OLS wage estimation equation (equation 4.3) as an extra explanatory variable, removing the part of the error term, U, that was initially in equation 4.3. By using the inverse Mills ratio, the sample selection bias is corrected and the wage estimation equation can therefore be given as:

$$W_i = \alpha + \sum \beta_1 S_{ik} + \beta_2 A_i + \beta_2 A_i^2 + \beta_3 Z_i + \beta_4 G_i + \lambda \qquad (4.5)$$

where λ is the inverse Mills' ratio or estimated expected error.

4.2.3 Financial Capital

Analysis in this section focuses on household income generation and diversification, access to financial institutions, access to credit and savings behaviour of households in the study area. Empirical evidence shows that access to financial markets can improve households' food security, when clientele with access to financial services make use of them. Credit enables the poor to tap finances beyond their own resources and take advantage of profitable investment opportunities (Zeller, et al., 1997). At the same time, microfinance programmes that reach out to poor women are an effective tool in improving women's status and overall household welfare (Schrieder, 1996; Zeller and Sharma, 2001).

Analysis of access to credit and savings behaviour of household members was carried out using descriptive statistics. Differences in savings behaviour by male and female household heads and by region are estimated using the T-test. In-depth analysis focuses on income diversification, since most of the households in the study area diversify their incomes as a risk-minimizing strategy and also as a way to raise their household incomes, and hence cope better with food insecurity, which is a challenge in the region.

4.2.4 Household Food and Nutrition Security

To determine food and nutrition security within the household, a combination of methods was used. These methods compliment each other, and information that was not captured by one tool was captured by the other. The tools are dietary assessment (dietary diversity and 24 hour food recall) and indices of household coping strategies. According to Hoddinott (1999), indices of household coping strategies directly capture notions of adequacy and vulnerability of households to food insecurity.

4.2.4.1   Indices of Household Coping Strategies

Household coping strategies during food scarcity are used to determine the household food security level. From the different strategies used by the household to cope when food is scarce in the household, a food security index is computed, which is then taken as a measure of the household food security level. This value is based on questions answered by respondents on the different coping strategies (see box) a household adopts during periods of food insecurity. The six strategies have weights that reflect the frequency of use by the household of each of the strategies. 'Often' is counted as four; 'from time to time' is counted as three; 'rarely' is counted as two; and 'never' is counted as one. A weighted sum of all the coping strategies used by households is carried out. The discrete score obtained from the summation is the cumulative food security index or score. The higher the sum, the more food-insecure the household is.

Using these data, the population is divided into four distinct categories of food security based on the experiences and behaviour patterns that characterize the severity of each strategy used by the household (Hoddinnot, 1999, Coates, 2003; Basiotis, 1992; Kennedy, 2004). The four categories are:

1. Food secure: little or no evidence of food insecurity
2. Food insecure without hunger: food insecurity is shown by households' concern about and adjustments to food management.
3. Food insecure with moderate hunger: food intake for adults is reduced, and adults are experiencing hunger owing to resource constraints.
4. Food insecure with severe hunger: households with children reduce the children's food intake to an extent that implies that the children experience hunger as a result of inadequate resources within the household, while adults show evidence of more severe hunger (e.g. going entire days with no food).

These four categories reflect increasing levels of severity as households move from food security to food insecurity and ultimately to severe hunger. The categorization reflects a continuum of progressively more severe levels of food insecurity from adjustments in the food budget to reduced food intake in adults to the final level of reduced food intake in children. Mostly, children are protected until the severe later stages of food insecurity within the household. This progression suggests a 'managed process' through successive stages of severity that is consistent with other earlier research (Basiotis, 1992; Radimer et al., 1992; Radimer et. al., 1990; Wehler, Scott and Anderson, 1992). The household food security index is used for further analysis.

Household coping Strategies during food scarcity (Adapted from Hoddinnott (1999)

The most knowledgeable woman in the household regarding food preparation and distribution within the household is asked a series of questions of the following form

Has the household consumed less preferred foods? (Circle the best response.)
1. Never 2. Rarely (once) 3. From time to time (2 or 3 times) 4. Often (5 or more times)

2. Have you reduced the quantity of food served to men in this household?
1. Never 2. Rarely (once) 3. From time to time (2 or 3 times) 4. Often (5 or more times)

3. Have you reduced your own consumption of food?
1. Never 2. Rarely (once) 3. From time to time (2 or 3 times) 4. Often (5 or more times)

4. Have you reduced the quantity of food served to children in this household in the last seven days?
1. Never 2. Rarely (once) 3. From time to time (2 or 3 times) 4. Often (5 or more times)

5. Have members of this household skipped meals in the last seven days?
1. Never 2. Rarely (once) 3. From time to time (2 or 3 times) 4. Often (5 or more times)

6. Have members of this household skipped meals for a whole day?
1. Never 2. Rarely (once) 3. From time to time (2 or 3 times) 4. Often (5 or more times)

4.2.4.2   Dietary Assessment

A combination of dietary diversity, the 24 hour food recall, and weighing of foods consumed were used. The 24 hour food recall and weighing food is a standard assessment technique. The food was weighed and recorded immediately before eating and again any leftovers were weight. Due to the probable accuracy, this method is the best for measuring food security. However, it was not possible to obtain food data from all households. For this reason, the other methods have been used. For children, a 24 hour recall combined with weighing of foods was used to collect information from all household with children under five years. Using the Nutri-survey software, amount of food consumed was transformed into specific nutrients and comparisons made with the recommended daily dietary intake.

Dietary diversity defined as the number of foods consumed over a given period of time, provides useful information on household food security. Consumption of a more diverse diet has positive nutritional outcomes. For example, it contributes to improved acquisition of micronutrients, improved haemoglobin concentrations, improved birth weight and reduced risk of death from cardiovascular disease and cancer (Hoddinott and Yohannes, 2002).

To analyse data on dietary diversity, the number of foods consumed are grouped into three categories depending on the nutrients in the food. The total number of different foods consumed from each category is added up, and the higher the number, the more diverse the household diet is.

4.2.4.3   Anthropometric Analysis

Anthropometry is a science or a technique that uses human body measurements to draw conclusions about the nutritional status of individuals and populations. The indicators utilized in the nutritional survey are based on measurement of height and weight for women and children. The child anthropometrics are presented as indices of height for age (stunting), weight for height (wasting), weight for age (underweight) (Cogill, 2003). The three anthropometric measures are generally used to explain the long-term and short-term nutrition situation of children between the age of 6 and 59 months. The measurements are compared with a standard reference population as defined by the World Health Organization (WHO).

The height for age index measures the degree of stunting (the failure to grow adequately in height in relation to age). This index is a cumulative growth deficit associated with chronic inadequate food intake, ill health, incorrect feeding practices and low socio-economic status. Children falling below the cut off point of minus two standard deviations (-2SD) from the median or sometimes 80% weight/height of the reference population[8] are classified as

---

[8] The reference population used is the international reference population defined by the U.S. National Centre for Health Statistics (NCHS). Since no comparable Kenyan/African standards have been developed so far, the NCHS is applied for the nutritional status assessment of children.

stunted. The height for age index reflects skeletal growth, and past or chronic malnutrition (UNICEF, 1998; Cogill, 2003).

The weight for height index measures the degree of wasting or acute weight loss. This is the failure to gain weight adequately in relation to height that reflects recent or acute undernutrition. Wasting results from a recent inadequate food intake and/or recent acute illness. It is also associated with seasonal morbidity and food availability. Children who are below two standard deviations (-2SD) from the median of the NCHS reference are regarded as wasted. This index is useful in emergencies when age is not known.

The weight for age index measures the degree of underweight caused by either wasting or stunting or a combination of both. The value for age index is composite of height for age and weight for height indices. Children whose weight for height index falls below minus two standard deviations (-2SD) are classified as underweight (WHO, 1995; WHO, 1999).

The anthropometric Z-score method is used to derive indications about the nutrition status of children under five. The Z-score is defined as the difference between the value of an individual and the median value of the reference population for the same age or height, divided by the standard deviation of the reference population (Cogill, 2003). Children can then be categorized based on their ranking in the Z scores as shown in Table 4.1 Analysis of the anthropometric Z-scores is done using the Nutri-survey software developed by the University of Hohenheim and also recommended for use by the World Health Organisation.

Table 4.1: Categories of malnutrition

Standard deviation (SD)	Category
<3SD	Severely malnourished
-3SD to < 2 SD	Moderately malnourished
-2 SD to -1 SD	Mildly malnourished
>-1SD to 2 SD	Well nourished

Source: UNICEF (1998)

4.2.4.4   Body Mass Index

To determine the nutritional status of the women, the body mass index (BMI) is used, which is a ratio of weight in kilograms divided by height in metres squared. BMI correlates with body fat, and is the main indicator used to assess women's nutritional status. Women's BMI is calculated and the measurements compared to the measurements from the Centers for Disease Control (CDC) and WHO. All women whose BMI measurements fall below 16 are underweight/suffer from severe malnutrition or chronic energy deficiency (CED), also known as grade 3 thinness; between 16.0 and 18.5 have moderate CED, while those with fewer than 16.0 have severe CED (UNICEF, 1998). A BMI of between 18.5 and 24.9 is considered normal for women, while a BMI of 25.0 to 29.9 is considered overweight, and women with a BMI of 30.0 and above are considered obese. Height is a measure of past nutritional status and in part reflects the cumulative effect of social and economic outcomes on access to nutritious foods during childhood and adolescence.

A comparison of BMI across different income groups and regions is carried out using the BMI categories. Pearson's correlation coefficient is used to establish a correlation between BMI and household food security. Associations between mothers' nutritional status and household dietary diversity and children's nutritional status are established. The health and nutritional status of women is one of the prime determinants of child nutritional status, since they affect the birth weight of the child, which later has an influence on a child's growth up to the age of seven years. For this reason, mothers' BMI will be used in further analysis of determinants of children's nutritional status.

4.2.4.5   Prediction of Malnutrition - Logistic Regression

Predictors of malnutrition were analysed using a binary logistic regression. Binary logistic regression is a type of regression analysis where the dependent variable is a dummy variable (coded 0, 1). The logistic regression model is a non-linear transformation of the linear regression. The logistic distribution is an S-shaped distribution function which is similar to the standard-normal distribution (which results in a probit regression model) but easier to work with in most applications (the probabilities are easier to calculate). Logistic regression can be used to predict a dependent variable on the basis of independents and to determine the percent of variance in the dependent variable explained by the independents; to rank the relative importance of independents;

to assess interaction effects; and to understand the impact of covariate control variables (Liao, 1994; Rice, 1974; Borooah, 2002).

Logistic regression applies maximum likelihood estimation after transforming the dependent into a logit variable (the natural log of the odds of the dependent occurring or not). In this way, logistic regression estimates the probability of a certain event occurring. It should be noted that the logistic regression calculates changes in the log odds of the dependent, not changes in the dependent itself as OLS regression does. OLS seeks to minimize the sum of squared distances of the data points to the regression line. MLE seeks to maximize the log likelihood (LL) which reflects how likely it is (the odds) that the observed values of the dependent may be predicted from the observed values of the independents (Liao, 1994; Borooah, 2002; Wright, 1995).

The logistic model can be specified as:

$$ln[p/(1-p)] = a + BX + e$$
$$or$$
$$[p/(1-p)] = exp(a + BX + e) \qquad (4.6)$$

where: ln is the natural logarithm, log_{exp}, where exp=2.71828...

- p is the probability that the event Y occurs, $p(Y=1)$
- $p/(1-p)$ is the "odds ratio"
- $ln[p/(1-p)]$ is the log odds ratio, or logit
- X is the vector of independent variables to be included in the model
- a is the constant
- B is the coefficient
- e is the error term

For this study, the dependant variable was the nutritional status of the child so that, $Y_i = 1$ if the child is malnourished and 0, otherwise. In households with more than one child below the age of five years, measurements and characteristics of all children was done, in order to ascertain whether there were differences in the nutritional status of children living in the same household. The independent variables are age of child, sex, socio economic status of the household.

4.2.4.6   Two-Stage Least Squares Estimation

Analysis of the determinants of child nutritional status is carried out using a two-stage least squares (2SLS) estimation regression analysis. The Z-scores of the dependent variable in the analysis and the explanatory variables include immediate and underlying causes of child malnutrition as discussed in section 3.4.2 and in the conceptual framework of this study. Due to the endogenous nature of the variables in the equation, the 2SLS estimation method is most appropriate for this analysis since it tends to solve the endogeneity problem of one or more explanatory variables by the method of instrumental variables. In addition to dealing with the endogeneity problem, the method of instrumental variables recognizes the presence of omitted variables, unlike the OLS method, which leaves the unobserved variable in the error term (Woolridge, 2002b). The method of instrumental variables works whether or not the independent variables are correlated with the error term. The availability of instrumental variables in the 2SLS estimation method ensures that the estimated parameters are consistent and reliable. The model is given as:

$$N = \alpha + \beta_1 edu + \beta_2 age + \beta_3 genHH + \beta_4 health + \beta_5 incomemum + \beta_6 incomeHH + \beta_7 childsex + \beta_8 Kcal$$
$$+ \beta_9 waterdummy + u \qquad\qquad (4.7)$$

where α, $\beta_{1,....,}$ β_9 are coefficients to be estimated;

$N =$	nutritional status of the child measured in terms of weight for height, height for age and weight for age z scores
$edu =$	education of household head
$age =$	age of mother
$genHH =$	gender of household head
$health =$	health of child (measured in terms of frequency of different illnesses)
$childsex =$	sex of child
$Kcal =$	caloric intake by each child
$Waterdummy =$	source of water (protected water source = 1, unprotected = 0)
$incomemum =$	income for mothers
$incomeHH =$	income for household head
$U =$	error term

The explanatory variables included in the model and how they relate to child nutritional status are discussed below.

The education of the household head and the education of the mother determine the care that children receive within the household. Care practices are strong determinants of children's nutritional status and are influenced by the level of schooling of the household head and mother. Care is considered in terms of child feeding practices, which are determined by knowledge of nutrition, and care practices such immunization and vaccination, which are important for the general health of the child. Gender of household head is included as a dummy to assess whether there are any differences in the nutritional status of children by gender of household head. The household head controls most of the resources within the household, especially time and income, and makes most of the decisions regarding how income should be spent, and the quality and type of health care children should receive. To measure the health of a child, frequency of illness is included as an indicator of a child's health. Frequent illnesses such as diarrhoea and malaria have a negative impact on the nutrition status of the child and his/her general health, and can contribute to short-term malnutrition as measured by weight for height Z scores.

The household's health environment is important, and an unfavourable health environment caused by inadequate water and sanitation can increase the probability of infectious diseases and directly cause malnutrition. The health environment is measured using indicators of source of water and latrine use. For water, the reference is the use of surface water and pipe water. Dummy variables for use of surface water and pipe water indicate safer water use. For latrine use, dummy variables for no latrine and presence of latrine indicate the prevailing sanitary conditions within the household. A dummy variable for the sex of the child is included in the model to capture any differences in nutritional status of male and female children within the household. Caloric intake has been included as one of the explanatory variables as a proxy for nutrition security for children. The age of the mother is included in the model, with the assumption that with increased age, women gain more childcare experience and hence provide better care for the children. The age of a child is important in the equation, since retardation in growth as measured by height for age is positively correlated with age, and other studies have shown an increase in malnutrition with an increase in the age of the child.

The above regression are run in turns with the different Z-scores for height for age (*haz*), weight for age (*waz*) and weight for height (*whz)*, as dependent variables. Height for age measures long-term nutritional status, while weight for height Z-scores measure short-term nutritional status.

4.2.5 Time Use Analysis

Analysis of gender division of labour in crop and household production activities took into consideration time used for off-farm and on-farm production, as well as household production. Descriptive analysis was done. The T-test was used to establish differences in time use for different activities by gender.

4.3   Research Design

This section describes provides a description of the study site, followed by the sampling procedure and finally the data. A brief overview of the research site is given to provide essential information required for the understanding of the research work.

4.3.1 Description of the Study Region

The study area, West Pokot district, is found in Rift Valley Province. It is situated along Kenya's western boundary with Uganda and borders with Trans Nzoia and Marakwet districts to the south, and Baringo and Turkana districts to the east and north respectively. The total area of land covered by the district is about 9100 km2, which is 5% of Rift Valley Province. The position of the district in relation to its neighbours is depicted in Figure 4.5 and that of the study sites in Figure 4.6. The distance from the district headquarters, Kapenguria, to the closest sizeable town, Kitale, is about 42 km. The distance to the provincial headquarters, Nakuru, is 250 km, and to Nairobi 435 km by road (GoK, 1996). The choice of the district as a study area was made on the basis of the following criteria:

1. Food insecurity: West Pokot district is one of the districts in Kenya that is particularly food-insecure. It is among the poorest districts in Rift Valley Province, with a high absolute poverty level and food insecurity. This region is prone to transitory and chronic food insecurity and relies heavily on food aid.

2. Gender inequality: it is one of the districts with hidden and obvious gender inequalities. Clear unequal representation of men and women in remunerated work and education exist, and there is low enrolment of

girls in schools as compared to boys (IEA, 2002). The traditional cultural practices as depicted in their norms tend to favour men as opposed to women.

3. Underdevelopment: in comparison to other districts in Kenya, West Pokot is one of the least developed districts in the country, both socially and economically. Although the underdevelopment can be attributed to the remoteness of the district, it is worth assessing whether existing gender inequalities in the district have contributed to this phenomenon.

Figure 4.5: A Map of Kenya

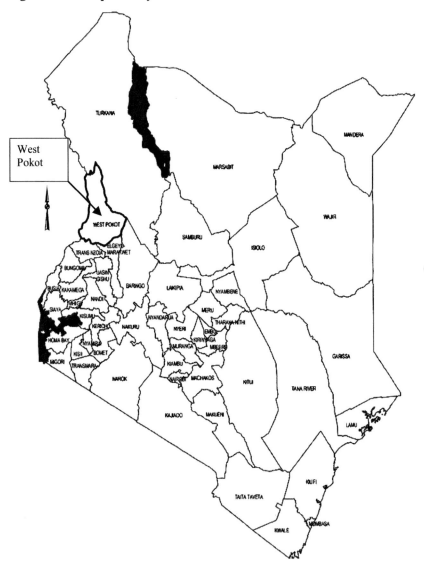

Source: GoK (1996)

Figure 4.6: A map of West Pokot

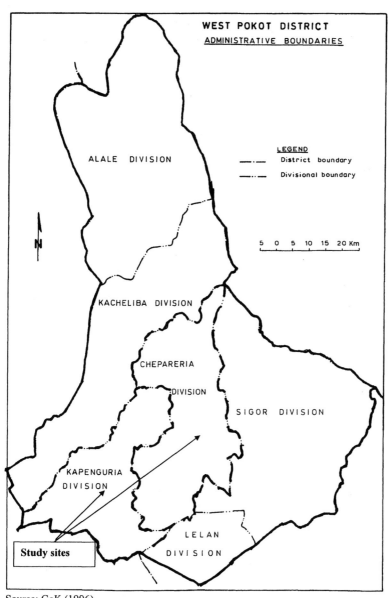

Source: GoK (1996)

4.3.2 Agro-ecological Characteristics of West Pokot District

The district has a great variety of topographical features. The south-east of the district is situated in the Cherangani hills with altitudes of over 3000 metres above sea level. The northern and north-eastern parts of the district, on the other hand, stretch towards the hot, dry plains of Turkana at altitudes of less than 900 metres above sea level. Several landscapes can be distinguished in West Pokot: high altitude, medium altitude and low altitude. The high-altitude area (more than 2100 metres above sea level) represents the largest proportion of the high potential lands in the district, where agriculture and livestock production are the major economic activities. Medium-altitude areas are at 1500 to 2100m above sea level. These areas have low rainfall and are predominantly pastoral lands. The low-altitude lands are all flat lands with an altitude of less than 1500m above sea level. The lowlands stretch throughout Alale, Kacheliba and parts of Sigor divisions (GoK, 2002; GoK, 1996).

The district has a bimodal type of rainfall. The long rains fall between April and August, with maximum rainfall being received in May. The short rains come between the month of October and February. There is, however, considerable variation in the amount of rainfall received in West Pokot district. A wide range of crops are grown, from drought-tolerant crops in the lowlands to temperate crops in the high altitudes of Lelan, although the main occupation of farmers is pastoralism, or pastoralism in transition to mixed farming (GoK, 2002; GoK, 1996).

Until 1996, West Pokot had six divisions, namely: Kapenguria, Lelan, Chepareria, Sigor, Kacheliba and Alale. By 2003, there were a total of ten divisions. These divisions are further subdivided into thirty-six locations. Kapenguria division, along with the lower parts of Chepareria and Sigor and Lelan division, fall within the high-altitude areas and are high potential resource areas in terms of soil quality and amount of rainfall, and therefore offer the best agricultural land and employment opportunities. The upper parts of Chepareria, Sigor and Kacheliba divisions fall within the middle-altitude area, while Alale division and upper parts of Kacheliba division fall within the low-altitude area. In 1999, the population was estimated at 308,086 with a population density of 34 people/km^2 (IEA, 2002; GoK, 2002). The extreme variation and rugged topography has made access to many of the district's resources difficult. The steep hills in some parts render the use of mechanized farming difficult.

4.3.3 Socio-economic Characteristics of West Pokot

The great variation in altitude and soil type in the district leads to considerable variation in the crops planted and livestock kept in West Pokot. Estimates from the ministry of Agriculture and Livestock Development indicate that 3% of the land area in the district has a high production potential, 6% has a medium potential, 28% is marginal land and 44% is considered rangeland. The remaining 19% of the land area is either covered by forests or is unsuitable for agricultural use. Land tenure in West Pokot is of two types: individual or private tenure, and communal ownership. Private ownership is to be found in the areas of higher agricultural potential of Kapenguria and Chepareria. Communal tenure is prevalent in the drier marginal areas, where land is owned and controlled communally (GoK, 2002).

Traditional farming methods are practised in the largest proportion (72%) of the district. Finger millet and sorghum are the main crops grown in this system. The most important crop in the potential lands of the district is maize. In potential areas of Chepareria and Kapenguria, maize is cultivated by most residents. In some instances, there is intercropping of maize and beans. Other crops grown in the region, but on a small scale, include cassava, bananas, potatoes, vegetables (kale, onions, tomatoes) and fruits (GoK, 2002; GoK, 1996).

Subsistence livestock farming is practised by the Pokot people dwelling in the lowlands. Almost one-third of the residents of the district are characterized as pastoralists. Their herds are composed mainly of cattle, goats and a few sheep. Movement of herds and access to seasonal grazing and water are essential to the survival of livestock in the traditional pastoral grazing system. To minimize the loss of livestock during drought, the pastoral Pokots practise an insurance system locally known as *tiliantany*. Through this system, cows are loaned to relatives or friends in the highlands in exchange for a steer (an ox less than four years old). The cow provides milk to the person who receives it, but the calves are the property of the original owner. The traditional system is declining, however, as the pastoral Pokot adopt a more sedentary lifestyle with a significant shift to agriculture incorporating crops such as millet, sorghum and, more recently, maize and beans (GoK, 2002; GoK, 1997; GoK, 1986).

Modern mixed farming (production of crops and livestock mainly for the market) dominates in Lelan, Kapenguria and Mnagei locations in the south of West Pokot. In the remainder of the district, the majority of households produce for their own consumption, either through cultivation of crops or keeping of livestock. A small surplus may be traded for cash or other goods (GoK, 2002).

4.3.4 Selection of Survey Sites

West Pokot district is divided into ten divisions, which spread through three agro-ecological regions – high, middle and low-altitude regions. The population in the region consists of non-farm households (entrepreneur and employee households), part-time and full-time farm households. All of these were included in the study. The population in the region is also categorized into pastoralist populations, agro-pastoralist populations and mixed farming populations. To ensure representativeness in the study, multi-stage sampling was carried out. Consideration was given to population distribution and density within the regions based on the 1999 population census statistics, which were obtained from the district administrative office. Regions with high population densities had larger representation in the sample population. The sampling was conducted as described below:

- First stage: purposive selection of two divisions out of the ten was carried out. The two divisions of Kapenguria and Chepareria were selected, since they had characteristics of all three agro-ecological zones, i.e. high, medium and low-altitude areas. Chepareria and Kapenguria are the largest divisions in West Pokot and have the highest population densities, with Chepareria having the highest number of inhabitants by the year 2002 (GoK/FAO - Early Warning System, 2003). In addition, the two divisions were easily accessible and relatively safe in comparison with the others, since human security is a major concern in this district.

- Second stage: random selection of four locations from each of the divisions was carried out. From Chepareria division, Kipkomo, Chepkopegh, Mwotot and Batei locations were randomly selected from the sixteen locations in the division. In Kapenguria division, Kishaunet, Kaisaget, Kapenguria and Mnagei locations were selected.

- Third stage: random selection of eight sub-locations from each of the locations was undertaken. In Kapenguria, Siyoi, Talau, Kamatira, Chepkono, Kishaunet, Serewo, Chemwochoi and Aramaget were randomly selected from the 14 sub-locations. A total of eight sub-locations were randomly selected. In Chepareria, Sopukwo, Propoi, Kerelwa, Morpus, Ortum, Chepareria, Mongorion and Ywalateke.

- With the help of the sub-chief of each sub-location, male and female-headed households were identified and a list of these households formed the sampling frame. The proportion of male and female-headed household was represented in the study as this ratio is in the total population. The SPSS sample selection function was used to calculate the sample size. The sample size was a function of population size, desired accuracy and level of confidence. Using a confidence level of 95% and the 1999 population size of the district, 200 households were randomly selected using this method.

Both women and men who were heads of households were interviewed. Women in male-headed households were interviewed separately.

4.4   Data Collection

A cross-sectional survey design was used in this study. Data was collected from households from a cross-section of three different agro-ecological regions, to ensure that the food security phenomenon in the region is well captured. Some parts of the region experience transitory food insecurity while others experience chronic food insecurity. The three agro-ecological zones also have different socio-economic and agro-ecological potential. The information base for this study consisted of both primary and secondary data. In the following sections, data collection procedures will be discussed.

4.4.1 Primary Data

The core information for the primary data consisted of a detailed household survey with the use of a standardized questionnaire. Group discussions were conducted to complement the primary data and also to provide some information that was not collected from the individual households. Additionally, a market survey was carried out to back up the household information on prices of inputs and outputs.

Household Survey

A household survey was carried out in all 8 of the selected locations. Male and female-headed households were included in the study. In addition, demographic information from both male and female household members residing in the household was collected. Information regarding children was also collected. The household survey was carried out with the help of a questionnaire, which consisted of the following sections:

*   Demographic and socio-economic characteristics of household members. All relevant information regarding household size, household member occupation and education was collected in this section.
*   Household asset base: land holdings, physical assets owned by household members
*   Financial characteristics: debt, credit and savings
*   Household expenditure: expenditure on food and non-food items.
*   Farm activities: data on crop and livestock production activities.
*   Division of labour within the household: time allocation to farm and off-farm activities as well as time allocation to household production activities.
*   Access to agricultural extension services
*   Health status of household members and access to health services

Food Consumption Survey

Dietary assessment of the households was done. Information collected in this section included: dietary diversity, weighing of food in combination with the 24 hour recall of all foods consumed. In addition to measuring household food security, dietary diversity can be used as a means for monitoring changes in seasonal food intake. A seven-day recall method was used, where respondents (mainly wives) responsible for preparing meals within the household stated the number of different foods that household members consumed while at home. Other household members who ate at home were also interviewed to provide additional information regarding the foods consumed. In some cases, adult members and children attending school ate outside the home. In such cases, this information was noted.

Information was collected regarding the amount of staple and non-staple food consumed in the last seven days of the study. Weighing of foods served to both children below five years was done. However, it was not possible to measure the amount of food served in all households, since in some households the interviews took place before the family meals were prepared. In some instances, on the day of the interview, no food was served to family members. Households from which food data was not collected are not included in the analysis on food consumption.

Information on indices of household coping strategies during food insecurity was also collected as an indicator of food security. The indices of household food security coping strategies directly capture notions of adequacy and vulnerability of households to food insecurity. Households using 'more severe' strategies are likely to be poor and more vulnerable to destitution (Hoddinott, 1999). Indices were given weights, and information was collected from the individual within the household responsible for serving family meals.

Anthropometric Survey Design

In order to determine the nutritional status of household members, anthropometric data was collected. Specific data collected included, weight, height, upper arm circumference and age of the child. Measurements for the weight and height of women were taken in order to determine their body mass index (BMI).

Market survey

Information regarding prices of agricultural inputs and outputs was collected by means of a market survey. Often, the heads of households and members did not know the exact price of the farm inputs. For this reason, it was necessary to carry out a market survey to ascertain the exact prices of inputs and outputs. The main local markets were visited on market days. In Chepareria division, the main market was held every Thursday of the week, in Kapenguria division, the market day took place every Friday of the week. Farmers and pastoralists from all over the district brought their farm products and livestock to sell at these two markets. Information on prices of goods and livestock was collected from shop traders.

4.4.2 Secondary Data

Secondary data was collected from international publications, national data from the Central Bureau of Statistics (CBS), Ministries of Agriculture, Health, Planning and National Development and various research institutions in Kenya (Kenya Institute of Public Policy Research and Analysis - KIPPRA and Institute of Policy Analysis and Research - IPAR). Secondary data concerning West Pokot was obtained from West Pokot district information centre.

5   INTER AND INTRA-HOUSEHOLD RESOURCE ALLOCATION

In the first section of this chapter descriptive statistics on demographic and socio-economic characteristics of the sampled households are presented, followed by results relating to household resource distribution along gender lines. Analysis of land as a production resource focuses on land use, distribution of land, crop productivity and labour use, all by gender. Results relating to human capital focus on education of household members, access to employment, division of labour and access to health care facilities. Financial characteristics within the household that are presented include sources of household income, savings behaviour and household expenditure. In the sections that follow, findings on household food and nutrition security are presented.

5.1   Household Characteristics

Table 5.1 presents the demographic and socio-economic characteristics of the sample households. The total sample size comprised 200 randomly selected households from Chepareria and Kapenguria divisions of West Pokot district. Out of these, 137 households were male headed while 63 were female headed. The average household size in MHH and FHH was about seven persons per household. More than 65% of household members in each category were adults. MHH had a high percentage of children (34%) in comparison to FHH (22%). FHH had a higher percentage of adults and labour force in comparison to MHH households. Labour force in this case is defined as members of the household aged between 15 and 65 years of age. The labour force in MHH was 76%, while that in FHH was 64%. There is a clear gender gap in schooling in favour of men. There exists a significance difference in years of school attended by male and female heads of households. Male heads of households had more years of schooling (on average 11 years) in comparison to female heads of households, who had only 6 years of schooling on average. Overall, there was no significant difference in the years of schooling for male and female household members in the two categories of households as can be seen from the T test results in Table 5.1. The heads of FHH were found to be younger than those of MHH, with an average age difference of 13 years.

Table 5.1: Household characteristics by gender of household head

Characteristic	Mean values of household characteristics		
	MHH (N=137)	FHH (N=63)	T- test
Household size	7.13 (2.89)	6.96 (2.46)	
Household composition			
% that is:			
Male	51.20 (34.27)	48.79 (22.62)	
Female	48.8 (12.25)	51.21 (20.66)	
Adults	66.42 (25.66)	78.47 (25.66)	
Children	33.58 (27.06)	21.53 (26.78)	
Average age of			
household head (years)	51.97 (9.980)	38.94 (9.43)	
Years of schooling:			
Head of household	10.55 (4.54)	6.11 (5.32)	0.001^{***}
Female household	10.32 (2.68)	10.23 (2.77)	0.17
members	12.01 (1.05)	12.30 (1.70)	0.19
Male household members	76	64	
Labour force (%)			

Source: Own survey data, 2003

Notes: Standard deviation in parentheses, ** indicates significance at level 1%

5.2   Land Tenure, Land Use

Land is undoubtedly one of the main production resources in Kenya. The land tenure system in West Pokot is of two types: individual or private ownership tenure, and communal tenure. Private tenure is found in the high agricultural potential areas of the district, where land is adjudicated under the Land Adjudication Act. Communal tenure is prevalent in drier marginal areas under the Trust Land Act. While land seems to be an abundant resource in the study site, a large portion of it cannot be used for farming purposes. In this section, findings on land holdings, land use and land productivity are presented.

5.2.1 Gender Differences in Land holdings

There were differences in land ownership by gender of the household head. Table 5.2 presents results relating to land ownership in the study region. About 51% of the women in MHH and 70% of women in FHH had access to and control over land. About 94% of men in MHH and 89% (n=56) of men in FHH had access to land. The FHH had acquired their land by purchase or accessed it through a male relative. Male heads of households had access to land through inheritance, buying or renting from others.

Although more than half of the women had access to land in both male and female-headed households, the amount they had access to was less than in the case of the men. On average, MHH owned more land (5.4 ha) in comparison to FHH (3.1 ha). However, the amount of land cultivated in MHH and FHH did not differ appreciably (only 2.43 ha and 2.18 ha in male and female headed households, respectively). In MHH larger portions of land were uncultivated, due to the larger number of livestock kept in these households. MHH rented land from other farmers in the region for cultivation purposes. Land was rented in areas that were considered to be more fertile and less prone to erosion. Comparison of land ownership by region revealed that a higher percentage of households in Kapenguria had access to land compared to households in Chepareria division.

Table 5.2: Land holdings and cultivation area in hectares

Land holdings	Type of household		Region	
	MHH (N=137)	FHH (N=63)	Chepareria (N=108)	Kapenguria (N=92)
Number of females with access to land	71 (51%)	44 (70%)	36 (35%)	22 (24%)
Number of males with access to land	129 (94%)	56 (89%)	72 (61%)	56 (62%)
Land owned by HH	5.40 (6.20)	3.10 (5.46)	2.98 (5.56)	7.41 (6.00)
Amount of land owned by women in ha	2.76 (5.23)	2.38 (1.69)	2.17 (5.35)	3.80 (5.46)
Area cultivated by household in ha	2.43 (2.68)	2.18 (1.67)	1.44 (0.99)	2.22 (2.31)

Source: Own survey data (2003)

5.2.2 Land Use

Land was used for both animal and crop production. The great variation in altitude and soil type in the district has led to considerable variation in the crops planted and the livestock kept. Only 3% of the land area in the district has a high production potential, 6% has medium potential, 28% is marginal land and 19% of the land area is either forested or unsuitable for agricultural use (GoK, 2002; GoK, 1985). In most households in the study site, a large portion of land was unsuitable for cultivation for one or more of the following reasons: the land was rocky and the soils were too shallow, and therefore not suitable for growing crops. In some instances, a large portion of the land was steep, making the soils prone to erosion. Table 5.3 presents results on crops grown in the region and the average area of land (in hectares) covered by each crop.

Maize is the main crop produced in the district, while production of beans is the second most important cropping activity. This crop is often intercropped with maize. Other crops grown on a small scale include potatoes (both sweet and Irish), cassava, kales, onions, tomatoes, millet and sorghum. Sorghum, millet and cassava are drought-resistant crops that are suitable for the lowlands of the district, since the lowlands receive small and unreliable amounts of rainfall. In many households, however, farmers have shifted from the cultivation of these traditional crops to cultivation of maize, which has a higher economic value. A large proportion of the land in both male and female-headed households was covered by the maize crop in comparison to the share of land on which other crops were grown.

Table 5.3: Crops cultivated and area of land in ha covered by each crop

Crops	Type of household	
	MHH (N=137)	FHH (N=63)
Maize	1.85 (2.38)	1.60 (1.79)
Sorghum	0.12 (0.70)	0.10 (0.23)
Millet	0.13 (0.71)	0.19 (0.51)
Beans*	1.52 (2.35)	1.60 (1.80)
Sweet potatoes	0.02 (0.07)	0.02 (0.93)
Irish potatoes	0.03 (0.11)	0.04 (0.13)
Cassava	0.07 (0.04)	0.04 (0.03)
Tomatoes	0.07 (0.68)	0.07 (0.04)
Onions	0.07 (0.68)	0.07 (0.05)
Kales	0.066 (0.14)	0.05 (0.1)
Total	2.43	2.18

Source: Own survey data (2003)
Notes: Standard deviations in parentheses
Beans are intercropped with maize; the amount of land covered is therefore not included in the total amount covered by all crops.

Table 5.4 shows the percentage of households that kept domestic animals and the average number of animals kept by households. A higher percentage of MHH kept cattle and goats – 54% and 44% respectively – in comparison to only 14 % and 9% of the FHH. There were larger herds of cattle and goats in MHH than in FHH. Livestock keeping is particularly important for men since livestock are necessary both for obtaining a wife and for subsistence. Extra male labour needed to take care of the herds is a constraining factor for FHH to keep cattle and goats, and the risk of losing livestock to livestock rustlers (raiders) was one reason given by female heads of households for not keeping cattle and goats. The initial capital needed to invest in livestock and the extra labour required could be contributing factors to the larger herds in MHH. Poultry was kept by more than half (54%) of FHH in comparison to 24% of MHH. This can be attributed to the fact that they enable households to generate income over a short period of time through the sale of poultry products. A small number of donkeys were kept by male and female headed households mainly for transportation purpose.

Table 5.4: Percentage of households keeping domestic animals

| Animal | MHH (N=137) | | FHH (N=63) | |
	% of HH	Average no. of animals	% of HH	Average no. of animals
Cattle	54	3.09 (4.07)	14	0.88 (3.17)
Goats	44	8.38 (16.58)	9	2.13 (4.12)
Sheep	9	4.33 (7.50)	9	1.97 (4.02)
Poultry	25	3.84 (25.33)	54	5.01 (7.85)
Donkeys	5	1.50 (0.49)	10	1.04 (0.56)

Source: Own survey data (2003)
Note: Standard deviation in parentheses

5.3 Human Capital

The following sections present findings on access to education, health facilities and division of labour in the study site.

5.3.1 Comparison of Education Level by Gender

The mean years of schooling for male heads of households were 11, compared to 6 years for the female heads of households. T-test results showed a significant difference in the years of schooling between the female and male heads of households at confidence levels 95% and 99%. There were no significant differences in years of schooling by male and female household members in the two categories of households. Data on years of schooling were categorized into various levels of education: no formal schooling, primary education, secondary, college and university. Figure 5.1 shows educational attainment in male and female-headed households. About 36% (n= 23) of the female heads of households had no formal education, compared to 6% (n=8) of the male heads of households. More than half the wives (57% (n=78)) in MHH had primary education compared to 32% of adult women in FHH. At higher levels there were no significant differences in education attainment of the FHH and the wives in MHH.

Figure 5.1: Education level by gender of household head

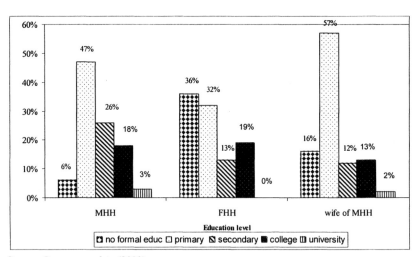

Source: Own survey data (2003)

Notes: N is equal to 137 for male headed households and 63 for female headed households

Comparison of education attainment by gender of household members was also done. Figure 5.2 shows the overall education level attainment of male and female household members in the study site. Overall, a higher percentage of men had formal education in comparison to women. For both primary and secondary education levels, a higher percentage of men had acquired these levels of education. At higher education levels (college and university), there was no difference in the educational attainment of women and men in the study site. This is because at the end of secondary school a national exam was done and only those who qualified in this examination could proceed to universities or qualify to enter into different training institutions. Lack of significant differences in the percentages of men and women who had acquired higher education points to the fact that girls and boys had the same capability and similar performance to qualify for higher learning.

Since the year 2003, primary education in all public schools is free in Kenya. Parents, however, still have to pay for school uniform and writing materials, and sometimes for the furniture to be used by their children. At secondary level, parents have to pay tuition fees as well as other school expenses. Children frequently have to walk long distances to get to school. Decision by parents to invest in a girl's education in the study region is more dependent on the price of education than in the case of boys. In addition, in most rural mixed schools in the study region, drop-out rates for girls tend to be high compared to those for boys. Contributing factors to the high drop out rate for girls are cultural practices (initiation[9] and early marriages), poor sanitary conditions so that once girls reach puberty, they cannot cope with the biological challenges that this stage brings, stereotypes by parents and sometimes by teachers and willingness of parents to pay for boys education than that of girls.

---

[9] Initiation was a practice that marked the end of childhood and beginning of adulthood. Girls were circumcised (often at the age of 14 years), after which they were expected to assume adult roles (marriage and child bearing).

Figure 5.2: Education level of male and female household members in West Pokot

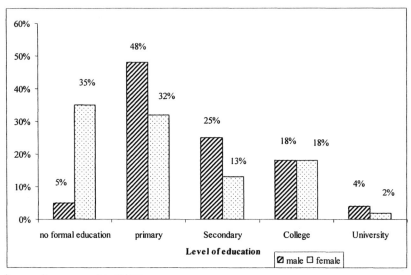

Source: Own survey data (2003)
Notes: N for male is 444 and 458 for women. N includes all children of school going age and adults living within all households

Access to education is important since it encourages people to move into more remunerative non farm employment, thus helping to increase household incomes (Heidhues, et al., 2004). In addition, education helps farmers to adopt more advanced technologies and crop management techniques. With less women having access to education in the study site, only few can move to the better paying non-farm remunerative jobs. In addition, agricultural productivity is likely to suffer, since the majority of women in the study site are actively involved in agricultural production.

5.3.2 Employment

Employment is a key to poverty alleviation since it provides the possibility for individual household members to earn an income and hence contribute to the welfare of the household. The survey revealed a low level of participation by women in non-farm formal employment and leadership positions (Table 5.5). About 20% of the women had formal jobs in the public sector (as teachers, secretaries and nurses) in comparison to 34% of the men who held positions in formal employment. About 10% of the women worked as casual workers, compared to 30% of the men. Casual jobs available in the region included working as cooks, cleaners, babysitters, housekeepers and security guards. Women who left school without qualifications (did not complete secondary or college education) were found to be economically disadvantaged, with many concentrated in the traditional low-paid jobs (e.g. employed as cooks, cleaners, waiters in restaurants and matrons). Many women experienced job segregation and pay discrimination due to their low levels of education. Highly remunerative jobs in Kenya require college and university education. Low representation of women in influential positions implies that women in the region have a low level of influence on policies affecting their welfare.

About 35% of women and 29% of men were involved in business activities. Engaging in business activities enabled individuals to generate extra off-farm income for their families. Off-farm activities women engaged in included trading in farm products such as vegetables, grains, pulses and eggs, collecting and selling firewood. Men engaged in activities such as carpentry, selling charcoal, trading in livestock, small-scale manufacturing of hides and skins, and activities in the transport business. More women (35%) than men 7% in the sample population did not have a non farm employment. Unemployed women were solely housewives, and participated in household production activities as well as in farming activities. Table 5.5 presents results on employment status in the study site by gender of respondents.

Table 5.5: Employment status by gender in %

Employment	Men (N=155)	Women (N=186)
Formal	34	20
Casual	30	10
Business	29	35
Unemployed	7	35

Source: Own survey data (2003)
Note: N for women includes women in male-headed households and N for men also include men from female-headed households.

5.4   Division of Labour

Labour is one of the important production factors both on the farm and within the household. The sections that follow describe division of labour in agricultural production as well as household production.

5.4.1 Labour Use in Crop Production

Table 5.6 presents the average labour use in hours by gender in the study area. Labour in both the highlands and lowlands of the district is female-dominated. Female labour dominated all cropping activities, while male labour was mainly used for land preparation. On average, during the cropping season, women spent seven hours and five hours on weeding and seeding respectively, while men spent two hours and three hours on average on these activities. Women spent more time (on average seven hours) on post-harvest activities in comparison to men (on average two hours). Significant differences exist in time used for crop production activities by male and female household members, with women working longer hours. Hired and borrowed labour (labour from neighbours and friends) played a big role during the peak cropping season for major crops (maize and beans). The findings in this study are in line with findings from other studies which indicate that women work for more hours than men do 8IFAD, 2004; UNDP, 2003). In Kenya, women and men spent 42% and 76% of their time on market oriented activities, respectively. Conversely, men spent less time (24%) on non market activities when compared to time spent by women (58%) on the same activities (UNDP, 2003).

Table 5.6: Average number of hours spent per day on cropping activities for the cropping season 2002/2003

Activity	Average amount of time used per day (in hours)	
	Male (N=155)	Female (N=186)
Land preparation	4.01 (2.15)	5.34 (2.1)
Seeding/planting	3.00 (4.94)	5.08 (2.3)
Weeding	2.75 (5.30)	7.47 (2.45)
Fertilizer application	1.67 (2.83)	3.18 (3.73)
Harvesting	2.23 (5.27)	5.40 (2.41)
Post-harvest activities	1.20 (2.1)	2.57 (3.67)

Source: Own survey data (2003)
Notes: Hours for each cropping activity indicate the average amount of time used by males and females in the study region during the 2002/2003 cropping season
N for males included males who participated in farming activities from male and female headed households. N for females includes females in female and male headed households. Children above the age of 14 and participated in these activities are included in the sample.

5.4.2 Labour Use in Livestock Production

The main types of domesticated animals in West Pokot are cattle, goats and sheep. Donkeys were domesticated and used for transportation of goods and water. Chicken were kept mainly for eggs, meat and for sale. In livestock production, male members of the household, especially boys, played an important role in taking care of animals, especially cattle and small ruminants. However, since the animals were left to roam in search of pasture, little household labour was needed to take care of them. Women were responsible for cleaning animal shelters, milking, and taking care of the chickens. On average, thirty minutes and four hours were spent per day on animal production activities by women and children respectively.

5.4.3 Labour Use in Household Production

All household activities were taken care of by women. The single activity which consumed most of the time was water collection. Empirical data shows that, on average, women worked up to fourteen hours in a day, with collection of water consuming most of the time. About 44% of the women used on average four hours for this task. Water points were often far away from the homesteads and women had to make several trips to get water. Other activities in which women engaged within the home are childcare, meal preparation and other household chores. Female children participated in these activities. Depending on their geographical location, women in the district participated in varied activities. For example, women in the highlands of West Pokot (Kapenguria region) built store-houses for family grain in addition to their household and farm activities. While women in the plains did most of the hard physical labour, including house building and herding, those in the highlands receive help from their husbands. Repairs within the home were done by men in Kapenguria division. In parts of Chepareria, women were responsible for thatching their huts. On average, men spent four hours on leisure in comparison to an average of one hour for women.

The survey reveals time poverty on the side of women resulting from multiple and competing productive and reproductive responsibilities. Most of their activities were performed without the assistance of labour-saving technology or adequate transportation means. This scenario has implications for the health of women, a situation that has contributed to the low life expectancy of women in the region.

5.5   Households' Financial Characteristics

In rural areas where the majority of the population relies on agricultural activities for their livelihood, increasing population pressure on land holdings and climatic conditions can have a major impact on economic well-being and production decisions. In response to insecure rural livelihoods, people in rural areas develop risk-management and coping strategies as a way to lessen or avert adverse conditions. One risk-management strategy used in rural households is to diversify incomes.

Diversification of incomes refers to an increase in the number of income sources of a household and the balance between them. This include on-farm income (subsistence, animal production and hunting), non-farm income (from local non-farm employment (wage and self-employment) and agricultural off-farm income (from agricultural wage labour away from own farm). Rural households diversify into the non-farm sector in order to increase income flows and asset stocks, smooth income flows that would otherwise fluctuate seasonally, reduce income risk, and to improve long-run income prospects by acquiring new skills (Buchenrieder, 2004; Möllers and Buchenrieder, 2004). Demand-pull and distress-push factors influence households to diversify into the non-farm sector. The term demand-pull is used to describe a situation where agricultural workers become more able to grasp more remunerative employment opportunities in the non-farm sector. The term distress-push describes a situation in which inadequate incomes in agriculture 'push' workers into often poorly paid non-farm diversification (Möllers, 2004). In this section, descriptive statistics relating to income generation and diversification in the study sample and their savings and borrowing characteristics are presented.

5.5.1 Income Distribution

Analysis on income was based on distribution of farm and non farm income within the households. Households were classified based on total income (income from farm and non-farm activity per month). There were no significant differences in farm income between the two categories of households. There were however, significant differences in the non farm income, with MHH having higher non farm incomes (on average KES 15,500 per month for men when compared to KES 3,750 for women). Given that individuals may not be honest about revealing how much income they earn, expenditure was taken as a proxy for income in the derivation of the poverty benchmark. The analysis of the mean monthly household expenditure was based on expenditure on food and non food commodities. Based on the household size, households that spent less than 3,500 KES (about 30 Euro) on food were classified as poor, those who spent up to 10,000 (up to 120 Euro) on food per month were classified under the middle income group, while those who spent over 10,000 KES (over 120 Euro) were classified as rich households. Based on both the food expenditure and monthly income, out of the 200 households, 138 households, representing about 69% of the total, were poor. About 22% (n=43) belonged to the middle socio-economic class, and 9% (n=19) were rich. More than half of male headed (n = 103 out of 137 MHH) and female headed households (n =35 out of 63 FHH) were poor. Both categories of households were affected by poverty.

5.5.2 Household Income Diversification

Households diversified their incomes by engaging in various activities. The activities ranged from farming and non-farm activities such as petty trade, to participation in formal and casual employment. In the analysis, sources of income were categorized into four groups: income from farming, non-farm self-employment, wage employment and unearned income, which included remittances from children and relatives, and pension benefits. Figure 5.3 gives an overview of income sources and their income shares in the total household income. In FHH, the highest shares of household income came from self-employment, followed by farming and then wage employment. In MHH, the highest share of household income was from wage employment, followed by income from farming and self-employment. Unearned income contributed a 15% share of the household income in FHH and 8% in MHH. Unearned income was in the form of money received from friends, relatives or children as gift or money received in form of pension. Participation in self employment included trading, carpentry and tailoring. Wage employment guaranteed the respondents of regular source of income in form of a monthly salary for those in formal employment (public/private) or casual employment. Income from farming was in form of sale of farm produce or payment for work done on the farm. It should be noted that wage earning is the only stable source of earnings in the study area; the other sources of income were unstable, since they depended on market prices that were unstable and subject to seasonal changes.

Figure 5.3: Sources of household income

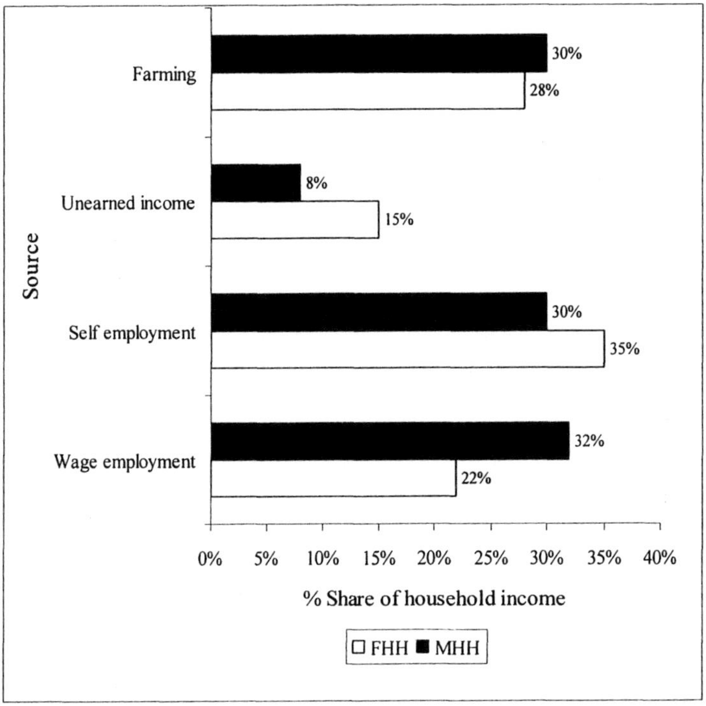

Source: Own survey data (2003)
Note: N = 137 for MHH and 63 for FHH

5.5.3 Savings

Both formal and informal institutions were important when it came to saving behaviour of the respondents. More than 78% of the 200 households had savings either in formal or informal savings institutions. Some individuals had savings in both formal and informal institutions. A larger number of women saved their earnings in informal institutions compared to those who saved in formal ones. Men had more savings than women. The average savings in formal institutions (banks, teachers' cooperative society and agricultural cooperative society) for all households amounted to KES 34,060 (equivalent to 425 euros). MHH had higher amounts of saving in comparison to FHH. The amount of money saved in informal institutions was relatively small. At present, West Pokot district has one commercial bank (Kenya Commercial Bank) and a cooperative for teachers.

There are 17 other cooperative societies in the district, but most are dormant (GoK, 2002). The informal institutions in the region are both registered and unregistered women's groups, and groups for men. Table 5.7 shows the savings situation in the study sample.

Table 5.7: Comparison of savings by gender

Type of savings	Male		Female		All	
	Frequency (N)	Average amount (KES)	Frequency (N)	Average amount (KES)	Frequency (N)	Average amount (KES)
Formal savings	38	35670	57	32450	97	34060
Informal savings	97	3950	104	2860	201	3405
No savings	22	0	58	0	80	0
Total	157	38620	219	35310	376	37465

Source: West Pokot, Kenya, own data (2003)
Note: The total number of female respondents (N) is 209 and includes women from male-headed households (143) as well as women from female-headed households (63). Some individuals save in several institutions at once, and so the total observations add up to 376 instead of 349. The approximate exchange rate in 2003 was 1 euro to KES 80.

Further analysis was carried out to ascertain whether husbands and wives maintain 'separate purses' and whether or not they pool their financial resources. Table 5.8 shows that more individuals preferred to have individual savings as opposed to joint savings. In most households in the study area, financial resources are not pooled. Not all households responded to this question.

Table 5.8: Type of savings

Type of savings	MHH		FHH		All	
	Frequency (N)	%	Frequency (N)	%	Frequency (N)	%
Joint savings	35	29	9	18	44	25
Individual savings	86	71	45	82	131	75
Total	121	100	54	100	175	100

Source: West Pokot, Kenya, Own data (2003)
Note: Not all respondents responded to this question

Individuals prefer to have separate savings (in the case of married couples), where they can control and monitor how the savings were used. It can be deduced from the findings that individual household members have different preferences, and hence use their incomes separately according to their preferences. Therefore, the unitary model, which assumes that the household has a single set of preferences and, with this, combines its goods, does not apply in more than 131 out of the 200 households in the study sample.

5.5.4 Access to Credit

The main sources for credit were informal financial groups and cooperatives. Table 5.9 gives an overview of the main sources of credit in the study site. A high percentage of MHH had access to credit from both formal and informal institutions. Borrowing from cooperative societies such as the teachers' cooperative or an agricultural cooperative society is limited to members or to those who have shares in the cooperatives. Borrowing from banks was not common in the study sample due to the high costs of processing loans and high interest rates charged. Informal financial groups and social networks played a big role in lending.

Table 5.9: Sources of credit

Source of credit	MHH		FHH		All
	Frequency (N)	%	Frequency (N)	%	Frequency (N)
Formal institutions					
Banks	9	7	5	8	14
Cooperatives	25	18	7	11	32
Informal institutions					
Financial groups	55	38	22	35	77
Individuals	20	14	5	8	25
Relatives	10	7	7	11	17
No credit	18	14	17	27	35
Total	137	100	63	100	200

Own survey data (2003)

Studies have shown that poor households with access to financial markets feel less need to sell their productive assets (such as animals or tools) and have been found to recover more quickly after periods of stress than households without access to the financial market. Their nutrition security also suffers less (Heidhues and Schrieder, 1997; Heidhues, 2000; Zeller and Sharma, 2001). Results relating to the borrowing behaviour of respondents are presented in Table 5.10. From the findings, a higher number of respondents used the loans for consumptive purposes, with up to 110 respondents borrowing mainly for payment of fees (ranked first). Almost 93 respondents borrowed in order to purchase food, and this reason was ranked second among the consumptive reasons for borrowing by respondents. An equal number of respondents in both MHH and FHH borrowed in order to purchase food.

Table 5.10: Borrowing behaviour by purpose and gender

Purpose	MHH	FHH	Total
	Frequency (N)	Frequency (N)	Frequency (N)
Productive			
Farm inputs and implements	18	7	25
House construction	6	1	7
Expanding business	24	16	40
Total	35	25	72
Consumptive			
Food	47	46	93
Health	22	21	43
School expenses	85	25	110
Clothing	12	10	22
Paying dowry	6	0	6
Social events	20	20	40
Other uses	12	12	24
Total	204	134	338

Source: Own survey data (2003)
Note: The numbers exceed the sample size for the study because heads of households used the loans for more than one purpose.

Among the productive reasons for borrowing, the highest number of respondents in this category borrowed in order to expand their businesses, followed by borrowing in order to purchase farm inputs. Borrowing for health reasons and for social events was ranked fourth and fifth respectively. Social events in the region include circumcision of girls and boys, weddings, funerals and resolution of conflicts between villages. During these social events, a lot of money was spent.

5.5.5   Access to Agricultural Extension Services

Overall, there was poor coverage by extension services in the region. Contributing factors to this were poor infrastructure, few agricultural personnel to cover the whole region and lack of sufficient funds to carry out agricultural extension work. Out of a sample of 200 households, only 31% (total N for MHH =137) of the male headed households and 12% (total N for FHH =63) of the female headed households reported to have access to agricultural extension services in the 2002/2003 agricultural year (Figure 5.4). Out of the farmers that received extension services a majority had high education. Many female farmers who had low levels of education were at a disadvantage in terms of accessing extension services. A chi square test showed significant difference in access to extension services by gender of household head. This finding is in line with Jiggins, et al. (1997) and Kiplangat (2003) who found out that there is a bias against women, in accessing extension services in Kenya.

Figure 5.4: Access to Agricultural Extension Services

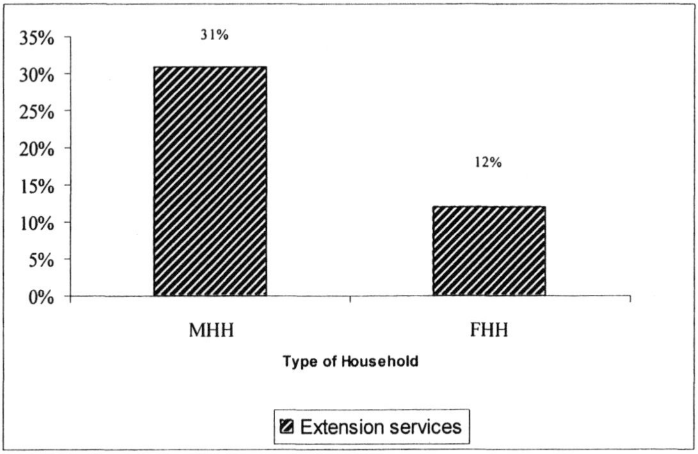

Source: Own Survey data (2003)
N is 134 for MHH and 43 for FHH. Not all households participated in farming. Only those who participated in farming needed agricultural extension services.

5.5.6 Decision making on Use of Resources

Control over the management of household finances, land and division of labour
are important components that determine household outcomes. Influence over
household decision making process has implications for household food security
and overall well being. In this study, it was found that women in FHH had large
decision-making role. In the absence of husbands (incases of migrant husbands))
some major decisions such as payment of school fees, purchase of farm inputs
sale of livestock had to be delayed, until the husband was consulted. In FHH
(widowed women, separated or those who never got married), women made all
decisions regarding overall well being of the household. In MHH women
reported to have a large influence on decision-making within the household,
although this was often 'behind the scenes', and therefore socially invisible. A
woman's decision-making within the household depended on her age and
household status. For example, all women with at least primary education
reported to participate in decision making on major issues affecting the
household. About 80% of women with a regular source of income, reported to
participate on how household finances should be managed. However, the final
decision on how the income was used was done by men. The adult married
women had the power to decide what household tasks were to be carried out and
who was to do them. In MHH, decisions regarding the crops to be grown,
sale/purchase of livestock or land were done by men.

5.6 Summary of Resource Allocation

The first objective of this study was to assess intra-household resource
allocation of land, human capital and financial capital along gender lines.
Findings on resource allocation reveal unequal access to land, education and
income in favour of men. Many households had no access to credit and
extension services in the entire study region. But they were the female headed
households that were at a disadvantage in accessing these two resources. It is
clear from findings that women have heavy work loads resulting from multiple
and competing reproductive and productive responsibilities, which are often
performed without labour-saving devices. Chi square and t-test results showed
significant differences between MHH and FHH in access to land, education,
income and agricultural extension. The findings confirm the hypothesis of the
study that there exists unequal access to land, human capital and financial

capital in the study site. The descriptive results on resource endowment set the stage for further analysis in the sections that follow.

5.7   Agricultural Productivity

5.7.1   Crop Production

Table 5.11 shows a comparison of the yields in kilograms of different crops grown in West Pokot. Maize is the main crop produced by both female and male-headed households. About 98% (N=134) of the MHH and 69% (N=43) of the FHH cultivated maize. Average yield was 1461.61 kg per ha of land for MHH and 1146.58 per ha of land for FHH. The average yield for maize in Kenya is 1500 kg/ha (Pingali, 2001), however most small holder farmers produced below the potential average of 4700 kg/ha (Hassan and Karanja, 1998).

Table 5.11: Yields of crops per ha of land by gender of household head

Crop	MHH (N=134)	FHH (N=43)	T-test
	Average yields	Average yields	
Maize	1461.61 (716.41)	1146.58 (235,80)	0.024*
Millet	34.82 (118.70)	30.25 (59.0)	0.773
Sorghum	36.42 (79.98)	28.57 (47.65)	0.471
Beans	136.22 (191.66)	186.77 (294.77)	0.011*
Cassava	10.175 (49.50)	5.5397 (20.15)	0.385
Banana	68.32 (375.43)	19.05 (93.03)	0.306
Sweet potatoes	3.97 (19.75)	6.98 (35.59)	0.444
Irish potatoes	77.52 (445.64)	91.43 (386.43)	0.831
Tomatoes	7.20 (27.55)	6.54 (14.14)	0.207
Onion	12.41 (50.65)	6.35 (35.35)	0.392
Kales	55.67 (231.51)	57.78 (250.19)	0.953

Source: Own survey data (2003)
Note: Not all households cultivated millet, sorghum, cassava, tomatoes and onions. N for millet, sorghum, cassava, tomatoes and onions is 25 for FHH and 75 for MHH.
* indicates significance at the 5 % level; Standard deviation are in parentheses.

T-test results in Table 5.11 show significant differences in the yields of maize and beans in male and female-headed households. Male-headed households had higher maize yields than female-headed households. FHH had higher yields in beans than MHH. There were no significant differences in the yield of all the other crops cultivated in both categories of households. In general, MHH had greater diversification in crops compared to FHH. This can be attributed to MHH having access to more land and labour.

5.7.2 Farm Inputs

Adequate and proper use of farm inputs determines farm productivity. A large percentage of households in the study region used neither fertilizer nor improved seed. Only 49% (n=21) of the FHH households used both fertilizer and hybrid seed. About 51% (n=22) used hybrid maize without using fertilizer. About 45% (n=60) of the MHH used fertilizer as well as hybrid seed, while 46% (n=61) of the MHH used hybrid seed without use of fertilizer. All households used manure and traditional seeds for millet, sorghum, and other crops grown. All households used household labour, and during peak periods hired labour was used. Table 5.12 presents amounts of farm inputs used by head of household. The findings reveal a weak statistical significance in fertilizer and hybrid seed use in the two categories of households. MHH households used more fertilizer (both basal and top dressing fertilizer) and improved seed in comparison to FHH. The average amount of fertilizer used in the study site is below the amount recommended by the ministry of agriculture, which is 50 kg per ha of land and above. The average intensity of fertilizer use in SSA has been reported to be low (roughly 8 Kg per ha). There has been an increase of fertilizer use in Kenya mainly on tea, sugarcane, horticultural crops and wheat, with minor increases on maize (Jayne, et al., 2003; Hassan and Karanja, 2003). There is no statistical difference as far as manure and traditional seed use are concerned. Three types of maize seed varieties were used by the farmers in the study area. These are: Katumi variety, with a maturity period of three months; 614 and 625 varieties. The statistical difference in maize yields in Table 5.11 above can be attributed to the use of inputs (fertilizer and hybrid seed) by MHH.

Table 5.12: Farm input use/ha of land

Input	MHH (N=134)	FHH (N=43)	T-test
	Average amount used per ha	Average amount used per ha	
Fertilizer (kg) –Basal	46.17 (28.88)	38.45 (24.54)	0.0342*
Top-dress fertilizer (kg)	45.56 (32.36)	40.48 (20.64)	0.625
Manure (kg)	34.82 (48.70)	30.25 (59.0)	0.773
Hybrid seed (kg)	11.10 (3.56)	7.656 (7.67)	0.0321*
Traditional seed (kg)	3.02 (3.57)	3.45 (3.54)	0.811
Hired labour (no of adult persons)	4.60 (4.271)	4.63 (4.20)	

Source: Own survey data (2003)

Notes: Not all households used fertilizer and improved seed. For that reason, N for amount of fertilizer used is 16 for FHH and 60 for MHH while use of seed N is 43 for FHH and 121 for MHH.

* indicate significance at 5% level

5.7.3 Gross Income per Hectare of Land

Overall, the average gross income per hectare for maize was KES 12,739.86 (approximately 159 Euros) in FHH, in comparison to KES 16,240.64 (approximately 203 Euros) for MHH. FHH had higher incomes from beans in comparison to male-headed households. Female-headed households cultivated beans because of their low input use in comparison to maize. Beans provide a cheap source of protein and were therefore cultivated for household consumption. The higher market prices of beans in comparison to maize contributed to FHH cultivating more beans. Table 5.13 shows the average income received from each crop by gender of household head.

Table 5.13: Comparison of average income received from each crop by gender of household head

	Male-headed households (N=123)		Female-headed households (N=63)		
	Average income (KES)	Std deviation	Average income (KES)	Std. Deviation	T-test
Maize	18240.64	7960.12	12739.86	13731.13	0.024*
Beans	2824.99	2785.27	4293.98	7316.49	0.041*
Irish potatoes	2937.96	11140.88	2285.71	9660.66	0.831
Sorghum	1056.93	3199.54	742.86	1905.99	0.471
Sweet potatoes	139.42	196.80	69.84	355.89	0.438
Tomato	215.95	826.57	76.19	424.16	0.207
Kales	834.98	3472.62	866.67	3752.85	0.953
Onion	186.13	759.76	95.24	530.19	0.392
Cassava	181.75	495.01	25.40	201.58	0.306
Banana	1708.03	9385.66	476.19	2326.96	0.382

Source: Own survey data (2003)
Note: 1,000 KES corresponded to 12.50 Euros at the time of the survey (2003)
1 Euro = 80 KES at the time of the survey

5.7.4 Household Food availability

All household reported to sell some of the yield at the end of the harvest period to meet other household expenditures. About 32% of the households reported that the amount of staple food (maize) produced was sufficient to meet their food intake for the whole year. About 56% of the households reported that their own production was not sufficient to carry them to the next harvest period. According to Pingali (2001) per capita consumption of maize which is the main staple crop in Kenya averages 103 kg/year. Given the large household sizes, own production alone was not sufficient to meet the yearly consumption needs. Therefore, these households had to depend on the market to compliment own production. About 12% of the households depended wholly on the market for the main staple food as well as other food commodities.

5.8   Household Food Security Analysis

In measuring household food security, a household food consumption survey was used. Data collected included: 24 hour food intake, weights of food consumed, food frequency data (giving frequency of common foods consumed) and indices of household coping strategies.

5.8.1 Indices of Household Coping Strategies

The person that was primarily responsible for serving family meals within the household was asked a series of questions regarding how the household responds during food shortages. Households using a higher number of strategies or using more severe strategies are likely to be poorer and more vulnerable to destitution. Hence, the higher the number of coping strategies, the more food-insecure the household is. Table 5.14 presents the results relating to household coping strategies during food scarcity by gender of household head. The results reveal that FHH used more severe coping strategies like reducing quantities served to children and women, and skipping meals. This can be deduced from the high mean of frequency of use of these three strategies. There were weak significant differences (at 10% level) in two strategies used for coping during food shortages: reduction of quantities served to children and women. Female-headed households reported using these two strategies more frequently than the male-headed households. Several studies (Radimer, Olson and Campbell, 1990; Wehler, Scott and Anderson, 1992; Hoddinott, 1999) have shown that children are protected until the severe later stages of food insecurity within the household. For this study, reduction of food served to children implies that the households were severely food insecure. All the other strategies used showed no significant differences in the two categories of households.

The weighted sum of the use of strategies was calculated by adding up all strategies used in the household and the frequency of use of these strategies. In calculating the severity of use of strategies, the strategies were given weights. A weight of 1 was ascribed to the strategies such as eating less preferred foods, and reducing the portion sizes of food served to men, children and women, and a weight of 2 to skipping meals and a weight of 3 to skipping meals for a whole day. The means for severity of strategies used and frequency of use are higher in female-headed households. There was a significant difference in the frequency of use or severity of strategies in the two categories of households with FHH using the more sever strategies than MHH.

Table 5.14: Indices of household coping strategies during food insecurity by gender of HH

Coping strategy	Type of Household		
	MHH (N=137)	FHH (N=63)	T Test
	Mean	Mean	
Consumption of less preferred foods	2.37 (0.97)	2.59 (0.75)	-1.556
Reduced quantity of food served to women	2.55 (1.18)	2.84 (1.13)	-0.436*
Reduced quantity of food served to men	2.19 (0.96)	2.25 (0.96)	-0.436
Reduced quantity of food served to children	2.20 (1.065)	2.51 (1.21)	-1.789*
Skipped some meals in a day	2.16 (1.26)	2.65 (1.21)	-0.995
Skipped meals for a whole day	1.42 (0.84)	1.57 (0.65)	0.427
Weighted sum reflecting use	12.86 (5.18)	15.71 (4.50)	-1.114
Weighted sum reflecting frequency and severity of use	17.85 (7.66)	19.83 (5.98)	-2.896**

Source: Own survey (2003)
Notes: * and ** indicate significance at 10% and 5 % level respectively; Standard deviation in parentheses

Table 5.15 presents results on the household coping strategies during food insecurity by region. There were significant differences in the means of all strategies used by households in the two regions (Chepareria and Kapenguria). Households in Kapenguria division were more food secure, since they had lower means for strategies used and hardly ever used strategies perceived to be severe, such as skipping meals for a whole day or skipping some meals in a day. On the other hand, households in Chepareria were more food insecure judging from the frequency of use of strategies perceived as severe. Results from crop productivity in the two regions, as discussed earlier, showed that households in Kapenguria division had higher productivity than those in Chepareria. Low agricultural productivity in Chepareria explains why households in this region were food insecure, as illustrated by their use of severe strategies during periods of food scarcity.

Table 5.15: Indices of household coping strategies during food insecurity by region

Coping Strategy	Categories of Households		
	Kapenguria (N=98)	Chepareria (N=102)	T Test
	Mean	Mean	
Consumption of less preferred foods	2.13 (1.03)	2.70 (0.70)	-4.583*
Reduced quantity of food served to women	2.18 (1.15)	3.04 (0.95)	-5.791*
Reduced quantity of food served to men	1.99 (1.10)	2.39 (0.79)	-3.020*
Reduced quantity of food served to children	1.78 (1.05)	2.73 (0.98)	-6.603*
Skipped some meals in a day	1.54 (0.95)	2.79 (1.17)	-8.158*
Skipped meals for a whole day Weighted sum reflecting use	1.45 (0.89)	1.36 (0.67)	0.834
	10.96 (5.02)	14.94 (4.19)	-6.107*
Weighted sum reflecting frequency and severity of use	15.26 (7.35)	20.56(6.07)	-5.589*

Source: Own survey data (2003)

Notes: Standard deviation in parentheses; *Indicates Significance at 10% level

Based on data on the weighted sum of use of strategies and frequency of use of strategies, the households were categorized into four groups: food secure, those suffering from mild food insecurity, the food insecure and those suffering from chronic food insecurity. This was done in order to get an impression about the households' food security situation. Table 5.16 presents the results for the food security categories in the study site. About 42% of MHH were food secure compared to about 29% of FHH. A higher percentage of FHH suffered from food insecurity. About 6% of MHH suffered from chronic food insecurity in comparison to only 2% of the FHH. A follow-up looking at other descriptive data showed that households suffering from chronic food insecurity were landless, did not engage in agricultural production and participated mainly in non-farm activities with no regular income, or the household head simply did not have any source of income. The household sizes of affected households were also large (up to 8 household members). Three households that were found to be food insecure engaged in agricultural production. However, these households sold most of the yield harvested, leaving the household with insufficient food until the next harvesting season. This indicates that sufficient food production does not automatically guarantee households of food security.

Table 5.16: Categories of food security by gender of household head

Category of food security		Type of household			
		Male-headed		Female-headed	
		Frequency	%	Frequency	%
Food secure		58	42.3	18	28.6
Mildly food insecure	food	34	24.8	22	34.9
Food insecure		37	27.0	22	34.9
Chronically food insecure	food	8	5.8	1	1.6
Total		137	100	63	100

Source: Own survey data (2003)
Notes: Food security – little or no evidence of food insecurity; mild food insecure – food insecurity without hunger; Food insecure - food insecurity with moderate hunger; Chronic food insecure - food insecurity with severe hunger (details in section 4.2.4.1).

Table 5.17 presents categories of food security in the study site by regions in West Pokot. About 53% of households in Kapenguria division were food secure, while 23% of households were food secure in Chepareria. Chepareria division had a higher percentage of households that were food insecure (mild food insecurity, food insecure, chronic food insecurity), when compared to Kapenguria division. About 77% of households in Chepareria were food insecure in comparison to 46% of households in Kapenguria division. The most affected locations in terms of food insecurity in Chepareria were the lowlands of Chepkopegh, Mwotot and Batei. In Kapenguria division, Aramaget, Kishaunet and Chemwochoi were the most affected by food insecurity. Households in these locations were found to be landless and household members had low levels of education, thus making it difficult for them to get meaningful remunerative jobs.

Table 5.17: Categories of food security by divisions in West Pokot

Category of food security	Division			
	Kapenguria		Chepareria	
	Frequency	%	Frequency	%
Food secure	52	53.1	24	23.5
Mildly food insecure	26	26.5	30	29.4
Food insecure	14	14.3	45	44.1
Chronically food insecure	6	6.1	3	3
Total	98	100	102	100

Source: Own survey data (2003)

Households were further divided into three socio-economic status groups based on their family income and the household asset base. Out of the 200 households, 138 households, representing about 69% of the total, were poor. About 22% (n=43) belonged to the middle socio-economic class, and 9% (n=19) were rich. Analysis of food security by household socio-economic status revealed that poor households were most affected by food insecurity in both categories of households (Table 5.18). Only 28% of the poor were found to be food secure, with the remaining 72% suffering from food insecurity (mild food insecurity to chronic food insecurity).

Table 5.18: Categories of food security by households' socio-economic status

Category of food security	Socio-economic status					
	Poor		Middle class		Rich	
	Frequency	%	Frequency	%	Frequency	%
Food secure	39	28.3	25	58.1	12	63
Mildly food insecure	44	31.9	10	23.3	2	10.5
Food insecure	50	36.2	5	11.6	4	21.2
Chronically food insecure	5	3.6	3	7.0	1	5.3
Total	138	100	43	100	19	100
Chi square	0.001**					

Source: Own survey data (2003)

The data revealed that the poor who were found to be food insecure, had a regular income (although low) and had small household sizes. A small number of households in the middle class and rich categories suffered from food insecurity compared to households belonging to the poor category. Middle and rich households that were found to be food insecure reported that most of the food crops produced were sold off immediately after harvest in order to meet other family expenditures such as payment of school fees. Chi-square results showed significant differences in household food security by socio-economic class.

5.8.2 Household Food Consumption

A 24-hour recall method in combination with weighing of food consumed was used to obtain information on the dietary intake of the household during the 24 hours preceding the interview/day preceding the interview. The information was used to characterize the mean caloric intake of members of a household. A 24-hour recall was done separately for children up to the age of five and adults living within the household. Data on food consumption for school-going children was not collected. The survey was conducted during the dry season preceding a harvest and went on until the end of the rainy season, when stocks of food were very low in most households. The results should therefore be interpreted with caution, since some households were worse off at the end of the rainy season as opposed to the end of the dry season (just after the harvest). The Nutri-survey software developed by the Nutrition Department of the University of Hohenheim was used to analyse the nutrient content of foods consumed. The main shortcoming associated with using this software was that some locally consumed foods in the region (local vegetables and fruits) are not included in the Kenya food data base of the software. Therefore, their nutrient content could not be accounted for. An attempt was made to solve this problem by selecting a food from the list of foods available in the software that was assumed to be close in nutrient content to the food consumed in other regions in Kenya. For example, for the case of vegetables such as cowpea leaves or *sukuma wiki* (kales), which are mostly consumed in Kenya, a vegetable such as spinach was selected from the list of vegetables in the software. For other vegetables such as *murele, lisutsa* and wild fruits, mixed vegetables and mixed fruits respectively were selected from the software to replace these foods.

Nutrient content of food may be altered depending on the method as well as the duration of cooking. This study only takes into account the different methods used to cook food by different households to a small extent. It does not take into account any losses in food nutrient as a result of other food preparation processes. Also, beyond the scope of this study is the individuals' ability to absorb nutrients. Individual requirements of each nutrient are related to a person's age, gender, level of physical activity and state of health. Some people will absorb or utilize nutrients less efficiently than others, while some may have difficulties absorbing some nutrients. For example, among older people, vitamin B12 absorption can be relatively poor (SCN, 2004). Sample groups for which dietary assessment was done are women aged 19 to 24 and 25 to 50, men aged over 19 years and children up to the age of five.

5.8.2.1   Dietary Diversity in the Household

There were differences in dietary diversity in the study area, with households in Kapenguria having more diverse diets than those living in Chepareria division. However, there was no significant difference in dietary diversity by head of household. Proportions of foods in daily dietary intake are shown in Figure 5.5. A high proportion of the dietary intake was composed of cereals, mainly maize and maize meal products. Roots and tubers (cassava, potatoes and arrowroots) formed part of the diet when maize products were not consumed. Traditional vegetables (*murele, cowpea leaves, managu*) were consumed on a large scale. Other common vegetables consumed were kales (commonly known as *sukuma wiki*), cabbage and spinach. During the dry season, some households reported consuming young cassava and sweet potato leaves. Also consumed were leaves from special trees. About 8% of the diet comprised milk products and eggs, vegetables and fruits. The most common kind of meat consumed in the region was goat meat. Beef was consumed on a few occasions and in many households offal from either cow or goat was consumed. All other categories of food were consumed in small quantities.

Figure 5.5: Proportional share of foods as % of all household food intake

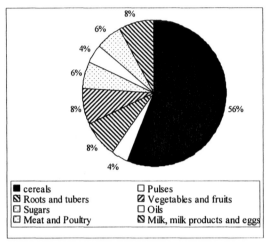

■ cereals	☐ Pulses
▨ Roots and tubers	▨ Vegetables and fruits
▥ Sugars	☐ Oils
▨ Meat and Poultry	▨ Milk, milk products and eggs

Source: Own data source (2003)

5.8.2.2   Dietary Assessment for Children

For infants under the age of six months, food and nutrition security implies exclusive breastfeeding of the child and utilization of preventive health services to ensure a healthy environment. Exclusive breastfeeding is the best strategy for ensuring food and nutrition security for the first six months and has numerous long-term advantages. Several studies have shown that infant morbidity and mortality is lower among breastfed than non-breastfed infants (WHO, 2002; Kramer and Kakuma, 2002; Jones et al., 2003). Of all the children aged 0 to 24 months in the sampled households (number of children in this age group = 69), about 58% (n = 40) were not breastfed during the time of the interview and about 42% (n = 29) were still being breastfed. For 56% of the women, exclusive[10] breastfeeding of their children went on for an average of four months and after this period other foods were introduced. The total range of exclusive breastfeeding was between 0 and 6 months. Women introduced

---

[10] Exclusive breastfeeding means that no other foods/fluids are given to the child except breastmilk and water or water-based drinks (WHO, 1996).

complementary[11] feeding at either the fourth or sixth month. During this period, women still continued breastfeeding. The average duration of breastfeeding was about 15 months and the range of breastfeeding was between 0 and 28 months as shown in Table 5.19.

Table 5.19: Child feeding practices for children aged 1 to 28 months

Parameter	Mean	Range	% of women
Exclusive/predominant breastfeeding in months	4.2 (2.7)	0 - 26	56
Average duration of breastfeeding in months	14.8 (10.8)	0 - 28	80

Source: Own survey data (2003)

Children were fed on various complementary foods. The starchy foods they were fed on included porridge, potatoes, rice and *ugali*. Among the protein foods, eggs, milk, goat meat and beans formed part of the menu, while traditional vegetables and fruits such as mangoes, oranges and wild fruits provided for their vitamin intake. A high proportion of the diet comprised carbohydrates, with 82% of the mothers reporting that they fed their children porridge every day. About 78% of the mothers fed their children potatoes and *ugali*.[12] The most popular animal protein food children were fed was milk and the most popular plant protein was beans. Children were seldom fed meat and eggs, partly because households could not afford to purchase meat, and even when households had chickens, they sold the eggs in order to obtain some income for the family.

Overall, there is uncertainty whether the household 24-hour recall was always complete, particularly for older children and other members of the household who stayed away from home during the day. Older children were likely to snack during their meals. These snacks included wild fruits, or simply fallen fruits from mango or guava trees, sweets and biscuits received from visitors or neighbours or begged from other children from well-off families. In the study site, the overall effect of the additional snacks would be an improvement in the micronutrient content rather than the energy content of the

---

[11] Complementary feeding means the introduction of other foods to the baby in addition to breastmilk.
[12] *Ugali* is the staple food in many households in Kenya. The main ingredients used to prepare *ugali* are water and maize meal.

diet. For children on breast milk, it was difficult to quantify how much milk the children fed on per day. The frequency of breastfeeding was taken into account and for each turn of breastfeeding, it was assumed that the baby consumed about 100 grams of milk.

Food composition analysis was carried out using the Nutri-survey software. The results relating to the nutrient intake of children of between 1 and 5 years reveal that carbohydrates composed the bulk of the nutrients consumed by children. Figure 5.6 and Table 5.20 show the nutrient intake of children aged 4 to 12 months and 13 to 49 months respectively.

Table 5.20: Nutrient intake analysis of children aged 13 to 49 months

Nutrient	Mean (Intake)	Standard Deviation	Recommended Level /day	Mean % Fulfilment
Calories	1433.6 kcal	256.5	1298.8 g	110
Protein	12.8 g	10.6 g	16.0 g	80
Fat	23.7 g	14.2	52.0 g	46
Vitamin A	371.3 µg	272.6	600 µg	62
Vitamin E	10.8 mg	8.25 mg		
Vitamin B 1	0.4 mg	0.6 mg	0.7 mg	59
Vitamin B2	0.4 mg	0.2 mg	0.8 mg	48
Vitamin B6	0.7 mg	0.3 mg	0.9 mg	78
Vitamin C	52.4 mg	28.6 mg	55.0 mg	61
Potassium	1144.5 mg	256.85	1500 mg	76
Calcium	198.6 g	150.5 mg	600.0 mg	33
Magnesium	150.4 mg	52.65 mg	140.0 mg	107
Phosphorus	330.4 mg	257.36 mg	800 mg	41
Iron	3.2 mg	6.8 mg	8.0 mg	40
Zinc	2.7 mg	5.8 mg	7.0 mg	38

Source: Own survey data (2003)
Note: Number of children aged 13 to 49 months = 156

On average, children aged 4 to 12 months and those aged 13 to 49 months consumed about 70% and 80% of the protein respectively. The caloric intake was adequate for the two age groups of children. The diet of children aged 4 to 12 months and 13 to 49 months was deficient in the core nutrients (fats and proteins) as well as in vitamins (except vitamin C), and in all minerals except magnesium. Deficiency in vitamins and micronutrients affects the overall health and development of the child. Iron deficiency, for example, leads to impaired cognitive development and lower school achievement (Grantham-McGregory and Ani, 2001). The high cost in terms of impaired cognitive development in turn has a large impact on economic productivity forgone.

Figure 5.6: Percentage Nutrient Intake for Children Aged 4 to 12 months

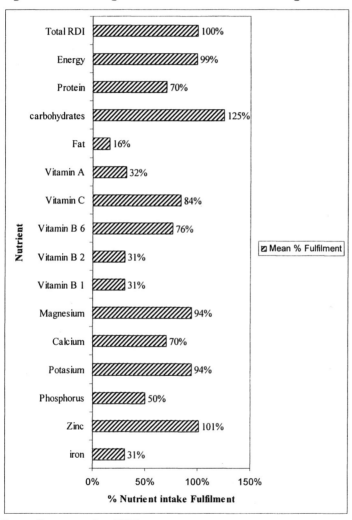

Source: Own survey data (2003)
Note: Number of children aged 4 to 12 months = 27

Iron deficiency is the most prevalent nutritional disorder reported by the World Health Organization. Zinc deficiency can lead to dwarfism, rough skin, poor immune system, mental lethargy and delayed puberty in adolescents. Deficiency in micronutrients such as vitamins and minerals can impair the body's ability to synthesize core nutrients such as carbohydrates, proteins and fats.

5.8.2.3   Nutrient Intake among Adults

Table 5.21 and Table 5.22 show the nutrient intake by women aged 19 to 24 and 25 to 50 in the study site. On average, women aged 19 to 24 consumed 1,958 kilocalories per day, and those aged 25 to 50 consumed 2,048 kilocalories per day, both measures falling below the recommended daily intake of 2197 and 2,270 kilocalories per day respectively. Daily intake of core nutrients such as carbohydrates, proteins and fat were below the recommended daily intake for women of these ages. Intake of micronutrients such as magnesium, vitamin A and B1 was satisfactory.

Table 5.21: Average nutrient intake for women aged 19 to 24 years

Nutrient	Mean (Nutrient Intake)	Standard Deviation	Recommended Level /day
Energy	1958.3 kcal	659.8 kcal	2197.9 kcal
Protein	47.7 g	25.6 g	48.0 g
Fat	47.0 g	23.2 g	72 g
Vitamin A	1890.5 µg	800 µg	236 µg
Vitamin E	23.7 mg	- mg	- mg
Vitamin B 1	1.3 mg	0.7 mg	1.2 mg
Vitamin B2	1.1 mg	0.6 mg	1.5 mg
Vitamin B6	1.9mg	0.6 mg	1.6 mg
Vitamin C	48.9 mg	25.8 mg	75.0 mg
Potassium	2300.1mg	651 mg	3500 mg
Calcium	558.0 mg	256.0 mg	1000mg
Magnesium	500 mg	126.4 mg	300mg
Phosphorus	1136.6 mg	256.3 mg	1500 mg
Iron	11.2 mg	6.8 mg	15.0 mg
Zinc	10.1 mg	7.0 mg	7.0 mg

Source: Own survey data (2003)

Notes: N=22 Female respondents

Whole maize meal commonly consumed in the form of *ugali* (a staple food in Kenya) was rich in micronutrients such as magnesium, zinc, potassium, and calcium, vitamin A as well as calories. However, due to the small quantities consumed, this food alone could not meet the required nutrient intake. The diet was deficient in vitamin C, vitamin B2 and B6, potassium, phosphorus, calcium and iron. Given that women aged 19 to 45 are in their child-bearing age, micronutrient deficiencies can lead to pregnancy complications and mortality among women (SCN, 2004). In addition, iron deficiency leads to anaemia, while calcium deficiency leads to the risk of hypertension.

Table 5.22: Average nutrient intake for women aged 25 to 50 years

Nutrient	Mean (Nutrient Intake)	Standard Deviation	Recommended Level /day
Energy	2048.1 kcal	469.8 kcal	2270 kcal
Protein	39.5g	25.6 g	48.0 g
Fat	35.1 g	25.0 g	77 g
Vitamin A	1326.5 µg	236 µg	800 µg
Vitamin E	6.5 mg	- mg	- mg
Vitamin B 1	0.9 mg	0.7 mg	1.0 mg
Vitamin B2	0.9 mg	0.6 mg	1.2 mg
Vitamin B6	0.8 mg	0.6 mg	1.2 mg
Vitamin C	71.0 mg	36.5 mg	100 mg
Potassium	2017.2 mg	651 mg	3500 mg
Calcium	203.6 mg	256.0 mg	1000mg
Magnesium	476.6 mg	126.4 mg	300mg
Phosphorus	1027.8 mg	256.3 mg	700 mg
Iron	8.9 mg	6.8 mg	15.0 mg
Zinc	9.8 mg	6.0 mg	7.0 mg

Source: Own survey data (2003)
Note: N=70 Female respondents

On average, the daily caloric intake of men aged 25 to 50 (2,186 kilocalories) was below the recommended daily intake of 2390 kilocalories, as can be seen from Table 5.23. Mean intake of protein, vitamin A, Vitamin B1, B2, B3, and B6 exceeded the recommended intake. However, the diets were deficient in fat, vitamin C and calcium. Men consumed a lot of goat meat that was rich in protein and got the largest share of all foods served. When the amount of meat available was limited, the men in the households still got the biggest share. Goat meat is rich in protein as well as Vitamin B1, B2, and B6. Measurement of micronutrient deficiencies in the sample population was out of scope of this study. However, nutrient intake analysis indicates that overall, a high percentage of the population may suffer from micronutrient deficiency related illnesses. Most affected by micronutrient deficiencies would be women and children as could be seen from their low micro nutrient intake presented earlier.

Table 5.23: Average nutrient intake for men aged 25 to 50

Nutrient	Mean (Intake)	Standard Deviation	Recommended Level /day
Energy	2186.3 kcal	506.4 kcal	2390.1 kcal
Protein	50.6 g	26.8 g	48.0 g
Fat	36.0 g	27.8 g	77.0 g
Vitamin A	841.3 µg	65.2 µg	800 µg
Vitamin E	14.5 mg		
Vitamin B 1	1.7 mg	0.5 mg	1.0 mg
Vitamin B2	1.7 mg	0.5 mg	1.2 mg
Vitamin B6	2.3 mg	0.8 mg	1.2 mg
Vitamin C	93.4 g	24.6 mg	100 mg
Potassium	2810.6 mg	265 mg	3500 mg
Calcium	689.1 g	375.6 g	1000 mg
Magnesium	561.4 mg	141 mg	310 mg
Phosphorus	817.4 mg	223 mg	700 mg
Iron	13.6 g	3.8 mg	15.0 mg
Zinc	14.5 mg	6.6 mg	7.0 mg

Source: Own survey data (2003)
Note: N=70 male respondents

5.9   Nutrition Security and Health Analysis

In this study, nutritional analysis is based on analysis of the body mass index (BMI) for women and child anthropometric measurements. According to Frankenberger and Maxwell (1992), anthropometric measurements may be viewed as the biological manifestation of nutrition security – a condition which combines having access to adequate food, being well cared for, and enjoying a healthy environment. The basic principle is that prolonged or severe depletion eventually leads to retardation of linear (skeletal) growth in children and loss of, or failure to accumulate, muscle mass and fat in both children and adults. Descriptive analysis of the children's health is carried out and presented in the sections that follow. Health of children is an important component in determining their nutrition status. For this reason, descriptive statistics on the health of the child are also presented.

5.9.1 Mother and Child Parameters

Women in the study area started the child-bearing process at an early age (16 years). Studies have shown that many teenage mothers are likely to give birth to underweight children and face higher health risks due to child-bearing complications. Results in Table 5.24 show that the average age of mothers in male and female-headed households was comparable. Male-headed households had a higher number of children in comparison to the female-headed households. The average number of children in both categories of households who had died before reaching their fifth birthday was the same in both categories of households.

Table 5.24: Mother and child parameters

Parameter	MHH (N=137)		FHH (N=63)	
	Mean	Range	Mean	Range
Age of the mother (years)	28 (6.4)	16 -49	29	14-49
Number of children born alive per family	3.7 (2.1)	1-11	2.7 (2.1)	1-7
Number of children under 5 per family	1.7 (0.6)	1-3	1.4 (0.6)	1-2
No. of children who have died under age five per family	1.28 (0.6)	0-3	1.28 (0.4)	0-3

Source: Own survey data (2003)
Note: Standard deviation in Parentheses

5.9.2 Access to Health Facilities

West Pokot district has limited health care facilities. There are two hospitals (Kapenguria district Hospital and Ortum Mission Hospital) in the district and four health centres/dispensaries (GoK, 2002). These facilities are inaccessible. The average distance to the health care facility is 15 Km, implying that patients have to walk for long distances to get to a health care facility. The patient doctor ratio is 1:84,528. The most prevalent diseases in the district are malaria, diarrhea and Urinary tract infections (GoK, 2002). The district is experiencing the negative effects of the HIV/AIDS pandemic especially in the economically active age cohort. It was not possible to get access to relevant documents relating to the HIV/AIDS infection rate in the district. The impact of this disease on productivity is therefore excluded in the analysis of this study.

5.9.3 Health of Children

Health-seeking behaviour includes both preventive and curative aspects. Infectious diseases such as diphtheria, tetanus, diarrhoea and respiratory infections are the leading causes of morbidity and mortality in young children. Numerous studies have demonstrated the relationship between low nutritional status and increased morbidity in children and vice versa. Smith et al. (2003) and UNICEF (1998) show the relationship between diarrhoea among children and increased severity of malnutrition. In a study by Yoon et al. (1997), low weight for age was a significant factor for diarrhoeal mortality in children under two years of age. Preventive measures such as immunization, timely and appropriate treatment are important care-giving practices for children.

The survey was conducted during the end of the dry season and went on until the rainy season. During the dry season, children in most households were not affected by common colds. The opposite occurred in the rainy season, with many children suffering from diarrhoea, common colds and malaria. From the study site, about 71 % (n=130) of the children had been sick during the two weeks prior to the interview or during the day of the interview. Table 5.25 shows the diseases the children suffered from according to their mothers' recall in the two weeks prior to the interview.

Table 5.25: Prevalence of illness among children under the age of 5

Disease	no of children in FHH N=54	no of children in MHH N=129	Total no of children (N=183)
Common cold	26	32	58
Diarrhoea	26	14	40
High fever	24	36	60
Malaria	24	22	46
Vomiting	10	6	16
Cough	16	12	28
Amoeba	4	1	5
Scabies	16	28	44
Pneumonia	6	6	12
Typhoid	1	1	2
Brucellosis	4	6	10
No illness reported	24	29	53

Source: Own data, West Pokot, 2003
Note: Multiple responses allowed

The top diseases children suffered from in the study site were the common cold, scabies, malaria, diarrhoea and high fever. Typhoid fever, brucellosis[13] and amoeba infections were prevalent in the study site due to poor sanitation and inadequate amounts of clean water for domestic use. There were no significant differences in the occurrence of illness among boys and girls in the study site. There was however, significance difference in occurrence of diarrhea in children in MHH and FHH households when a Pearson Chi square was run (P= 0.00252). There was no significance difference in occurrence of other illnesses. A high proportion of the children (>70%) received some treatment from local health care services, especially children who suffered from typhoid fever, brucellosis, pneumonia and malaria. Mothers also reported to have administered traditional herbs to treat some of the illnesses, especially for high fever, coughs and alimentary tract infections (vomiting and diarrhea). Given the high cost of

---

[13] Brucellosis is an infectious disease caused by the bacteria of the genus *Brucella*. Various *Brucella* species affect sheep, goats, cattle, deer, pigs, dogs, and several other animals. Humans become infected by coming in contact with animals or animal products that are contaminated with these bacteria. In humans, brucellosis can cause a range of symptoms that are similar to the flu and may include fever, sweats, headaches, back pains, and physical weakness. Severe infections of the central nervous systems or lining of the heart may occur.

medical care and inaccessibility of the health care centres, mothers opted for traditional diagnosis and medicines to treat the illness.

5.9.4 Nutritional Situation of Children

Anthropometric measurements from a total of 183 pre-children were used to carry out the analysis on the nutrition status of children. Overall, a high percentage of children in West Pokot suffered from wasting, stunting and underweight in comparison to the national estimates of the three anthropometric indices. Figure 5.7 compares the prevalence of malnutrition in West Pokot and the national estimates for three indices (weight for height, height for age and weight for age) for the year 2003. About 12% and 40% of children in the study region suffered from wasting and stunting respectively. These estimates are higher when compared to the national estimates of 6% and 37% for the same indices in the same year (2003). A higher percentage of children in West Pokot suffered from underweight (24%) compared to the national estimate of 23% for the same index.

The high prevalence of malnutrition in the study region points to an insufficient intake of nutrients by children, a poor health environment and poor care given to the children. The health environment is particularly compromised during both the rainy and dry seasons. In the dry season there is insufficient water, thus making it difficult to keep the living environment clean and prepare food in hygienic conditions. In the rainy season, most water points are shared by both humans and animals, thus exposing humans to water-borne diseases. Children in households whose source of water was unprotected – well/pond, rain-water, river, or public tap/borehole had a high prevalence of stunting, underweight or wasting. Members of households with private piped water are less likely to suffer from water-borne diseases during the rainy season. However, during the dry season the taps were dry and households were forced to purchase water from vendors. The safety of water being sold was questionable and such water posed health risks to its users.

Nutrition surveys carried out by the Welfare Monitoring Survey in 1997 and 2000, and by the Institute of Economic Affairs (IEA) indicate that semi-arid and arid regions of Kenya are most affected by malnutrition. West Pokot is one of the affected districts in the semi-arid regions of Kenya, recording a high prevalence of malnutrition and child mortality in both studies (GoK, 2001; GoK, 2002; IEA, 2002). At national level, the prevalence of stunting was highest

(42.3%) for children belonging to poor households in 1997. This pattern of child malnutrition holds true for children in rural and in urban areas. A high percentage of malnourished children in urban areas are from households residing in slum areas where sanitation is compromised.

Figure 5.7: Prevalence of malnutrition in children under 5 years in 2003

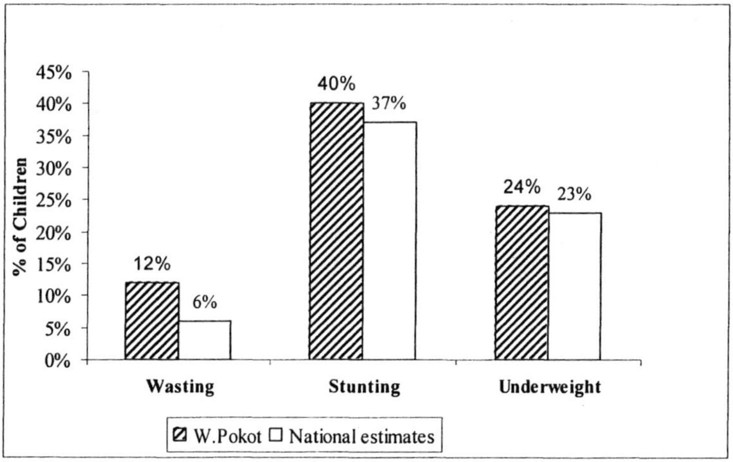

Source: Own survey data, 2003; source of national estimates: UNICEF, 2004

Table 5.26 shows the percentage of undernourished children (mean Z-score and t-values) obtained from the analysis. On average, the children in male-headed households were healthier than those in female-headed households, as can be deduced from the higher mean Z-scores for weight for height (WHZ) and weight for age (WAZ) in this category of households, in comparison the same indices in the female-headed households. Weight for height and weight for age Z-scores measure wasting and underweight respectively. Despite their poor performance on the WAZ and WHZ indices, children in female-headed households performed better on the height for age Z-score (HAZ), which measures stunting. Due to slight differences in percentage occurrence of the three anthropometric indices, a 2-tailed t-test was run to test if there was any statistical difference in the Z-scores of children in the two categories of households. T-test results showed no statistical difference in the means of Z-scores in MHH and FHH. This implies that children in the two categories of households were affected in the same way by malnutrition. Proper nutrition for children comprises a number of factors: adequate nutrient intake, healthy environment as well as caring practices. Women have a direct influence on all the three factors through their roles as care takers. Therefore lack of significance difference in the nutrition status of children in the two categories of households is an indication that women in both households have similar status in terms of education attainment, decision making capability and ability to carry on their child care roles.

Table 5.26: Percentage of undernourished children by household head

(-2SD reference as cut-off point)

Indicator	Type of Household		T-Value
	MHH (N=129)	FHH (N=54)	
	Mean	Mean	
Weight for height Z-scores	2.961(3.95)	0.860 (4.513)	0.921
Height for age Z-scores	-1.977 (4.809)	-2.245 (3.28)	1.404
weight for age Z-scores	0.0981 (4.575)	-0.793 (1.35)	1.198

Source: Own survey data (2003)
Note: N = number of children in each category of household

5.9.4.1   Prevalence of Malnutrition by Age and Sex

Table 5.27 shows the prevalence of malnutrition by sex and age of children in the study site. A higher percentage of girls (13.3%) suffered from wasting (acute malnutrition) in comparison to boys (9.7%). Stunting and underweight affected both girls and boys in the same way. Overall, girls and boys were affected by malnutrition in a similar way. The chi-square results showed no statistical differences in the nutritional status of boys and girls in the study site. Other studies have shown that girls in some regions, such as India, are more disadvantaged in terms of their nutrition status, i.e. more girls suffer from malnutrition. This is not the case in this study.

The occurrence of malnutrition was highest among children aged less than 12 months. A high percentage of children in this age category suffered from acute malnutrition (wasting), stunting (chronic malnutrition) as well as from underweight (a combination of the two). Other age categories that were most affected by stunting and underweight were ages 36 to 48 months and 49 to 60 months. According to the Academy for Educational Development (1999), children between the ages of 6 and 23 months are at highest risk of nutritional deficiency and growth retardation. The results of this study confirm this statement but also indicate that older children are still at risk of nutritional deficiency.

Table 5.27: Prevalence of malnutrition by sex and age of children in the study area

Parameter	Indicator of malnutrition					
	WAZ <-2SD		HAZ < -2SD		WHZ < 2SD	
	F	%	F	%	F	%
Male children (n=93)	22	23.7	38	40.1	9	9.7
Female children(n=90)	22	24.4	35	38.9	12	13.3
Age in months						
< 12 months (n=27)	10	37	15	55.6	4	14.8
12 – 24 months (n=42)	5	11.9	10	23.8	5	11.9
25 - 36 months (n=30)	6	20	11	36.7	6	20
37 – 48 months (n=43)	12	27.9	19	44.2	5	11.6
49 - 60 months (n=41)	11	26.8	18	43.9	1	2.4

Source: Own survey data (2003)

Using the WHO (1999) classification scheme, children were classified into those that were severely malnourished (-3SD) and those that suffered from moderate malnourishment (-2SD). Overall, a higher percentage of children had moderate malnutrition, as can be seen from all three indices used to measure malnutrition in Figure 5.8.

According to Groenewold and Tilahun (1990), the degree of malnutrition is positively related to the risk of mortality in respiratory tract patients. Other studies have attributed the high death rates in children in developing countries to mild to moderate malnutrition (SCN, 2000; Smith et al., 2003; SCN, 2004). These studies stress the importance of early intervention, even before the child has reached a severe status of malnutrition. In the study site, diseases were a potential risk factor for a child to become malnourished due to increased requirements and/or loss of appetite.

Figure 5.8: Severe and moderate malnutrition

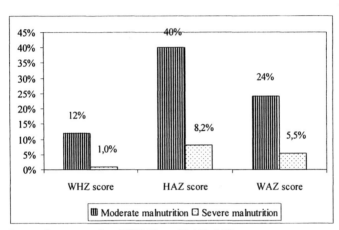

Source: Own survey data (2003) Note: N=183 children

5.9.4.2   Prevalence of Malnutrition in Children by Household Head

About 13% and 11% of children in female and male-headed households respectively were found to suffer from wasting, indicating a recent and severe process of weight loss, which is often associated with acute starvation and/or severe disease. Consequently, 30% and 22 % of the children in the female and male-headed households respectively were found to be underweight. About 46% and 37% of the children in female and male-headed households respectively were found to have stunted growth. Stunting reflects a process of failure to reach linear growth potential as a result of sub-optimal nutritional and/or health conditions. The higher prevalence of wasting, underweight and stunting in the female-headed households indicates that these households had poorer access to and utilization of food. Figure 5.9 compares the percentage of undernourished children by head of household.

Figure 5.9: Prevalence of malnutrition in MHH and FHH

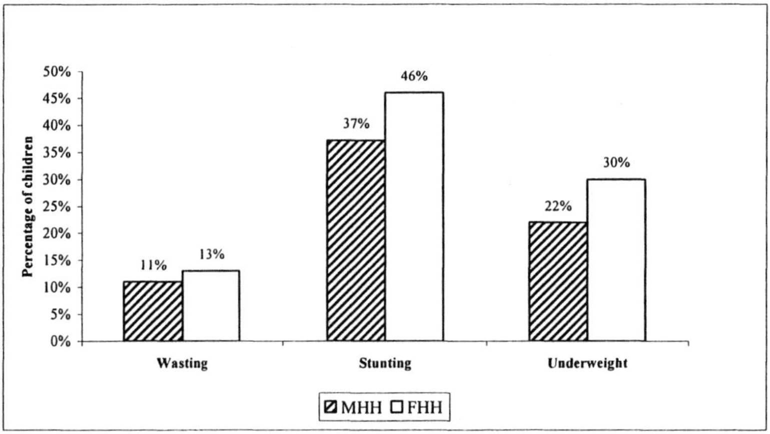

Source: Own survey data, 2003
Notes: Number of children in male and female headed households is 129 and 54 respectively

Table 5.28: Percentage of undernourished children (-2SD reference as cut-off point) by region

Variable	Division			
	Kapenguria (N=78)		Chepareria (N=105)	
	Frequency	%	Frequency	%
Wasting	8	10.3	13	12.4
Stunting	28	35.9	36	34.3
Underweight	17	21.8	27	25.7
Mean weight for height Z-scores	4.97(3.95)		0.341 (3.054)	3.664[***]
Mean height for age Z-score	-4.72 (7.051)		2.821 (3.382)	1.221
Mean weight for age Z-score	0.382 (6.865)		-0.793 (1.35)	1.281

Source: Own survey data (2003)
Note: ***significance at 1% level

Table 5.28 shows the percentage of undernourished children in the study region by division. A higher percentage of children in Kapenguria were stunted in comparison to children in Chepareria who suffered from the same. Chepareria division had a higher percentage of children who suffered from wasting and underweight. Results of a two-tailed t-test showed significant differences at the 1% level in the occurrence of underweight (WHZ) in the two regions, with children in Chepareria division being worse off as regards WHZ. There were no significant differences, however, in HAZ and WAZ in the two divisions.

5.9.5 Nutritional Situation of Women

Overall malnutrition is the main contributor to illness and disease in the world (Ezzati et al., 2004 and Ezzati et al., 2002), comprising risk factors related to undernutrition, excess consumption of certain dietary components (e.g. calories and fat), and low consumption of others (e.g. vitamins and fruits). Table 5.29 presents the body mass index of women in MHH and FHH households. BMI is the most commonly used anthropometric index to assess the nutritional status of adults. In this study, BMI was categorized into four groups: severe chronic energy deficiency (BMI of below 16), moderate chronic energy deficiency (BMI 16.0-18.5), normal/within the optimal range (BMI of 18.5-24.9) and overweight (BMI of over 25) based on FAO body mass index estimates. Results reveal that about 24% of women in MHH suffered from both severe and chronic energy deficiency in comparison to about 42.8% of women from FHH. More than half (60%) of the women in MHH had a normal BMI compared to about 41% of the women in FHH. Yet T-test results showed no significant difference in the mean BMI of women in the two categories of households. Lack of significant difference in the BMI was due to the inclusion of about 27 women who were overweight in the two categories of households. A T-test was run with the exclusion of the overweight women, and it showed a significant difference in the BMI, with women in MHH being better off. Maternal underweight is a key risk factor in low birth weight children. This in turn is a risk factor for child stunting and underweight (SCN, 2004).

Table 5.29: Comparison of BMI for women by gender of household head

Category of BMI	Type of household			
	MHH (N=111)		FHH (N=55)	
	Frequency	%	Frequency	%
Severe CED	3	2.7	2	3.6
Moderate CED	24	21.4	22	39.2
Normal	67	60.36	23	41.1
Overweight	18	16.1	9	16.1
Total	112	100	56	100
Mean BMI	21.025 (3.257)		20.599 (3.743)	

Source: Own Survey data, West Pokot, (2003)
Note: Standard deviation in parentheses,
N in MHH is 111 and not 137 and 55 in FHH and not 63. Measurements were not taken for all women in all households.

Comparison of BMI for women by division is presented in Table 5.30. More than half of the women had a normal BMI as per the FAO classification. About 53% and 54% of women had a normal BMI in Chepareria and Kapenguria divisions respectively. In Chepareria division, a higher percentage – about 40% – of women suffered from moderate chronic energy deficiency in comparison to about 15% of the women in Kapenguria division. T-test results showed a significant difference in the mean BMI at the 1% level, although the means for both regions fall within the 'normal' BMI category.

Table 5.30: Comparison of BMI for women by region

Category of BMI	Type of household			
	Kapenguria (N=83)		Chepareria (N=83)	
	Frequency	%	Frequency	%
Severe CED	2	2.4	3	3.6
Moderate CED	13	15.3	33	39.8
Normal	45	52.9	45	54.2
Overweight	25	29.4	2	2.4
Total	85	100	83	100
Mean BMI	22.363 (3.702)		19.366 (2.282)	
T-test value	6.298[***]			

Source: Own survey data, 2003
Note: [***] Significant at level 1%; CED = chronic energy deficiency

5.10 Summary

The second objective of this study was to determine the food security situation in the study region and make comparisons based on the gender of the household heads and access to the main production resources – land, financial capital and human capital. There were higher maize yields in MHH in comparison to FHHs. MHHs practiced more crop diversification due to access to land and more labour. During food insecurity, FHHs used more severe coping strategies such as skipping meals and reducing quantities of food served to children and women. Households that produced their own food were found to be more food secure as opposed to those who depended on the market for the main staple food (maize). However, results also show that sufficient own food production does not always guarantee food security for some households. What was important was the amount of food stored for future use and ability of households to access food from the market through purchase. The economic status of the household was most important in determining household food security, as could be seen from the strong significance that emerged according to the economic status of the households. Poor households were most affected by food insecurity. In terms of nutrient intake, neither male nor female respondents met the recommended dietary intake for their age. However, most at risk of micronutrient deficiencies were women and children.

A higher percentage of children in female-headed households were undernourished in comparison to undernourished children in male-headed households. Overall, there was a high frequency of illness in the study site. Most children suffered from alimentary and respiratory diseases. More than half of the women in the sampled households were found to be healthy as per the BMI. The descriptive statistics in this chapter are the basis for the econometric analysis in Chapter 6 of this work.

6 EFFECTS OF RESOURCE ACCESS & OWNERSHIP ON HOUSEHOLD WELFARE AND FOOD SECURITY

Land, human capital and financial capital are important factors that affect the food and nutrition security situation within households. Access to and control over these resources is important in determining household food security. Access to these resources also determines many other household characteristics such as living standard, expenditure patterns, health-seeking behaviours and overall welfare of household members. The relationship between access to these three resources, household food security and other household socio economic characteristics is the central research issue of this study. Access to land, human capital and financial capital is hypothesized to: increase agricultural productivity; improve nutrition status of household members as a result of improved access to food and purchasing power. Specifically, access to education is also hypothesized to: improve the nutrition status of household members; increase household income (both agricultural and non-agricultural incomes) and; reduce child morbidity and fertility rate in women.

The first section of Chapter 6 analyses the determinants of household income, followed by analysis of the determinants of nutrition status of children. The sections that follow, deal with analysis of the determinants of maize productivity, and food security. Finally, an analysis of the relationship between education and a number of household characteristics is undertaken.

6.1 The Two Stage Heckman Procedure: Determinants of Household Income

In this section, the determinants of a household's farm and non-farm incomes are analysed. A particular focus is given on the evaluation of the effects of the farm size and human capital variables. The income determination functions were estimated for farm and non-farm incomes using a two-stage Heckman procedure. This procedure is used to avoid the sample selection bias caused by a large number of non-participants in either farm or non-farm income.

The two-stage Heckman procedure involves two stages. The first stage estimation was a probit function in which the dependant variable was the probability that an individual participated in non-farm/farm employment. The dependant variable was 1 if the individual was a participant in non-farm activities, and 0 if not. The independent variables used include individual characteristics such as age, schooling, size of land, region and gender dummies to represent differences in rates of participation in non-farm employment.

Stage 1

$$prob(y_i = 1) = \alpha + \sum \beta_1 S_{ik} + \beta_2 A_i + \beta_3 Z_i + \beta_4 G_i + u_i \qquad 6.1$$

where

y   1 if a person participated in non-farm employment, 0, otherwise

$\beta_1.....\beta_4$ coefficients to be estimated
A age
Z region dummy
G gender dummy
S_k schooling to education level k

    In the probit analysis, the effects of explanatory variables on farm/non-farm employment participation are estimated. The main interest is the effect of the unmeasured characteristics of the respondents on the employment participation decision. Information on the effect of these unmeasured characteristics is not available in the coefficients of the explanatory variables. However, in the residuals of the probit analysis, it is. In the Heckman procedure, the residuals of the selection equation are used to construct a selection bias control factor which is equivalent to the inverse Mills ratio (Smits, 2001; Batzlen, 2000). This factor reflects the effects of all unmeasured characteristics which are related to unemployment. The value of this factor (inverse Mills ratio) is saved and added to the data file as an additional variable. Using the SPSS syntax, the inverse Mills ratio (lambda) was calculated using the procedure detailed by Smits (2001).

    Stage 1: First a logistic regression was carried out, after which the predicted residual for the explanatory variables were saved. Next, transformation of the predicted residuals was transformed into probit scores as follows:

IPS = Probit (predicted residuals)

Where: IPS = individual probit scores

Next, the inverse Mills ratio (lambda) was computed as follows:

Lambda = ((1/SQRT (2*3.141592654))*(EXP(-ips*ips*0.5))) /CDFNORM(ips). In the second stage of the Heckman procedure, an ordinary least squares regression is done in which the effects of education on income is taken into consideration. Yearly non-agricultural income is used as the dependant variable for the non-farm income function. The dependant variables included are those pertaining to individual characteristics, including the dummies for gender and region. The predicted inverse Mills ratio/selectivity correction obtained from the first equation is used as a regressor in the second-stage equation. Due to the presence of the control factor in the analysis, unmeasured characteristics that are also related to employment are taken care of, and other predictors in the equation are freed from the effect of unmeasured characteristics. The regression analysis produces unbiased coefficients for the other predictors in the equation.

Stage 2

$$W = \alpha + \sum \beta_1 S_{ik} + \beta_2 A_i + \beta_3 Z_i + \beta_4 G_i + \lambda \qquad 6.2$$

Where:

w	yearly earnings from non-farm employment
$\beta_1 \ldots \beta_4$	coefficients to be estimated
A	age
Z	region dummy
G	gender dummy
S_k	schooling to education level K
λ	inverse Mills ratio

Equation 6.2 gives us an estimate of the rate of return to schooling for individuals in wage employment (non-farm employment). In addition, it gives the contribution of other parameters included in the equation to earnings in non-farm employment. The same procedure was repeated for the farm income function, with the inclusion of household characteristics in the second stage of the equation (OLS equation) as independent variables. Household characteristics are included, since it is presumed that individuals' decision to work in the farm sector is affected not only by individual characteristics but also by the characteristics of other household members. Thus, the number of working members of the household aged 15 to 65, regardless of type of job and household size is included. A vector H, containing the household characteristics is introduced in the equation. It is expected that the returns to schooling for those in farm employment and non-farm activities will differ due to personal and

household characteristics (average education of household members, age, and dependency ratio). In addition, size of land (L) a household owns is included in the regression, since land is an important production resource which may contribute significantly to farm income. The dependant variable is the farm income. It includes revenue from all crops and livestock production, and revenues from lending farm resources minus all farm expenses for that year (expenses from inputs and services for crop and animal production, rent of land, and expenses for transportation of farm inputs). The farm revenue was for the year 2002/2003. The function for farm income can be formulated as follows:

$$W_i = \alpha + \sum \beta_1 S_{ik} + \beta_2 A_i + \beta_3 A_i^2 + \beta_4 Z_i + \beta_5 G_i + \beta_6 H_i + \beta_7 l_i + \lambda \qquad 6.3$$

6.1.1 Estimation Results

Table 6.1 shows the probit estimates for participation in non-farm income. The probit coefficient for age is positive (0.0125) for male respondents but negative (-0.0014) for female respondents. This implies that with increasing age, males increased their chances of participating in non-farm employment, while the chances for non-farm employment decreased for women with increases in age.

The probit coefficients for all education levels are positive. Male and female respondents with college education had a higher likelihood of participating in non-farm employment as opposed to those who had only primary or secondary-level education. The results also show that an increase in an individual's education from one level to the next increased his/her probability of participating in non-farm income.

The probit coefficient for the gender dummy is negative for the female probit function and positive for the male probit function, an indication that participation in non-farm employment is influenced by the gender of the household head. Both female and male members of the household were less likely to participate in non-farm employment if the household head was female. This can be attributed to the low levels of education among members of female-headed households in comparison to those in male-headed households. With a low level of education, participation in non-farm employment was limited.

Table 6.1: Probability of participating in non-farm income

Parameter	Probability of participating in non-farm income for men (probit) (N=156)	Probability of participating in non-farm income for women (N=197)
Constant	-4.514	-0.759
Age	0.0125	-0.0014
Education of HH		
Primary dummy	0.813	0.052
Secondary dummy	1.319	0.494
College dummy	1.522	1.407
HH Gender dummy	-0.768	-0.645
Region dummy	-1.245	-0.812
Ratio of working HH members	0.0196	0.032
Size of land	0.0076	0.0011
Pearson goodness of fit chi-square	265.318	6250.65
DF	147	188
ρ	0.00	0.000

Source: Own survey data (2003)

Note: Dependant variable was participation in non-farm employment: 1 = participant in non-farm employment and 0 = non-participant

The region dummy is negative for both males and females. The region in which an individual lived greatly influenced his/her participation in non-farm employment. Individuals in remote parts of West Pokot, where infrastructure was poor and access to markets limited, had less chance of participating in non-farm employment. The size of the land influenced participation in non-farm employment, although not significantly, as can be seen from its weak coefficient. The Pearson goodness of fit Chi-square is significant, indicating that there were significant differences between male and female respondents as far as participation in non-farm employment was concerned.

6.1.2 Farm and Non-Farm Incomes

The OLS estimates for determinants of farm and non-farm income are presented in Table 6.2 and Table 6.3 respectively. Both the standardized and non-standardized coefficients are reported. The coefficients for region dummy, household non-farm income, education and age are significant for both men and women. The region dummy has a negative coefficient (-0.582) and led to a reduction in farm revenue when one moved from Kapenguria to Chepareria division. The reduction in farm revenue as one moves from one division to the next can be attributed to the more favourable climatic conditions in Kapenguria in comparison to Chepareria, which were not the main focus of this data. Data on these two variables are not included in the analysis. In addition, differences could be attributed to differences in farm input use in the two regions.

Schooling contributes positively to farm income for both men and women. For women, all three levels of education for women contributed significantly to farm income. Secondary education has the most significant contribution to farm income for both men and women. Secondary education of women contributed significantly to farm income, as could be seen from the high coefficient, which was significant at the 99% level. For the women and the men, attaining college education contributed significantly to non-farm income, but its contribution to farm income is weak, as can be seen from the weak significance of the coefficient. Many individuals with college/university education are employed in the public or private sectors in Kenya. For farm income, secondary school level education seemed to contribute significantly, since many secondary school graduates were employed in the farm sector. College education did not contribute significantly to farm income, as can be seen from the low coefficient, which was not significant. The OLS results provide evidence that schooling has a significant impact on both farm and non-farm income, as can be deduced from the positive and significant coefficients of education in both the farm and non-farm income functions.

From the coefficients of the different levels of education it can be seen that returns to primary, secondary and college education in the farm/agricultural sector are higher for women than for men. On the other hand, returns to the non-farm sector are lower for women with primary and secondary education when compared to returns for the same level of education for men. Thus, it is more beneficial for those with primary education to work in the agricultural/farm sector than in the non-farm sector, and it is more beneficial for those with college/university education to work in the non-farm sector than in the farm sector. Those with secondary education benefit more by working in the farm sector than in the non-farm sector, while those with college/university education lose when employed in the farm sector.

Coefficients for off-farm income are significant for both men and women. Off-farm income is important since it can be used to purchase inputs to be used on the farm, thus increasing the farm productivity. Age does not seem to exert any significant impact on farm incomes for men. The coefficient for age for men is negative, implying that with an increase in age, farm revenue was likely to fall. However, the coefficient for age for women was positive, implying an increase in farm revenue with an increase in women's ages, which can be attributed to the experience that women gain over time. Thus, with an increase in age, they have more experience of farming and therefore achieve higher returns. In non-farm employment, it is assumed that with an increase in age, an individual gains more experience. There is therefore a yearly increment on an individual's salary each year they are in public/private-sector employment. Age squared was dropped from the analysis due to collinearity.

OLS coefficients for the gender dummy are negative in the farm income function but are not significant. With a female head of household, the farm income is likely to be lower, although not significant. Lack of significance in the coefficients implies that women tend to contribute to farm income as much as men do. However, in the non-farm income function, the coefficient for the gender dummy is negative for the income function for women and positive for the income function for men. The weak statistical significance in the gender dummy coefficient for both men and women indicates that men contribute more to non-farm income than women. These findings can be attributed to a higher number of men in well-paid jobs due to their higher levels of education, as well as their involvement in lucrative business activities that are more economically rewarding. In addition, income from migration may have been a factor contributing to this phenomenon, since men were more likely to migrate in search of well-paid jobs than women, thus raising their incomes.

The coefficient for the region dummy is negative and significant for both farm and non-farm income, indicating that the region where the HH lived greatly determined their levels of both farm and non-farm incomes. Better infrastructure and proximity to the market contribute to the differences in incomes in the two divisions in the study region, with households in Kapenguria division being better off. Size of farm has a positive coefficient for farm income, which is statistically significant for the coefficient for the men, an indication that the size of the farm does contribute significantly to farm income. However, the coefficient for farm size in the income function for women is not significant. With greater access to land, the men had the possibility to diversify their farm activities, and hence earn more income from the different activities. The women, on the other hand, had limited access to land, which also limited the activities they could carry out on the farm. There is no statistical significance on the coefficients for the ratio of working household members, either for farm or non-farm income. Lack of significant coefficients for non-farm income could be due to the fact that a large proportion of working members have already moved from home (they may reside in the same compound but live in their own houses) and only make small remittances to their parents. The coefficients for the selection control variable are positive and highly significant in the non-farm income function for men, an indication that the characteristics of those participating in non-farm income are different from non-participants. In addition, the significance of the selection control factor implies that the selection bias of not including non-participants in either income function was large for men. For the women, the selection control variable had positive coefficients but was not significant, an indication that although these factors contributed positively to the OLS regression, they were not significant.

About 83.1% and 62.2% of the variation in the non-farm income function for men and women respectively could be explained by the model. The adjusted r^2 was 0.831 and 0.622 for men and women respectively. About 41.3% and 37.2% of the variation in the farm income function for men and women respectively could be accounted for. The adjusted r^2 values for these functions are low, and this is due to other factors such as soil quality, climatic conditions in the region which were not included in the data base and hence are not in the model. Other factors that may contribute to non-farm income which did not form part of the data base contribute significantly to non-farm income. Such factors include unobserved characteristics such as individual ability, quality of school an individual attended and individual family background, which may have an impact on the individual's level of performance and hence their future earnings.

Table 6.2: Determinants of farm income by gender (two-stage Heckman's procedure estimates)

Variable	Farm income for men		Farm income for women	
	Unstandardized coefficients	Standardized coefficients	Unstandardized coefficients	Standardized coefficients
Constant	12747	2.131*	19973.87	2.829**
HH gender dummy	182.52	0.045 (1.784)	-5158.87	-0.044 (-0.246)
Region dummy	-7717.985	-0.142 (-1.887)*	-5784.75	-0.240 (-2.019)*
Farm size	2641.332	0.649 (6.313)***	2306.796	0.184 (1.971)*
Schooling of HH Primary dummy Secondary dummy College dummy	1586.70 9704.09 6268.40	0.029 (0.175) 0.150 (1.022)* 0.098 (0.520)	13640.9 19539.6 6143	0.667 6.534)** 0.860 6.584)** 0.219 (1.534)*
HH size	690.142	-0.043(-0.583)	-1038.082	-0.015 (-0.270)
Age of adult male	40.915	0.035 (0.222)	1026	0.004 (0.172)
Schooling of adult Female (if not HH) Primary Secondary College	10310.45 10733.13 11680.93	0.190 (1.929) * 0.120 (1.313)* 0.166 (2.189)**		
HH off-farm income	1853	0.292 (3.438)**	631	0.456 (3.981)**
Selection control variable	18.800	0.380 (0.008)	-17.5	-0.176 (0.702)
Adjusted R²	0.413		0.372	
Number of observations	156		196	

Source: Own survey data (2003)

Notes: Dependant variable: farm revenue

Numbers in parentheses are t-statistic values for each variable. The dependant variables for the OLS functions are yearly earnings from farm employment. The signs *, ** and *** indicate significance at the 10%, 5% and 1% level respectively.

Table 6.3: Determinants of non-farm income by gender

Variable	Non-farm income for men		Non-farm income for women	
	Unstandardized coefficients	Standardized coefficients	Unstandardized coefficients	Standardized coefficients
Constant	63305.02	(4.381)***	12988.9	(4.031)***
HH gender dummy	1616.31	0.118 (1.23)*	-20746.66	-0.181 (-0.78)
Region dummy	-83901.79	-0.582 (-11.17)***	-11920.55	-0.111(-0.49)***
Schooling of men				
Primary	20903.45	0.146 (0.959)		
Secondary	48291.55	0.515 (3.87)**		
College	88792.12	0.753 (5.47)**		
Schooling of women				
Primary			1364.90	0.054 (0.58)
Secondary			5941.60	0.098 (1.55)*
College			13143	0.327 (3.45)**
Age	-504.30	-0.075 (-2.06)*	778.506	0.136 (2.73)***
Selection control variable	122654	0.774 (12.75)***	43819.621	0.292 (0.85)
Number of observations	123		114	
Adjusted R^2	0.831		0.648	

Source: Own survey data, 2003

Dependant variable: non-farm income

Notes: Numbers in parentheses are t-statistic values for each variable. The dependant variables for the OLS functions are yearly earnings from non-farm employment. The signs *, ** and *** indicate significance at the 10%, 5% and 1% level respectively.

6.2 Logistic Regression: Determinants of Child Nutrition Status

A logistic regression was used to analyze the probability of a child being undernourished or not. Two logistic regression analyses were performed separately, i.e. for female-headed households and male-headed households. This was done to establish whether household characteristics in the different households affected the nutritional status of children living in these households differently. The logit model was estimated as follows:

$$prob(y_i = 1) = f(X_1, X_2, X_3, X_4, X_5, X_6, X_7, X_8, X_9)$$ 6.4

Where

$Y_i = 1$ if the child is malnourished and 0 otherwise

f = coefficient to be estimated

X_1 = economic status of household

X_2 = education level of household head

X_3 = education level of mother of child if not household head

X_4 = age of the child

X_5 = caloric intake

X_6 = availability of toilet facility

X_7 = availability of water

X_8 = frequency of illness

X_9 = age of the mother

As can be seen from Table 6.4, the logistic regression analysis identified education of household head, education of mother, economic status of the household, age of the child, and caloric intake as determinants of stunting among children in both male and female-headed households. Children in households where the household head had only primary education were 1.25 and 1.44 times likely to be stunted in male and female-headed households respectively. Children in households where the household head had no formal education were 1.36 and 1.89 times likely to become stunted in male and female-headed households respectively. Children whose mothers had primary education had a lower probability of being malnourished compared to those whose mothers had no formal education at all. Some studies have shown that parental education is associated with efficient management of limited household resources, greater utilization of available health care services, better health-promoting behaviours, lowered fertility and more child-centred caring practices, all factors associated with better child health and nutrition (Smith, 2003; Haddad, 2002). Studies in developing countries have also shown the importance of maternal education for child nutrition (Jones et al., 2003; Quisumbing, 2003; SCN, 2000).

The economic status of the household was important in determining the nutritional status of the children. Children from poor households were 2.48 and 2.01 times more likely to be malnourished in male and female-headed households respectively. Children from middle and rich families had a lower likelihood of being malnourished, i.e. 1.24 and 1.87 times for middle class children in male and female-headed households respectively. The economic status of the household was measured in terms of income and asset base of the household. The results indicate the association between household economic status and household food security in general and nutrition status of children in particular. Poor households often do not have enough money to purchase nutritious food for their children or pay for their health care.

The findings of this study showed that the risk of stunting increases with age. This is not surprising, since stunting is a cumulative process that occurs as a result of inadequate dietary intake and/or risk of illness. Children at a lower age (0-12 months) were at significantly lower risk of stunting compared to children in the older age groups. This low risk of stunting may also be due to the protective effect of breastfeeding. A high prevalence of malnutrition in older age groups may be an indication of either inappropriate food supplementation in quantity and quality during weaning, or exposure to diseases. However, it should be noted that, after the age of 12 months, the method of height measurement changed from lying down to standing. Due to change in measurement mode, children may appear shorter, resulting in an increase in stunting.

Dietary assessment of children based on 24-hour recall (frequency of meals and nutritional content of the meals served to children) was included in the analysis as a measure of food adequacy/availability. Children in food-insecure households were 1.07 and 1.02 times more likely to be malnourished. The odds ratio for this variable, however, did not show any statistical significance in the two categories of households. This indicates that malnutrition is not just about food deprivation but a combination of food deprivation and other factors such as care and health. Consequently, children in households with an unprotected water supply are 1.45 and 1.95 times more likely to be stunted in male and female-headed households. And children in households without a toilet facility have a 1.24 and 0.94 chance of being stunted. Availability of safe drinking water and toilet facilities are not significant in the regression analysis. This is because water and toilet facilities are not only environmental measures but also proxies for economic status. Households with high socio-economic status tend to have private piped water and ensure that the water is treated.

Table 6.4: Probability of a child suffering from undernutrition

	Male-headed		Female-headed	
	Odds ratio	Wald χ^2 statistic	Odds ratio	Wald χ^2 statistic
Education of HH				
No education	1.36	3.256*	1.89	3.213*
Primary	1.25	1.056	1.44	3.024*
Secondary +	1.00		1.00	
Education of the mother	1.94	2.091*	1.53	7.982**
No education	1.59	5.568**	1.90	3.178**
Primary	1.00		1.00	
Secondary +				
Economic status of HH				
Poor	2.48	2.990*	2.01	6.821**
Middle	1.240	1.156	1.87	3.878*
Rich	1.00	0.056	1.00	
Child's age in months				
6-12	1.00		1.00	
13-24	1.98	3.450*	3.68	6.481**
25 – 36	1.96	2.582*	3.37	6.248**
37 – 59	1.27*	3.213*	3.77	4.277**
Sex of child				
Female	1.20	0.56	1.08	0.44
Male	1.00		1.00	
Caloric intake				
Food insecure	1.07	0.82	1.02	0.78
Food secure	1.00		1.00	
Availability of toilet facility				
No facility	1.24	1.842	0.94	1.13
Facility available	1.00		1.00	
Source of water for the household				
Unprotected	1.45		1.09	0.832
Protected	1.00		1.00	
LR	53.625		44.737	
p-value	0.00		0.00	
Nagelkerke R-square	0.495		0.553	

Source: Own survey data (2003)   Notes: ** Significant, unmarked = not significant; Dependant variable (nutrition status dummy: 1 if child is undernourished, 0 = otherwise)

Height for age Z scores used to categorise children into undernourished and not nourished

6.3   Two-Stage Least Squares: Determinants of Stunting, Wasting and Underweight in Children

The results of the logistic regression show the likelihood of a child being malnourished. To be able to estimate the contribution of each of the variables to the child Z-score, analysis using the two-stage least squares estimation method (2SLS) was carried out. The 2SLS estimation method was used due to the endogenous nature of the explanatory variables. The 2SLS procedure involves first regressing each of the endogenous variables on all the exogenous variables in the system in order to calculate the estimated values of the endogenous variables. In the second stage, the estimated values are used as regressors in an ordinary least squares regression. The 2SLS regression was done using the SPSS software which does the first and second steps of the analysis in one go. The height for age, weight for age and weight for height Z-scores were used as the dependent variables in separate regression analysis. The model can be estimated as follows:

$$N = \alpha + \beta_1 edu + \beta_2 age + \beta_3 genHH + \beta_4 health + \beta_5 incomemum + \beta_6 incomeHH + \beta_7 childsex$$
$$+ \beta_8 kcal + \beta_9 waterdummy + u$$

where α, $\beta_{1,....}$, β_9 are coefficients to be estimated;
edu   education of household head
age   age of mother
genHH   gender dummy of HH
health   health of child (measured in terms of frequency of illnesses)
childsex   sex of child dummy
kcals   caloric intake
waterdummy   source of water (protected water source = 1, unprotected = 0)
Incomemum   income for mothers
IncomeHH   income for household head
U   error term

The explanatory variables included in the model and how they relate to child nutritional status are discussed in detail in Chapter 4 of this study. Variables that are assumed to be exogenous to the household and that are used as instrumental variables are household assets, household characteristics such as size of household, religious affiliation, ecological region, home gardening participation, and mean price of the main food groups consumed in the region. Some of these variables may be affected through unobserved household characteristics, making them inappropriate for use as instruments. To test for exogeneity of instruments, the generalized method of moments specification test was used. The method was used to test whether the instruments are uncorrelated with the error term. This test examines the existence of correlation between the instruments and the estimation residuals, by assessing how close the cross products of instrumental variables and residuals are to zero when evaluated at the estimated parameter value. The specification test is general in that rejection can occur not only because of endogeneity of variables, but also because of omitted variables. The statistics are low for all the models, indicating a weak statistical evidence of endogeneity of instrumental variables used. Results of the test are reported and labeled as chi square statistic in the result tables.

The determinants of nutritional status as obtained from the two-stage least squares regression analyses are presented in Table 6.5, Table 6.6 and Table 6.7. Education of the mother, frequency of illness and caloric intake of the child emerge as the main determinants of nutritional status in the study site, as can be seen from the coefficients of the three variables. The coefficients for these variables are highly significant at the 99%, 95% and 90 % levels. Using years of schooling would give an exaggerated improvement in the child Z-scores with each additional year of school. For this reason, years of education were transformed into levels of education to give primary-level education, secondary-level education and college-level education. So, 1 = if an individual completed primary education, 0 = otherwise; 1 = if an individual completed secondary education and 0 otherwise; 1 = if an individual completed college or university education and 0 = otherwise.

The standardized coefficient for the primary dummy is 0.0983 (t-value =1.946) and is significant at the 90% confidence level. The coefficient for the secondary school dummy is 0.332 (t-value = 5.609), which is highly significant at the 99% level, and that for the college dummy is 0.395 (t-value = 4.648) and is significant at the 99% level. College and secondary education emerge as the levels of education that contributes most significantly to an improvement in the HAZ score. A child of a woman with primary education has 0.0983 height for age Z-score points higher than a child of a woman with no education. The score for a child whose mother has secondary education is 3.5 times higher than that of a child whose mother has primary education. The HAZ scores for a child whose mother has college education is 4.2 times higher than that of a child whose mother has only primary education and 1.2 Z-score points higher than a child whose mother has secondary education. This finding confirms that an increase in the mother's education has an effect on the child's nutrition status.

Education of the household head had a positive impact on the nutritional status of the children but was not significant.

The coefficient for caloric intake of children is significant for all of the three indices used to measure the nutritional status of children. A 1% increase in caloric intake of the child would increase the HAZ score by 0.4203, WAZ by 0.0137 and WHZ score by 0.155 Z-score points. On average, children in the study site were served three meals a day. In some cases, older children received only two main meals, which were not adequate to meet their nutritional needs. The highest proportion of the meals was composed of carbohydrates, with limited protein, vitamins and micronutrients.

A high frequency of illness reduced the HAZ score of the child by 0.2527, the WHZ score by 0.347 and the WAZ score by 0.173. The diseases considered in determining the frequency of illness are diarrhea and malaria, which were common in the region. Other variables that showed weak significance for the Z-scores were the gender of the household head and the income for mothers. Total household income had a positive coefficient, indicating a positive impact on the Z-scores. However, the t-value for this coefficient was not significant. Various studies have shown that it is not so much the total household income that may have the greatest impact on the nutritional status of the household members, but who earns and controls that income (Haddad et al., 1997; Smith et al., 2003; Quisumbing, 2003). When the variable for total household income was omitted from the analysis and instead replaced by the individual non-farm incomes for the household head and the income for mothers, coefficients for non-farm income going to the household head and that going to mothers were significant at the 95% and 90% levels respectively. The low coefficient and weak significance of the mothers' income indicates the low contribution of mothers' income to the nutrition status of children. Mothers earned less on average, and therefore the impact of such income cannot be great compared to that of the household heads who, on average, earned higher incomes.

An increase in the age of the mother had a negative impact on the Z-scores, an indication that with advancement in age of the mother, the child's nutritional status deteriorated by 0.0861 Z-score points for the HAZ. Although it can be argued that an increase in the mother's age should lead to improved nutritional status of the children due to experience gained over time, this is not the case for this study. The underlying reason for this occurrence, derived from the descriptive statistics of this study, is that women in the study site had more children with advancement in age. With many children (on average six children), coupled with the various tasks they had to do within the household and on the farm, women did not have enough time for their children. The quality of care given to children was therefore compromised since they were left in the care of young siblings. In addition, with more children, those that were slightly older (more than 2 years of age) were not given adequate care. This is confirmed by the increasing occurrence of malnutrition among children with increasing age that can be seen from the logistic regression results discussed earlier. In the 2SLS analysis in Table 6.5, an increase of one month in the age of the child negatively affected the HAZ score by 0.0353 Z-score points. Therefore, an increase in age of one year would decrease the HAZ scores by 0.4236 Z-score points, and the WAZ score by 1.368 Z-score points. Studies in developing countries have shown that child nutritional status declines significantly from the first year of a child's life to the second and remains low in the third (Smith et al., 2003; Smith and Haddad, 2001). The findings of this study are consistent with these findings for the HAZ measure used in the regression analysis as the dependent variable.

Table 6.5: 2SLS estimates of determinants of stunting in children

Parameter	Unstandardized coefficient	Standardized coefficient	T-value
Constant	-4.434		-1.196*
Age of mother	-0.039	-0.0861	-1.714*
Age of women squared	0.0002	0.0316	0.093
Education of mother			
Primary dummy	0.6599	0.0963	1.946*
Secondary dummy	1.962	0.332	5.609***
College dummy	2.5854	0.395	4.648***
Education of HH			
Primary dummy	0.472	0.0881	1.391
Secondary dummy	0.678	0.1079	1.533
College dummy	0.817	0.1371	2.196**
HH gender dummy	-0.5919	-0.200	-3.953***
Frequency of illness	-0.6180	-0.2527	-4.729***
Age of child	-0.0005	-0.0350	-1.858*
Caloric intake	1.0458	0.4203	7.107***
Sex of child	-0.101	-0.0192	-0.457
Income of Household head	5.137E-06	0.0923	1.7153*
Mothers' income	2.567E-06	0.0544	1.654*
Water dummy	0.5401	0.1037	1.711*
R-squared	0.7231		
Adjusted R^2	0.7053		
Chi square statistic	0.005		
Number of observations	183		

Source: Own survey data (2003)

Notes: Height for age Z-scores is the dependent variable.

The signs *, ** and *** indicate significance at the 10%, 5% and 1% level respectively.

Table 6.6:   2SLS estimates of determinants of underweight in children

Parameter	Unstandardized coefficient	Standardized coefficient	T-value
Constant	0.2349		0.070
Age of mother	-0.2735	-0.7904	-1.336
Age of women squared	0.00492	0.9082	1.534
Education of mother			
Primary dummy	0.02633	0.00714	0.054
Secondary dummy	1.6472	0.416	2.881***
College dummy	2.1761	0.5016	2.965***
Education of HH			
Primary dummy	0.952	0.145	1.017*
Secondary dummy	0.7539	0.1812	1.863*
College dummy	0.4859	0.2107	2.577**
HH gender dummy	-0.396	-0.1039	-1.218
Frequency of illness	-0.3218	-0.1733	-1.886**
Age of child	-0.0113	-0.114	-1.161
Caloric Intake	0.0272	0.0137	0.142
Sex of child	-0.131	-0.0374	-0.509
Income of Household head	4.016E-06	0.0016	0.018
Mothers' income	2.016E-06	0.0544	0.431
Water dummy	0.0152	0.0044	0.048
R squared	0.588		
Adjusted R^2	0.346		
Chi square statistic	0.004		
Number of observations	183		

Source: Own survey data (2003)
Note: Dependent variable is the weight for age Z-scores. The signs *, ** and *** indicate significance at the 10%, 5% and 1% level respectively.

Table 6.7: 2SLS Estimates of determinants of wasting in children

Parameter	Unstandardized coefficient	Standardized coefficient	T-value
Constant	5.03107		1.251
Age of mother	-0.106	-0.303	-0.416
Age of women squared	0.00185	0.3280	0.451
Education of mother			
Primary dummy	0.1674	0.0166	0.840
Secondary dummy	0.3827	0.0871	0.9692
College dummy	0.5642	0.1170	1.118*
Education of HH			
Primary dummy	0.055	0.0114	0.098
Secondary dummy	0.5327	0.115	1.106
College dummy	1.0511	0.258	2.390
HH gender dummy	-0.531	-0.142	-1.970
Caloric intake	0.2581	0.155	1.970*
Age of child	-0.2009	-0.1909	2.105**
Frequency of illness	-0.0384	-0.347	-3.299***
Sex of child	0.0651	0.0191	0.281
Income of Household head	5.137E-06	0.044	0.412
Mothers' income	2.417E-06	0.055	0.439
Water dummy	0.764	0.194	1.694
R square	0.522		
Adjusted R^2	0.273		
Chi square statistic	0.085		
Number of observations	184		

Source: Own survey data, 2003
Notes: Dependent variable is the weight for height Z-scores; the signs *, ** and *** indicate significance at the 10%, 5% and 1% level respectively.

6.4   Determinants of Maize Productivity

Maize emerges as the only crop cultivated by more than 75% of households in the study site. It is also the only crop that showed a strong statistical difference in yields in the male and female-headed households. For this reason, further analysis is undertaken to establish the determinants of maize productivity with regard to access to resources.

The model used for investigating the determinants of maize productivity is specified in equation 6.5. In the regression model, the natural logarithm of revenue from maize (total yield considered when calculating revenue) is the dependent variable and is assumed to be a linear function of various production resources (land, labour input, education, income, age of the household head). The assumption behind this model formulation is: socio-economic characteristics of the household head and household members such as age and education level influence crop productivity; access to financial capital, extension services and markets positively affects agricultural productivity. In other words, the closer the farmers are to the market, the higher their productivity. Dummy variables for gender of the household head and region, and an error term to capture random deviations are included in the model. The hypothesis to be tested in this analysis is:

- There is no significant difference in maize productivity in male and female headed households. Presence of differences in productivity in the two categories of households is attributed to differences in access land, education, income, credit and extension services.

The specific model is estimated as follows:

$$lnY = \alpha + \beta_g D_g + \beta_r D_r + \beta_e D_e + \beta_c D_c \sum \beta_1 lnx_1 + \beta_2 lnx_2 + \beta_3 lnx_3 + \beta_4 lnx_4 + \beta_5 lnx_5 + u$$
6.5

Where
ln is the natural logarithm
β and α are coefficients to be estimated,
Y is the dependent variable – maize yield for the cropping season 2002/2003
x_1 is area of land cultivated
x_2 is labour input
x_3 is education measured in terms of years of schooling
x_4 is household non farm income
X_5 is age of household head
D_g is a dummy variable for gender of household head
D_r is the dummy variable for region
D_c access to credit dummy (1= access to credit, 0, otherwise
D_e access to extension services dummy (1=access to extension services, 0= otherwise
u is the error term to capture random variations.

The variables included in the model are further defined in section 4.2.1.1 of this work. Tests were carried out to determine whether variables $x_{1...5}$ are correlated. This was done by looking at the variance inflation factor (VIF) or tolerance of variables. There was a weak correlation between non-farm income and education as measured by years of schooling. The VIF for non-farm income was 2.093 and that of education was 2.018. The two VIF values for the two values were not too high (below the acceptable range of 10 VIF value). Both variables were therefore included in the regression analysis, since access to income and education is the main focus of this study.

Multiple regression results of the determinants of maize productivity are presented in Table 6.8. The coefficients for size of land cultivated, education, labour input and non-farm income are positive. The estimated coefficient for size of land cultivated is 0.173 and significant at the 1% levels, an indication that land is an important production factor in the study area. The amount of land put under cultivation therefore made a big difference to the output in the study site. The coefficient for education (0.139) is significant at the 5%, an indication that the education of the heads of households has a positive impact on farm productivity. This finding is in agreement with findings by Pannin and Brümmer, (2000). Labour contributes positively to productivity, as can be seen from its positive coefficient which is also significant. A 1% increase in labour input caused a 0.63% increase in maize yield. Labour in the study site was needed for tilling the land given the rugged topography in the region.

The coefficient for household income is positive and statistically significant, an indication that access to non- farm income by the households was a great determinant of maize productivity since, with income, households are able to access farm inputs, hire labour and pay for farm machinery use.

The estimated region dummy is negative and highly significant. A negative region dummy indicates that productivity declined when one moved from Kapenguria to Chepareria. Kapenguria division is expected to have higher productivity than Chepareria due to the better soil quality and more favourable climatic conditions in the region. The coefficient for the gender dummy is positive and significant, indicating that there is a significant difference in maize yields between male and female-headed households. The difference can be attributed to differences in access to education, income and land in favour of male-headed households. In addition, differences in yields can be attributed to differences in accessing farm input such as improved seed and fertilizer. Male-headed households who had high incomes would have been better able to pay for farm inputs compared to the female heads of households. Differences in yields can also be attributed in technical inefficiencies. Analysis on technical efficiency between male and female managed farms is done in the in section 6.4 of this work.

The estimated coefficient for age of household head is negative (-0.169) but statistically insignificant. This means that as the age of the household head increases, per hectare yield tends to decline, but not significantly. Therefore, the assumption made in this study and in other studies that an increase in age has a significant positive impact on productivity as a result of increasing experience does not hold for this study. What this implies is that younger farmers who have had the chance of a better education are better off in terms of productivity (at least in this study).

Table 6.8: Multiple regression estimates of determinants of maize productivity

Parameter	Standardized coefficient	Standard Error	T-value
Constant	5.605	0.060	9.270***
Gender dummy	-0.285	0.19	-1.934*
Region dummy	-0.323	0.142	-2.32***
Farm size	0.173	0.081	2.123***
Education of HH	0.139	0.061	2.276**
Labour	0.639	0.037	1.712**
Age of HH head	-0.169	0.084	-019
HH non-farm income	0.361	0.046	7.795**
Education of HH members	0.141	0.052	0.027
Credit	-0.758	0.018	-0.411
Extension services	-0.438	0.064	-0.068
Adjusted R^2	0.758		
F test	27.44***		
Number of observations	167		

Source: Own survey data (2003)
Notes   The dependent variable is the log of total revenue from maize
Note: Dummy for gender (0=female; 1=male), Region dummy (0=Chepareria; 1=Kapenguria)
The signs *, ** and *** indicate significance at the 10%, 5% and 1% level respectively.

The adjusted R^2 is 0.758, an indication that on average, about 75% of the variance in the dependent variable could be explained by the independent variables included in the regression equation. About 25 % of the variance cannot be explained by independent variables. The unexplained variance can be attributed to other factors such as soil quality, climatic conditions, and differences in farm input use, which were not included in the regression model and hence not included in the analysis. The standard error is low at 0.0642 and indicates that, on average, each respondent was about 0.6 points away from the regression line. The F-Test is significant at 27.44. There exists a significant difference between male and female households in maize production. The null hypothesis that there are no significant differences in maize productivity between male and female headed households is rejected. Therefore the alternative hypothesis that there are differences in education attainment, access to income and land which contributed to differences in yields between the two categories of households is accepted.

6.5   Technical Efficiency (TE) Analysis in Maize Production

In this section, analysis dwells on TE between female and male managed farms. The aim of this analysis is to establish whether there are differences in technical efficiency in the two categories of farms. Inefficiency in farm production may be as a result of internal or external inefficiency factors. Internal factors that determine production efficiency include a farmer's education level, age and experience. These individual characteristics are important since they influence his or her ability to use and manage the available resources. External factors that affect production include the physical (soil and weather conditions) and institutional environments that affect farmers' incentives for production. Institutional environment includes access to markets, financial institutions for agricultural credit and agricultural extension services.

The descriptive results in this study have shown that gender differences in resource ownership exist in the study site. In the regression analysis on determinants of maize productivity, there are significant differences in yields of maize in male and female-headed households. The gender differences in yields can be attributed to differences in resource ownership, access to farm technologies and managerial skills of the female and male farmers. The hypotheses to be tested in this section are:

- There are no significant differences in TE of MHH and FHH farmers given the same farm technologies and managerial skills by farmers. Any significant differences would be attributed to differences in farm technology use.
- There is no joint significant effect of the variables that influence the technical efficiency of maize farmers

6.5.1 Evaluation of Technical Efficiency in Maize Production

The Cobb-Douglas production function is the appropriate model for the technical efficiency analysis. There are two approaches for estimating the model: the single-stage approach and the two-stage approach. The single-stage approach is a frontier where the efficiency effects are expressed as a function of the vector of the farm-specific variables and a random error. The assumption behind this approach is that there is interaction between farm-specific variables and input variables (Battese and Coelli, 1995). The estimation procedure consists of estimating the production frontier and the technical efficiency effects model simultaneously.

The two-stage/neutral stochastic frontier has two stages: the first stage involves specification and estimation of the stochastic frontier production function and prediction of either the inefficiency effects or the level of technical efficiency of the farms in terms of various explanatory variables and an error term. This step is done using the maximum likelihood estimation method. The second stage involves specifying the regression model where the technical efficiency indexes are dependent variables and the farm characteristics are independent variables. The second step uses the ordinary least squares technique. Due to the inconsistency in the assumption about the independence of the inefficiency effect in the two-stage approach, this study makes use of the single-stage approach (Battese and Coelli, 1995).

The stochastic frontier approach has advantages in modelling output growth in terms of evaluating the effects of policy changes. First, it allows the filtering out of random effects caused by weather changes and measurement errors. Second, the estimates of a firm's technical efficiency can be obtained by comparing observed and predicted output; and third, it allows for a functional specification of the production technology and a test of its statistical properties (Battese, 1992; Battesse and Coelli, 1995).

6.5.2 The Model

The inputs in the model are: area of land covered by the maize, labour input in hours, expenses on seeds, expenses on fertilizer, quantity of manure, age, education of household head, region dummy; dummies for access to credit and extension services as well as physical infrastructure to proxy market access are also included. The general Cobb-Douglas model is specified as:

$$InY_1 = \beta_0 + \sum_{j=1}^{k} \beta_j Inx_{ji} + u_i \qquad\qquad 6.6$$

The specific equation for the study is derived from equation 6.6 as follows:

$$InY = \beta_0 + \beta_1 InX_1 + \beta_2 InX_2 + \beta_3 InX_3 + \beta_4 InX_4 + \beta_5 InX_5 + \beta_6 InX_6$$
$$+ \beta_7 InX_7 + \beta_8 InX_8 + \beta_8 D_r + \beta_{10} D_c + \beta_{11} D_e + u \qquad\qquad 6.7$$

where:

In	the natural logarithm
Y	total maize revenue for the agricultural year 2002/2003
β_0	In of the constant term
$\beta_1 .. \beta_{11}$	input elasticity for variable in the model
X_1	area of land covered by maize
X_2	labour input
X_3	amount of seeds (per hectare)
X_4	amount of fertilizer (per hectare)
X_5	quantity of manure used
X_6	age of household head
X_7	education of household head
X_8	amount of manure
D_r	region dummy
De	access to extension services dummy (1= access to extension services; 0= otherwise)
D_c	access to credit dummy (1= access to credit; 0= otherwise)
u	error term

The production functions for male and female managed farms were estimated separately. Another production function for the pooled regression (for all households) was also done with an inclusion of a dummy variable for the gender of farm manager (or household head). The analysis is aimed at carrying out an accurate diagnosis of whether sources of productivity differences, between male and female managed farms exist, so that important policy interventions for increasing productivity and welfare can be made. The software package LIMDEP 7.0 was used to carry out maximum likelihood estimation of the parameters of the stochastic frontier production function. A brief description of these variables is given as follows:

Farm size: Land covered by maize crop was taken into consideration in the analysis, but not the total size of land owned by the farmer. Farm size is expected to have different effects on farm efficiency. Several studies have shown that small farms are more efficient than large farms in terms of costs and transaction costs (luibrand, 2002).

Education: In many studies on technical efficiency, education of the farmer is taken into consideration since it affects the ability to use farm resources. In this study, the education of the household head is included in the analysis. In addition, the education of other household members such as wives and adult children living in the household is taken into consideration, since the education level of other members of the household may contribute to how the farm is managed or how resources are used on the farm. Educated members of the household can provide information to the household head regarding the farm inputs on the market and give advice on timing/when to carry out different farm operations.

Age: Age of the household head is used to proxy experience. Farmers who are advanced in age are expected to have more experience accumulated over a long period.

Access to credit: Availability of credit to a farmer boosts the farmer's ability to obtain inputs at the right time. In turn, this has an impact on the technical efficiency of the farm through the use of modern inputs. Farmers may also use credit for consumptive purposes. In this case, if the credit is used to purchase food, then it has an effect on TE through its effect on labour productivity.

Access to agricultural extension services: Access to extension services is expected to improve farmers' production efficiency. Agricultural extension agents provide information to farmers regarding modern technologies to use on their farms as well as markets for farm inputs and sale of produce.

Region dummy: Farm location is important, since farms may operate under different climatic or altitude conditions, and have different soil quality. A region dummy is included in the analysis to capture the effect of agro-ecological differences on farmers' technical efficiency. The physical infrastructure can also differ regionally. Physical infrastructure such as roads affects access to markets, transport services and information. The longer the distance from the main road, the higher the transaction costs. There is also poor access to information with increasing distance from the main road (Tadesse, 2004).

Other variables included in the model are amount of seed, fertilizer, labour input. Total labour included hired and household labour. Input use variables are included in the model to capture the effect of the level of intensification on the technical efficiency. Due to the rugged topography in the study region, households needed a lot of labour to till the land.

Parameter estimates of the technical inefficiency effects stochastic frontier model employed to identify the factors influencing farmers' level of technical inefficiency are presented in Table 6.9. These estimates are elasticities. According to the results, age of household head, access to credit, gender and region dummies have negative coefficients in the analysis where all household were included . The coefficients for gender and region dummies are significant. A negative and significant gender coefficient implies that, there were differences in TE for maize production in FHH and MHH. TE in FHH was much lower than that in MHH. MHH seem to have made good use of inputs.

A negative and significant coefficient for the region dummy in all the three analysis implies that as one moved from Kapenguria to Chepareria divisions, TE of farmers improved. Farmers in Kapenguria division were more technically efficient in terms of use of inputs. There was a negative and significant coefficient for amount of seed used in all the three regression analyses. A negative coefficient for the amount of improved seed used indicates an overuse of seeds due to lack of proper knowledge on usage of amounts of seed per unit of land. This finding is in line with findings of similar studies conducted in Vietnam and Ethiopia (Luibrand, 2002 and Tadesse, 2004) which found a negative impact due to overuse of hybrid seeds.

The age of the farmer was used as a proxy to measure experience. Age of the household has a negative coefficient that is significant for the first round of analysis. It would be expected that the older the farmer gets, the more experienced he gets hence improved use of inputs. However, this is not the case for this study. Older farmers lacked knowledge on how to use farm inputs as can be deduced from the negative coefficient with advancement in age. In this case, younger farmers with better education may be well versed on use of farm inputs. The coefficient for the age household head in the analysis for male headed households is positive and significant, implying that for the males, with increase in age, the farmers gained experience and therefore improvement in TE. While advancement in age improved TE for male farmers, the opposite was true for female managed farms. The male farmers had the possibility to share information through village meetings which they attended often as opposed to female farmers. In a study on TE analysis between female and male managed farms in Botswana, Pannin and Brümmer (2000) found that with advancement in age, farmers were less technically efficient.

Access to credit enables farmers to purchase farm inputs. Accessing credit was a constraint to most farmers in the study site and thus negatively affected their technically efficiency. Coefficient for credit dummy were negative for all the three regression analyses, implying that credit access was a constraint for male as well as female farmers. From descriptive statistics of this study, only 25% and 19% of MHH and FHH had access to credit from formal financing institutions.

Education of the household head and labour input had positive effects on TE. Highly educated farmers are likely to be more technically efficient than their less educated counterparts. This is true for the three regression analyses. This finding is in line with findings of Pannin and Brümmer (2000) in their TE study among male and female farmers in Botswana. In terms of labour, a 1% increase in labour input in man hours caused 0.44% increase in maize revenue. Maize production was labour intensive and so an increase in labour input was likely to cause an increase in yield. Labour in the study region was used for tilling the land (in the mountainous regions where use of farm machinery was not possible), weeding, harvesting. An increase in labour during tilling increased the amount of land that was covered by the crop.

The estimate on farm size show that TE tended to increase with an increase in farm size leading to increase in yields. Access to big farms allowed use of farm machinery and more input. Farmers who owned big farms were likely to be members of cooperatives and could easily obtain farm inputs on credit and the size of the farm could then be used as collateral. This finding concurs with Morrison (2000), who argues that larger farms are advantageous since they attain economies of size by spreading fixed costs over more land and output, by getting volume discounts for purchased inputs, or by achieving better market access and higher prices for large volumes delivered.

Table 6.9: Maximum likelihood estimates of determinants of inefficiency in Maize production

Parameter	All Households (Regression 1)		MHH (Regression 2)		FHH (Regression 3)	
	Standardized coefficient	T-value	Standardized coefficient	T-value	Standardized coefficient	T-value
Constant	10.600	10.438***	7.569	8.880***	8.975	6.219***
Gender dummy	-0.869	-5.551***	...	...	...	
Region dummy	-0.742	-4.818***	-0.460	-4.759***	-0.368	-2.490**
Farm size	0.553	4.879***	0.725	10.081**	0.524	3.619***
Education of HH	0.158	1.762**	0.341	1.669*	0.220	2.295**
Age of HH head	-0.229	-0.840	0.350	2.79***	-0.129	0.402
Distance	0.123	0.425	0.122	0.222	0.102	0.132
Labour	0.440	0.430	0.154	3.589***	-0.189	-0.151
Fertilizer	0.135	1.646*	0.957	2.165**	0.248	2.298**
Seed	0.033	0.408	-0.597	-0.491	-0.277	-1.631
Credit	-0.0379	-0.290	-0.052	-0.013	-0.612	-0.409
Manure	0.086	0.219	0.035	0.123	0.065	0.
Extension services	0.0875	0.577	0.141	1.335	0.079	0.05
Log Likelihood function	-80.2348		-67.85		-13.763	
Number of observations	167		120		47	
Variance parameters						
Sigma-squared - σ^2 (v)	0.6120		0.041		0.022	
Sigma-squared - σ^2 (u)	0.782		0.439		0.328	

Source: Own survey data (2003)

Note: ... indicates variable not included in the analysis

***; ** and * indicates significance at 1%, 5% and 10% levels respectively

Estimates for distance to the main road and access to extension services had positive effects on TE although not statistically significant. TE was likely to improve with access to extension services. Access to the main road implies easy access to the market and hence access to farm inputs by farmers. Prices of farm inputs tend to be lower with decreasing distance to the market.

It is evident from the estimates of the variance parameters that technical inefficiency effects were present in both categories of households. The parameter responsible for the inefficiency effects is the variance of u (which is the variance of the output below the frontier). In the analysis involving all households, the value of the variance of u is approximately 1.27 times the variance of v (the variance of the frontier), a confirmation of the presence of inefficiency effects in both categories of households.

In testing the hypotheses, the log likelihood ratio is used. The log likelihood for the regression of all households is used (regression 1). The estimate for the log-likelihood is negative and significant. The model jointly tests the joint effect of all variables in influencing technical efficiency. The null hypothesis that there is no technical inefficiency effect for all parameters is therefore rejected. The parameters in the model jointly affect technical efficiency of the farmers. In testing the hypothesis related to the effects of individual variables on TE, the model found the absence of individual effects of age of household head, labour, distance, seed, access to credit and extension services not having a significant effect on TE. The hypotheses are therefore accepted.

6.6   Determinants of Household Food Security

One of the most commonly accepted definitions of food security is adequate access to food at all times. Access is ensured when all households and all individuals within those households have sufficient resources to obtain appropriate foods for a nutritious diet (Heidhues, 2000). Access to food is dependent on the level of household resources - capital, labour, and knowledge to ensure sufficient production and on income for purchasing power. Adequate access can be achieved without households being self-sufficient in food production. More important is the ability of households to generate sufficient income which, together with own production, can be used to meet food needs. At individual level, individual food security requires consideration of two factors: how food is allocated within the household; and biological utilization. In households where distribution is unequal, it is possible for aggregate access to improve and for some individuals to experience no change in their food security status. Utilization entails the ability of the human body to take food and translate it into either energy that is used to undertake daily activities or be stored. Utilization requires not only an adequate diet, but also a healthy physical environment (so as to avoid disease) and an understanding of proper health care, food preparation, and storage processes as presented in the conceptual framework of this study.

In the sample population of this study, results of the analysis on nutrient intake within households showed that there were differences in nutrient intake for men, women and children as discussed in Chapter 5 of this work 8(section 5.7.2). On average both men and women did not meet their daily dietary intake, however the women were most disadvantaged. In this section, analysis of determinants of food security is going to be based on the caloric and protein intake. The dependant variable in the OLS regression will therefore be the energy (Kcal) and protein availability for children below five years of age. The independent variables included in the model are household size, food cost per month and female education. A gender dummy is included in the model to capture any differences in nutrient intake in the two categories of households. The variables included in the model have been reported to influence food security in other studies determining food security (Weinberger, 2001; Girma and Genebo, 2002). The hypothesis to be tested is that: there are significant differences in caloric and protein intake among children (proxy for food security) in male and female headed household due to differences in expenditures on food in these households. Food expenditures depend on available household income.

The model used in the analyses can be specified as follows:

$$y = \alpha + \beta_1 X_1 + \beta_1 X_1 + \beta_2 X_2 + \beta_3 X_3 + \beta_4 X_4 + D_g + u_1 \qquad\qquad 6.8$$

where,
y=dependent variable (caloric intake -Equation 1; Protein Intake –equation 2)
$\beta_1 ... \beta_4$=Coefficients to be estimated
X_1 = Household size
X_2 = Education of women
X_3 = food cost per month
X_4 = Amount of staple food kept stored for home consumption
D_g = gender dummy
U = unobserved variability

Household food expenditure, amount of food stored and women's education emerge as the factors that positively contribute to nutrient intake and in turn food security as can be seen from Table 6.10. The coefficients for food costs per month and amount of food stored for home consumption are positive and significant at the 1% level for both the caloric and protein intake. An increase in the amount of food expenditure contributed to an increase in caloric and protein intake for children. Also, increased storage of food caused an increase in caloric intake. The coefficient for food stored is high for the regression where caloric intake is the dependant variable than for protein intake, an indication that available food stores were mainly rich in calories. In low income households, protein rich foods such as eggs were sold in order to obtain income to purchase the main staple food (maize). Households that had less food stores were likely not to meet the caloric requirements.

The coefficient for household size was negative and significant indicating that with an increase in household size, individual caloric as well as protein intake was likely to reduce. Education of women residing within the household had a positive impact on both caloric and nutrient intake. Women are responsible for food preparation and distribution within the household and women with high education are likely to have higher nutrition knowledge thus contributing to preparation of a balanced diet. Education of women plays an important role at all these stages. Findings of this study are in line with findings of Weinberger (2001) who studied nutrient intake among adults in India. Weinberger (2001) found that education had a positive effect on fat, iron and Vitamin B1 intake.

The coefficient for the male headed household dummy was positive and significant for protein intake, while that of the female headed household was positive but weakly significant. This finding gives an indication that a difference in protein intake in the two categories of households exists. Children in male headed households consumed more protein foods than female headed households. However, for caloric intake of children the coefficients for both household heads was not significant, indicating no significant difference in caloric intake in the two categories of households. From the descriptive statistics, more than half of the male headed households had livestock; therefore household members had access to milk from the cows. Access to more income in the male headed households enabled them to have access to more protein foods such as meat and eggs from the market. With income being a constraint, the female headed households even sold the protein rich foods such as eggs to be able to purchase maize.

The variance in the dependant variables (caloric intake and protein intake) could be explained by about 42% and 34 % for the two regression analyses respectively. The results indicate that expenditure on food was one of the most important determinants of calorie and protein intake. With increase in income, households are likely to spend more on food hence causing an increase in nutrient intake resulting into improved household food security.

Table 6.10: Determinants of Caloric and Protein Intake (OLS Estimates)

Variable	Standardized Coefficients (Caloric intake Dependant variable)	T- value	Standardized Coefficients (Protein intake as dependant variable)	T- value
Constant		10.036***		0.273
Household size	-0.469	-4.835***	-0.245	-.3.126***
Food expenditure	0.316	4.473***	0.386	3.437**
Amount of food stored	0.320	4.476***	0.126	1.852*
Education of women	0.134	1.437*	0.155	2.306**
Female HH dummy	0.112	0.857	0.148	1.112*
Male HH dummy	0.142	0.945	0.176	2.562**
F-value	27.925		18.779	
Adjusted R^2	0.428		0.344	
Number of observations	183		183	

Source: Own survey data (2003)

6.7 Relationship between Access to Education, Child Morbidity and Fertility Rate

The relationship between education and child morbidity (as measured by frequency of illness) and fertility (as measured by number of births per woman) is presented in Table 6.11. Two simple regression analyses were run, with frequency of illness and number of children as dependent variables. In each case, the education of the mothers and men (fathers) was the explanatory variables. The coefficients for education of both women and men were negatively associated with child morbidity. With increase in education, the frequency of illness in children decreased. With access to more years of schooling, women and men gain access to better paying jobs and earn more income. Therefore, their living standards are likely to improve as a result of an increase in income. Hence, households have the possibility of accessing food and living in a healthy environment. Poor sanitation is one of the main causes of illness. Poor households are likely to live in poor living conditions, thus increasing the chances of children becoming sick. The negative relationship between education and child morbidity can also be explained in terms of the health care-seeking behaviour of educated individuals in the event of illness in comparison to those who have no education. Educated women are also better informed about the importance of antenatal care for the child. Many educated women would take their child for immunization against diseases, thus preventing some diseases from occurring. In addition, educated women with higher incomes are able to pay for health care services, thus maximizing the preventive as well as the curative aspects of health.

The coefficient for education is negative in the regression between education and number of births per woman. The negative relationship between women's education and the number of births per woman implies that an increase in education reduced the number of births. Education of men has no significant impact on the number of births per woman in the study site.

Table 6.11: Impact of education on fertility rate and child morbidity (OLS estimates)

Parameter	Fertility rate	Child morbidity
	coefficient	coefficient
Constant	7.520 (26.94)***	1.53 (7.779)**
Women's education	-0.427 (-6.377)***	-0.223 (-3.071)***
Men's education	0.0125 (0.859)	-0.285 (-3.526)***
Adjusted R^2	0.178	0.144
Number of women	165	165

Source: Own survey data (2003)

Notes: T-values in parentheses; *** and ** indicates significance at 99% and 95% confidence levels respectively

Analysis of variance (ANOVA) to test whether there were significance differences in number of children according to the level of education completed by women showed that women who had secondary school education (12 years of schooling), had one child less on average than those who did not attend school at all, or had only completed lower primary education (3 years of schooling). And women who had had college or university education (more than

13 years of schooling) had two fewer children than those with no schooling or only lower primary education (3 years of school). Women with college education also had one child less than those with secondary education (12 years of schooling)

Staying in school longer enabled women to get married at a later age, thus having children later. Also, with education at least up to secondary level, women had acquired knowledge about family planning. Women in the study site had six children on average. Women started the child-bearing process at an early age, and hence it was possible for them to have more children. In addition, due to the fact that women had a low level of education, and hence limited access to income, not many of them could afford the family planning services offered in health care clinics. Moreover, the government clinics were not easily accessible for the majority of the women. West Pokot has only three government hospitals where women could access free family planning services. The private clinics to be found in major trading centres in the district charged exorbitant fees, making the services affordable only to a minority of women. This finding is in agreement with findings from other studies which show that an increase in women's education has an impact on both fertility and child morbidity.

Table 6.12: ANOVA results – relationship between women's educational level and number of children

Parameter	Number of children	F-Value
	Mean number of children	
No schooling to 3 yrs of school	6.845	
Upper primary (7-8 yrs)	6.158	
Secondary education	5.680	
College/university	4.789	
Total	5.869	
		13.690***

Source: Own survey data (2003)
Note: *** indicates significance at 99%

6.8 Summary of Analytical Regressions

Variables	Two Stage Heckman Procedure: Non farm income	Two Stage Heckman Procedure: farm income	Logistic regression: Nutritional Status	2SLS: HAZ (dependant Variable)	2SLS: WHZ (dependant Variable)	2SLS: WAZ (dependant Variable)	OLS: Food security	Multiple regression (OLS)	Technical efficiency	OLS: Morbidity and Fertility
Gender of HH	√	...	√	√	...		...	√	√	n.a
Education of HH	√	√	√	√	...	√	n.a	√	√	n.a
Education of the mother/wife	n.a	√	√	√	√	√	√	n.a	n.a	√
HH Income (farm and non farm)	n.a	n.a	√	n.a	...	...	√	n.a	n.a	n.a
HH non farm income	n.a	√	n.a	n.a	n.a	n.a	n.a	√	n.a	n.a
Mother's income	n.a	n.a	n.a	√	...	n.a	n.a	n.a	n.a	n.a
Land	n.a	√	n.a	n.a	n.a	n.a	n.a	√	...	n.a
Access to credit	n.a	n.a	n.a	n.a	n.a	n.a	n.a	n.a	...	n.a
Extension services	n.a	n.a	n.a	n.a	n.a	n.a	n.a	n.a	...	n.a
Labour	n.a	n.a	n.a	n.a	n.a	n.a	n.a	√	...	n.a
Seed	n.a	n.a	n.a	n.a	n.a	n.a	n.a	n.a	√	n.a
fertilizer	n.a	n.a	n.a	n.a	n.a	n.a	n.a	n.a	n.a	n.a
Household size	n.a	n.a	n.a	n.a	n.a	n.a	n.a	n.a	...	n.a
Region	√	√	n.a	n.a	n.a	n.a	n.a	...	√	n.a
Region	√	√	n.a	n.a	n.a	n.a	n.a	...	√	n.a
Age of HH	n.a	n.a	n.a	√	...	n.a	n.a	n.a	n.a	n.a
Age of the mother	n.a	n.a	...	√	...	...	n.a	n.a	n.a	n.a
Caloric Intake	n.a	n.a	...	√	√	...	n.a	n.a	n.a	n.a
Sex of Child		...		...	√		n.a	n.a	n.a	n.a
Age of Child				√	√	√	n.a	n.a	n.a	n.a
Frequency of illness	n.a	n.a	n.a	√		√	√	n.a	n.a	n.a
Source of Water	n.a	n.a	n.a	√			n.a	n.a	n.a	n.a
Food stored	n.a	n.a	n.a	n.a	n.a	n.a	√	n.a	n.a	n.a

Note: √ = explanatory variable significant in regression; ...= explanatory variable NOT significant in regression

n.a. = explanatory variable not included in regression

6.9 Summary

Education and income emerged as the most important factor for determining farm productivity, nutritional status of children and in reduction of child morbidity. Households where the household head had a higher level of education had more non-farm income. The region dummy was also important in determining household incomes. Households in Kapenguria division had higher incomes for both farm and non-farm employment. This was due to better infrastructure and proximity to markets in Kapenguria division compared to Chepareria division. Access to non-farm income contributed significantly to farm income. With non-farm income, households were able to gain access to farm inputs and hence increase their productivity. The hypothesis that access to education increases household income (both agricultural and non-agricultural income) is accepted. For farm income, the hypothesis that access to financial capital increases agricultural productivity was also accepted.

The amount of land owned played a significant role in agricultural productivity and hence farm income, as could be seen from the statistical significance of the coefficient for land size in the regression analysis. Therefore, the hypothesis that women's limited access to land leads to lower household agricultural productivity can be accepted.

Education of the household head and that of mothers was an important determinant of the nutritional status of children in both male and female-headed households, as can be seen from the results of the two-stage least squares regression analysis. Income going to the household head contributed significantly more to the nutritional status of the child than income going to mothers, as could be seen from the coefficients. With their low education level, women earned less in the non-farm sector. Therefore their contribution to total household income was not significant. The hypothesis that women's limited access to education and financial capital leads to poor nutritional status of household members is accepted. Increase in mother's age had a negative impact on child nutrition status. With increase in age, women had more children hence an increase in their work burden, leaving them with inadequate time for child care.

Education of the women also played an important role in reducing the frequency of illness in children and reducing the fertility rate in women. The findings show that education, income and land are very important for agricultural productivity, access to food and improving the nutrition security of household members. In addition, education of women is important for reducing child   morbidity   and   number   of   children   per   women.

7 SUMMARY, CONCLUSIONS AND POLICY RECOMMENDATIONS

Kenya's current food supply situation and outlook give cause for serious concern. The food situation is particularly dire in arid and semi arid regions of the country. The prevailing food insecurity situation has consistently been blamed on erratic climatic conditions, poor planning, poor agricultural policies and post-harvest wastage in most parts of the country. What has not been taken into consideration is the role that prevailing gender biases in resource access has played in the food insecurity phenomenon and related effects. The overall objective of this study is to assess gender-based differences regarding access to and control of land, financial and human capital, and the consequences this has on household food security and household socio-economic welfare. This study was conducted in West Pokot district, a region that lies in the arid and semi-arid lands of Kenya. The purpose of this chapter is to summarize the major findings of the study, derive policy recommendations and suggest areas that would merit attention in future research.

7.1 Summary and Conclusions

The first objective of this study was to assess inter and intra-household resource allocation of land, human capital and financial capital along gender lines. Findings on resource allocation reveal unequal access to land, education and income in favour of men. Male respondents in the study region had more access to education at primary and secondary school levels. At higher levels of education – college and university – there was no significant difference in attendance by male and female heads of households. As regards access to land, women were at a disadvantage: women could only access land through a male relative, by purchase or rental. Direct access through inheritance was not acceptable in this region, as in many parts of Kenya. With their low levels of education, women had lower incomes since they could not access formal jobs that were better remunerated. A high percentage of the male respondents had access to credit from formal institutions compared to women. Men had access to land and other assets, such as livestock, which they could use as collateral to obtain credit. A high percentage of women borrowed from informal institutions including women's groups, private moneylenders and organizations. The amount borrowed from these institutions was small in comparison to that borrowed from formal institutions by male respondents.

In terms of division of labour, findings reveal that women are engaged in both household and farm production activities. Due to their multiple and competing responsibilities, often carried out without the assistance of labour-saving devices, or adequate transportation means, the women in the study site suffered from time poverty.

The second objective of this study was to determine the food security situation in the study region and make comparisons based on the gender of the household head and access to main production resources – land, financial capital and human capital. Household food security was measured in terms of availability, access and utilization of food by household members. In terms of availability, the analysis was based on household food production, amount of harvest sold and amount stored for home consumption. Households that produced their own food and stored enough for home consumption were found to be food secure. Male-headed households produced more maize than the female-headed households, and had a greater diversity of crops. In contrast, those that relied on the market for their supply of the main staple food (maize) were found to be food insecure.

In terms of use and utilization of food, data were gathered on food consumption including 24-hour food recall, dietary diversity and weighing of food. Results on nutrient intake reveal that on average neither male nor female respondents met the recommended dietary intake for their age and level of activity. Nutrient intake for children was also insufficient. Foods were lacking in protein, vitamins and micronutrients as well as primary nutrients (proteins, carbohydrates and fats), which is detrimental to health. Findings show unequal distribution of food with women and children being at high risk of micronutrient deficiencies.

Anthropometric analysis was done to determine nutrition security within households. Results on nutritional status of children indicate a high incidence of malnutrition among children in the study site. There was a high incidence of stunting (40%), wasting (12%) as well as underweight (24%) among children. In terms of age, children most affected by stunting and underweight were aged 36 to 47 months and 48 to 60 months. Children between the ages of 6 and 12 months were most affected by wasting and underweight. Incidence of underweight, stunting and wasting among children in female-headed households was high, an indication of poor access to and utilization of food in these households. A higher percentage of children in female-headed households were undernourished in comparison to children in male-headed households.

For women, the body mass index (BMI) results showed that more than half the women of child-bearing age had a normal BMI. About 30% of the women were found to be underweight, with women from female-headed households being most affected. Maternal underweight is a risk factor in low birth weight children, which in turn is a risk factor for child stunting and underweight. Low BMI could have been a result of poor nutrition coupled with energy demanding hard work within the household and on the farm done by women.

Results on the strategies used by households to cope with food scarcity revealed that female headed households used more severe strategies to cope with food scarcity in comparison to male headed households. Such strategies include: skipping meals and reducing quantities served to household members. Household coping strategies during food shortages were used to determine a food security index, which was then used to classify households according to various food security categories. Using the food security index as a measure of food security, there was a weak significance difference in households' food insecurity based on the gender of the household head. However, female-headed households seemed to be worse off when the households were ranked according to economic status. The economic status of the household was most important in determining household food security, as could be seen from the strong significance that emerged between poor, middle-income and rich households of the chi square results. The poorest households often had a deficiency of cereals because of the small size of their land holdings. One of their main survival strategies was therefore the sale of foods with higher economic and nutritional value, such as eggs, chicken, pulses and legumes, in order to purchase lower-value cereals (maize). At middle and high-income levels, household food security was stable in both female and male-headed households, an indication of the ability to purchase food in the event of their own production being insufficient. Few households in the middle and high-income categories were affected by food insecurity. Follow-up analysis of the data revealed that these households produced enough food for their own consumption but sold most of the food, confirming that production of food alone is not enough to secure food security for households

Overall, there was a high frequency of illness in the study site. Diarrhoea among children was one of the prevalent illnesses reported, pointing to poor health and sanitation conditions in most households in the study site. Other diseases prevalent among the children are alimentary and respiratory diseases. High incidence of disease, coupled with inadequate dietary intake and poor sanitation in most households in the study site contributed to the poor nutritional status of the children. The econometric analysis in this study focuses on analysing the determinants of farm and non-farm incomes, technical efficiency analysis in male and female-managed farms, determinants of household food security, and nutritional status in children. A two-stage Heckman procedure is used to analyse the determinants of farm and non-farm incomes. Education emerges as the most important factor determining farm and non-farm incomes. There were higher returns for women with primary and secondary education in the farm sector compared to returns for women with same level of education in the non-farm sector. With college-level education, there were higher returns for both women and men in the non-farm sector. The region dummy was also important in determining household incomes. Households in Kapenguria division had higher incomes from both farm and non-farm employment. This was due to better infrastructure and closer proximity to markets in Kapenguria compared to Chepareria division. Access to non-farm income contributed significantly to household income. With non-farm income, households were able to gain access to farm inputs and hence increase their productivity. The hypothesis that access to education increases household income (both agricultural and non-agricultural income) was accepted. For farm income, the hypothesis that access to financial capital increases agricultural productivity was also accepted.

Overall, farm productivity in the study site was low. The amount of land owned played a significant role in agricultural productivity, as could be seen from the statistical significance of the coefficient for land size in the ordinary least squares regression analysis. There were differences in agricultural productivity in male and female-headed households, with male-headed households having higher yields.

To establish the extent to which technical efficiency, total labour and intensity of input use affect farm productivity, analysis of male and female-managed farms was carried out using a stochastic Cobb-Douglas production function. The argument behind this analysis is that, given the same level of technology use, farm input use and education, farm productivity in male and female-managed farms should not be significantly different. Any differences in productivity are attributed to differences in the amount of inputs used and as a result of unequal access to resources such as education, income, credit and agricultural extension services. Given the different climatic and soil characteristics in Chepareria and Kapenguria divisions, a region dummy was included to capture any differences in the two divisions. Analysis of male and female-managed farms is carried out separately. The main factors that tended to contribute significantly to technical efficiency are education of the farmer, access to credit, fertilizer use and distance of the farm to the main road. Education of the farmer had a positive and highly significant impact on the efficiency of maize production. This indicates that farmers with more years of schooling exhibited higher levels of technical efficiency. Accessing credit was a constraint to most farmers in the study site and thus negatively affected their technically efficiency. With credit, farmers are able to purchase farm inputs and pay for farm machinery use and modern technology. From descriptive statistics of this study, only 25% and 19% of MHH and FHH had access to credit from formal financing institutions. The distance of the farm to the main road was statistically significant at the 5% level, implying that technical efficiency tends to increase with the proximity of the plot to the main road.

The OLS regression analysis on determinants of food security revealed that household food expenditure, food stores and household size were the most important factors in determining caloric and protein intake among children (used as proxy of household food security). Amount of income spent on food influenced both caloric and protein intake positively, while with an increase in household size, intake of these nutrients tended to decline. The coefficient for food expenditure was larger for the caloric intake regression than for protein intake regression analysis, an indication that most of the food budget went to purchase of high energy giving foods/ cereals in this case maize. A larger amount of food stored for home consumption contributed to higher levels of caloric consumption.

Results of the two-stage least squares regression analysis of the determinants of nutritional status of children show that education of the household head and that of mothers were important determinants of the nutritional status of children in both male and female-headed households. Children whose mothers had no formal education had a higher probability of being malnourished (logit regression results). Secondary and college education contributed significantly to reducing stunting, wasting and underweight. Income going to the household head contributed significantly to the nutritional status of the child compared to income going to mothers. With their low educational level, women earned less in the non-farm sector, and therefore it is no wonder that the coefficient for income going to mothers has a weak significance in comparison to the coefficient for income going to the household head. The hypothesis that women's limited access to education and financial capital leads to poor nutritional status of household members was confirmed by the data and is accepted.

OLS regression results show that education of women is important for reducing child morbidity and fertility rate in women. Women with secondary education (12 years of school) had one child less than women who had no formal schooling; while women with college and university level of school (> 13 years of school) had two children fewer than those with no formal education. The magnitude of the reduction in fertility in women can be attributed not only to education but also to other positive effects of education, such as job opportunities and knowledge of contraceptive use.

In conclusion, there is clear evidence that access to human capital, financial capital and land have an impact on household food and nutrition security and on the socio-economic well-being of household members. Households where the household head and household members had a good combination of access to education, land and income were food secure in terms of availability, access to and utilization of food. Due to limited access to land, education, income, credit and extension services, female-headed households were disadvantaged in terms of agricultural productivity and their ability to purchase food from the market was constrained by limited income. This leads to poor nutrition of household members, manifested in poor nutritional status of children. There is also a link between education and fertility rate in women, an indication that an increase in education for women will reduce the number of children per woman in the study region.

Food insecurity in West Pokot district, therefore, cannot be blamed solely on erratic climatic conditions in the region. Existing gender biases in accessing major productive resources play an important part in contributing to the food security phenomenon. Given that women play multiple roles in sustaining society, it is difficult to achieve sustainable food security in all its dimensions in this region without addressing the existing, culturally-perpetuated biases against women. In addition, it would be difficult to achieve sustainable economic growth in this region without promoting equal education opportunities for girls and boys. Education of girls is important in addressing the poverty-related problems in the region, such as high fertility rates, child morbidity, poor nutrition and health and hence low productivity.

7.2   Policy Recommendations

Based on the results of this study, the following recommendations are made for policy interventions.

7.2.1 Investment in Education and Health Care Services

The study consistently shows the overridingly important role played by education in nutrition, agricultural production, non-farm activities and overall well-being of the households. The government needs to invest in teachers, schools and health care facilities so that more women in rural areas can have access to education and health services. Primary and secondary school attendance should be made mandatory for all children. Access to education, especially for women, is likely to significantly reduce the fertility rate, child morbidity and mortality in the study region. Overall, it seems clear that investing in education should be the key element in tackling poverty and its related effects, such as food insecurity, poor nutrition and high morbidity rates, in West Pokot. Approaches to promoting gender equality in education might include reducing prices and increasing physical access to schools; improving the design of service delivery; and investing in time-saving infrastructure.

Data obtained on school enrolment and drop-out indicates high drop-out rates for girls. Reasons contributing to the high drop out rate were high school expenses (uniform, writing material, furniture), long distance to school and unfavourable stereotypes. To improve continued school attendance by girls, it is recommended to reduce school expenses, provide school stipends for girls, better train staff, review and revise school curricula and educate parents to ensure that gender stereotypes are not perpetuated in the classroom and in the community. Investment that reduces the distance to school and investment in basic water and energy infrastructure can boost female enrolment rates in part by reducing the opportunity cost of schooling for girls as this study has shown.

Data shows poor access to health care facilities in the study region. Increasing access to health care facilities may reduce the time women and girls need to spend caring for sick family members. Investment in this area means fewer interruptions to women's paid work and to girls' schooling.

7.2.2 Eradicating Discrimination in Land Ownership

The study reveals inequalities in access to land and other economically productive assets, with women being the most disadvantaged. Legislation is needed to guarantee women's right to inherit and own land. The government of Kenya should include clear-cut laws on land ownership and inheritance in the Constitution, taking into consideration women's right to land. This will help to eliminate the existing conflict between customary land rights and land laws laid down in the old Constitution of Kenya. The new Constitution (still being drafted) should put in place a legal framework and statutory provisions to strengthen women's entitlements to guarantee equal rights in land inheritance. Such a legal framework would increase the enforceability of laws on land ownership and women's claims to natural and physical assets in the event of separation or divorce or death of the husband.

7.2.3 Financial Support for Women

The study shows limited access to credit by women. Women need both fixed and working capital for agricultural production and for their non-farm activities. There is a need for investment in rural finance and credit lending institutions by the government and private investors. This study has shown that food security, especially in female headed households is closely linked to the size of the farm, income and labour efficiency. Therefore, these institutions should target women entrepreneurs and farmers to enable them to start or enlarge their enterprises. In this way, household income under the control of women will increase, bringing an increase in access to food by household members through purchase or increased production. As a result, nutrition of household members will improve. With access to credit, women can also invest in small ruminant rearing (an activity that many women in the study region would like to start) – and this can help increase their household income through sale of the animal products. Consumption of animal products such as milk and meat can contribute to improving nutrition. Access to sustainable and effective financial markets by poor households may enable these households recover more quickly after periods of stress than those without access to financial markets. Not just this study could show that under this circumstance, their nutrition security also suffers less.

7.2.4 Nutrition and Agricultural Extension Campaigns

The results of the study reveal inadequate access to extension services for farmers, especially female headed households. There is a need to strengthen extension service programmes. Extension services should be oriented to meet the needs of both female and male farmers. One way of doing this is by promoting community radio, through which extension workers can pass on information to all farmers. Given that most women farmers in the study region are illiterate or have low levels of education, promotion of extension services using the local Pokot language would be extremely helpful in meeting the needs of the less well-educated farmers and would not result in additional costs for the government.

In the light of the inadequate intake of micronutrients revealed by this study, nutrition programmes need to be promoted in the region. Again, community radio could provide a useful vehicle for this. Such programmes could include promotion of home gardens/kitchen gardens for growing vegetables and fruits, leading to improved nutrition.

7.2.5 Micronutrient Supplementation

It is clear from the food consumption data analysis that consumption of micronutrients is inadequate in the region, a situation that can lead to micronutrient deficiencies. The results reveal that women and children were at most risk of micronutrient deficiencies. Children under five years of age and women should be provided with iron and multivitamin supplements at local clinics. For school age children, foods provided through the on going school feeding programme by the government of Kenya and World Food Programme should be fortified with essential nutrients such as iron, calcium and Vitamin A.

7.2.6 Labour-Saving Technologies

Women in the study region carry the heavy burden of work. Developing technologies to ease the workload of rural women would be appreciated. Examples of such technologies include labour-saving stoves that use less firewood, and water-harvesting techniques. Women can be taught how to construct the stoves for themselves so that the technology does not represent a financial burden. Water harvesting during rainy seasons can help women have sufficient amounts of water during the dry season. These two technologies can reduce the workload of women, especially given that a considerable amount of women's time is spent on fetching water and collecting firewood as was revealed by this study. Labour-saving technologies can free up more time for child care or for income-generating activities thereby improving their food security position.

7.2.7 Development of Rural Infrastructure

Given the poor infrastructure in West Pokot, most private banks and private agricultural businesses avoid this region. With no private investors to provide agricultural seeds, fertilizers, farm machinery or credit, coupled with lack of extension agents to introduce better technology to farmers, it is difficult to achieve higher agricultural yields in West Pokot district. Therefore, there is need for the government of Kenya to invest in physical infrastructure in West Pokot and other rural areas; this will facilitate economic growth and in turn contribute to food security in the country.

An obvious recommendation, although not directly based on the study is related to the erratic rains in West Pokot and other arid and semi-arid regions. The government should also invest in water reservoirs for irrigation. Rainwater can be harnessed from rivers in the region that flood during the rainy season. Storage of this water would enable the inhabitants of these regions to grow irrigated crops. In addition to providing water for irrigation, water from the reservoirs could be used for drinking, energy and industrial use. Due to the considerable financial resources needed to realize this goal, the government needs to collaborate with NGOs working in the region to find ways of funding the irrigation water project and expand existing ones.

7.2.8 Training and Labour market Participation

The study reveals that 32% and 13% of women in the study area had primary and secondary school education. With these levels of education, it is difficult for these women to enter high income non farm employment. The government should put mechanisms in place to ensure that labour markets are available to such women by encouraging vocational training. Employers should promote and encourage vocational training (both basic and in-service training), to enable women with up to secondary education to participate more effectively in the labour market.

Women's self-help groups run most community-based projects in West Pokot and most rural parts of the country. These projects are mainly income-generating activities. Women groups should be given technical assistance and training to ensure that their income-generating activities are export-oriented – for example, this could be the production of high-quality curios or handicrafts for sale in large markets in the main cities and for export. The government needs to support such projects that complement household income and eventually translate into increased food purchases and meet the health, nutritional and educational needs of children.

7.2.9 Rural Development Activities

Levels of education in the study area are low, an indication that individuals are unable to obtain well-paid jobs in the formal public employment sector. This has led to high unemployment in West Pokot. The government and NGOs working in the region can implement public work programmes to increase the incomes of poor unemployed and underemployed people. The government can benefit by tapping available labour in the region, and the people involved in such programmes may be paid in cash or in kind (e.g. food). In addition to increasing the incomes and purchasing power of people and, eventually, their access to food, such programmes can create assets through the economic activities of the people employed such as rural roads, dams, and land conservation. If well targeted, such programmes are likely to benefit those people who have no alternative source of income and employment in the region.

Current emergency relief projects (e.g. general food aid distribution) providing temporary food to people in the region should focus more on food-for-work or cash-for-work schemes where people can be encouraged to work on their own farms. Such programmes will ensure that both men and women work to boost their household food supplies as well as income.

7.3   Research Implications

It is clear from the findings of the study that, due to their low level of education, most women worked in the agricultural sector, which provides low returns. While returns to education are higher in the non-farm sector, there is a need to improve incomes of those who remain in the agricultural sector. To achieve this, agricultural research should be directed toward technologies that increase returns to women's labour. This could include technologies that make women's labour more productive, such as technologies to improve the efficiency of food processing or fuel collection, or new crops that are more profitable and offer a higher return to women's labour.

Given the low nutrient intake in the study region, there is need to conduct research on micronutrient deficiencies that may have adverse effects on the health and development of people in the region and find ways to eliminate them. With inadequate intake of micronutrients, there is a high probability of children as well as adults suffering from micronutrient deficiency related diseases that lead to cognitive retardation, blindness or even death. Without addressing the micronutrient deficiency problem, advocating for policies such as improving access to education may be counter productive. Children with cognitive retardation may have low performance which eventually leads to low returns to education.

The analysis has shown a low domestication of livestock in female headed households. The results also show a low nutrient intake in the study region. Livestock keeping can lead to consumption of animal products such as milk and meat, thus improving household food and nutrition security. Research should be done to find out whether access to formal financial institutions can encourage women farmers to increase their livestock herds for improved household food security.

Zusammenfassung, Schlussfolgerungen und Politikempfehlungen

Die gegenwärtige Nahrungsmittelversorgung Kenias und deren Perspektive sind Besorgnis erregend. Die Nahrungsmittelsituation ist besonders prekär in den trockenen und halbtrockenen Gebieten des Landes. Das unberechenbare Klima, die schlechte Agrarpolitik und Nachernteverluste (z.b. durch Lagerung und Transport) wurden immer wieder für diese unsichere Ernährungslage verantwortlich gemacht. Die Rolle der bestehenden geschlechterspezifischen Ausrichtung beim Zugang zu Ressourcen in Bezug auf die unsichere Ernährungslage und deren Auswirkungen wurde dabei bisher nicht beachtet. Das übergeordnete Ziel dieser Untersuchung ist es, die geschlechterspezifischen Unterschiede zu erfassen bezüglich Zugang zu Land, Finanz- und Humankapital und die Auswirkungen dieses Zugangs auf die Nahrungsmittelsicherheit und das sozioökonomische Wohl der Haushalte zu bewerten. Diese Untersuchung wurde im Distrikt West Pokot in Kenia durchgeführt, einer Region, in der halbtrockenes bis trockenes Klima vorherrscht. In diesem Kapitel werden die wichtigsten Ergebnisse dieser Untersuchung zusammengefasst, Politikempfehlungen daraus abgeleitet und Themen aufgezeigt, die bei zukünftigen Untersuchungen berücksichtigt werden sollten.

Zusammenfassung und Schlussfolgerungen

Erstes Ziel dieser Untersuchung war, die Zuteilung von Land, Human- und Finanzkapital an die Haushalte geschlechterspezifisch zu erfassen. Bei der Ressourcenallokation ergibt sich ein ungleicher Zugang zu Land, Erziehung und Einkommen zugunsten der männlichen Bevölkerung. Die männlichen Befragten in der untersuchten Region hatten einen größeren Zugang zu Grund- und weiter führender Schulbildung. Bei der höheren Schulbildung (College und Universität) war kein signifikanter Unterschied zwischen den Geschlechtern festzustellen. Was den Zugang zu Land anbelangt, so waren Frauen benachteiligt: Sie konnten Land nur durch Kauf oder Pacht über einen männlichen Verwandten erwerben. Der direkte Zugang zu Land, etwa durch Erbschaft, war in dieser Region nicht zulässig – wie in vielen Teilen Kenias. Auf Grund ihrer durchschnittlich schlechteren Schulbildung hatten Frauen niedrigere Einkommen, da sie keinen Zugang zu besser bezahlten, Arbeitsplätzen im formellen Sektor hatten. Verglichen mit Frauen, hatte ein hoher Prozentsatz der männlichen Befragten Zugang zu Kredit von formellen

Institutionen, wie Banken. Männer hatten Zugang zu Land und anderen Vermögenswerten, wie beispielsweise Vieh, das sie als Sicherheit angeben konnten, um einen Kredit zu erhalten. Ein hoher Prozentsatz von Frauen besorgte sich Kredite von informellen Institutionen, z.b. von Frauengruppen und privaten Geldverleihern. Die von diesen Institutionen ausgeliehenen Summen waren gering im Vergleich zu denjenigen, die männliche Befragte bei formellen Institutionen ausgeliehen hatten.

Was die Arbeitsteilung anbelangt, so zeigen die Ergebnisse, dass Frauen sowohl im Haushalt als auch bei der Feldarbeit tätig waren. Auf Grund ihrer vielfältigen und gewissermaßen auch konkurrierenden Tätigkeiten (oft ohne arbeitssparende Hilfs- oder Transportmittel), litten die Frauen des Untersuchungsgebietes unter Zeitnot.

Das zweite Ziel dieser Untersuchung war, die Lage der Nahrungsmittelsicherheit in der untersuchten Region zu erfassen und Vergleiche anzustellen, basierend auf dem Geschlecht des Haushaltsvorstandes und seinem Zugang zu den wesentlichen Produktionsfaktoren Land, Finanz- und Humankapital. Die Nahrungsmittelsicherheit der Haushalte wurde gemessen an Hand von Verfügbarkeit, Zugang und Nutzung der Nahrungsmittel durch Haushaltsmitglieder. Hinsichtlich der Verfügbarkeit basiert die Analyse auf der Nahrungsmittelproduktion pro Haushalt, der Menge des verkauften Ertrags sowie der Menge, die für den Eigenbedarf zurückbehalten wurde. Haushalte, die ihre eigenen Nahrungsmitteln produzierten und genügend für den Eigenbedarf zurückhielten, wurden als nahrungsmittelsicher befunden. Dabei zeigte sich, dass Haushalte mit männlichen Haushaltsvorständen mehr Mais produzierten und eine größere Erntefruchtvielfalt hatten als Haushalte mit weiblichen Haushaltsvorständen. Als nahrungsmittelunsicher wurden Haushalte bezeichnet, die ihr Hauptnahrungsmittel (Mais) ausschließlich über den Markt bezogen.

Bezüglich Zugang und Nutzung von Nahrungsmitteln wurden Daten erhoben über den Nahrungsmittelverbrauch auf einer 24-Stunden-Basis, der Nahrungsmittelvielfalt und der Nahrungsmittelmenge. Es zeigte sich, dass im Durchschnitt weder weibliche noch männliche Befragte die empfohlene Vielfalt an Nährstoffen ihrem Alter und ihrer Tätigkeit entsprechend aufnahmen. Auch die entsprechende Nährstoffaufnahme bei Kindern war unzureichend. Den Nahrungsmitteln fehlte es an Proteinen, Vitaminen, Mikronährstoffen sowie Kohlenhydraten und Fett, was der Gesundheit abträglich ist.

Um die Ernährungssicherheit innerhalb der Haushalte zu bestimmen, wurde eine anthropometrische Analyse vorgenommen. Dabei wurde eine signifikante Häufigkeit von Unterernährung bei den Kindern in der Stichprobe festgestellt. Gehäuft traten Unterentwicklung (40%), Auszehrung (12%) und

Untergewicht (24%) bei Kindern auf. Am meisten betroffen von Unterentwicklung waren Kinder zwischen 36 und 48 Monate und Untergewicht (zwischen 48 und 60 Monate). Kinder zwischen 6 und 12 Monaten waren am häufigsten betroffen von Auszehrung und Untergewicht. In Familien mit weiblichen Haushaltsvorständen war die Häufigkeit von Untergewicht, Unterentwicklung und Auszehrung unter Kindern groß, ein Hinweis auf schlechten Zugang zu und Gebrauch von Nahrungsmitteln in diesen Haushalten. Ebenso war in diesen Haushalten ein höherer Prozentsatz an Kindern unterernährt im Vergleich zu Haushalten mit männlichem Haushaltsvorstand.

Mehr als die Hälfte der Frauen im gebärfähigen Alter hatte einen normalen „Body Mass Index" (BMI). Ungefähr 30% der Frauen waren untergewichtig, wobei Frauen in Haushalten mit weiblichem Haushaltsvorstand stärker betroffen waren. Untergewicht bei Müttern führt zur Geburt untergewichtiger Kinder, was wiederum ein Risikofaktor für spätere Unterentwicklung und Untergewicht des Kindes ist. Ein niedriger BMI kann das Resultat einer schlechten Ernährung, verbunden mit schwerer körperlicher Arbeit im Haushalt und auf dem Feld sein.

Um einer Nahrungsmittelknappheit zu begegnen, benutzten Haushalte mit weiblichen Haushaltsvorständen striktere Strategien als Haushalte mit männlichen Vorständen. Solche Strategien enthielten: Wegfall von Mahlzeiten und Reduktion der Nahrungsmengen für Haushaltsmitglieder. Die Strategien der Haushalte während der Nahrungsmittelverknappung wurden verwendet zur Definition des Nahrungssicherheitsindexes, welcher dann benutzt wurde, um die Haushalte in verschiedene Nahrungssicherheitskategorien einzustufen. Der Nahrungssicherheitsindex als Maß für die Nahrungssicherheit zeigte nur eine schwache Abhängigkeit vom Geschlecht des Haushaltsvorstands. Allerdings schnitten Haushalte mit weiblichem Haushaltsvorstand schlechter ab, wenn die Haushalte nach ihrem wirtschaftlichen Status bewertet wurden. Der wirtschaftliche Status eines Haushalts war für die Nahrungssicherheit am bedeutendsten, was an Hand der Chi-Quadrat-Resultate zwischen armen, mittleren und reichen Haushalten belegt werden konnte. Die ärmsten Haushalte hatten oft einen Mangel an Getreide (insbesondere Mais) auf Grund der geringen Größe des von ihnen bewirtschafteten Landes. Eine ihrer wesentlichen Überlebensstrategien war deshalb der Verkauf von höherwertigen Lebensmitteln, wie z.B. von Eiern, Hühnern, Hülsenfrüchten und Gemüse, um davon geringerwertige Lebensmittel, wie beispielsweise Mais, zu kaufen. Bei den mittleren und höheren Einkommen war die Nahrungssicherheit sowohl in Haushalten mit weiblichen als auch männlichen Haushaltsvorständen gleichermaßen gesichert; ein Hinweis darauf, dass hier bei unzureichender

Eigenproduktion Lebensmittel hinzugekauft werden konnten. Nur wenige Haushalte mit mittleren und höheren Einkommen waren von der Nahrungsmittelunsicherheit betroffen. Weitergehende Analysen dieser Daten zeigten, dass diese Haushalte genügend Nahrungsmittel für den Eigenbedarf produzierten, das meiste davon aber verkauften. Dies bestätigt, dass die Nahrungsmittelproduktion alleine nicht ausreicht, um Nahrungssicherheit der Haushalte zu gewährleisten.

Insgesamt gab es eine hohe Krankheitsrate in der untersuchten Region. Diarrhöe bei Kindern war die am weitesten verbreitete Krankheit, über die berichtet wurde, was auf schlechte Gesundheit und schlechte sanitäre Bedingungen in den meisten Haushalten der Region schließen ließ. Andere weit verbreitete Krankheiten bei Kindern waren nahrungsbedingte Erkrankungen und Erkrankungen der Atemwege. Diese Häufigkeit von Krankheiten, verbunden mit Mangelernährung und schlechten sanitären Bedingungen in den meisten Haushalten der untersuchten Region trugen zu dem schlechten Ernährungszustand der Kinder bei.

Die ökonometrische Analyse dieser Untersuchung konzentriert sich auf die Faktoren des landwirtschaftlichen und nicht-landwirtschaftlichen Einkommens, die technische Effizienz-Analyse in von Männern bzw. Frauen geführten landwirtschaftlichen Betrieben, die Faktoren der Nahrungsmittelsicherheit der Haushalte und den Ernährungszustand der Kinder. Ein zweistufiges Heckman-Modell wurde angewandt, um die Faktoren des landwirtschaftlichen und nicht-landwirtschaftlichen Einkommens zu analysieren. Ausbildung ergab sich als der bedeutendste Faktor, der das landwirtschaftliche und nicht-landwirtschaftliche Einkommen bestimmt. Frauen mit Grund- und weiterführender Schulbildung erzielten einen höheren Ertrag im landwirtschaftlichen Sektor als Frauen mit der gleichen Ausbildung im nicht-landwirtschaftlichen Sektor. Bei höherer Schulbildung (College) erzielten sowohl Frauen als auch Männer höhere Erträge im nicht-landwirtschaftlichen Sektor. Der Regionaldummy war ebenfalls wichtig zur Bestimmung der Einkommen der Haushalte. Haushalte im Gebiet Kapenguria hatten ein höheres Einkommen sowohl aus landwirtschaftlichen als auch aus nicht-landwirtschaftlichen Tätigkeiten auf Grund der besseren Infrastruktur und der größeren Nähe zu den Märkten im Vergleich zum Gebiet von Chepareria. Der Zugang zu nicht-landwirtschaftlichem Einkommen trägt wesentlich zum landwirtschaftlichen Einkommen bei. Mit nicht-landwirtschaftlichem Einkommen hatten Haushalte die Möglichkeit, landwirtschaftliche Investitionen zu tätigen und dadurch die Produktivität zu steigern. Die Hypothese, dass Zugang zu Ausbildung das Haushaltseinkommen steigert (sowohl im landwirtschaftlichen als auch nicht-landwirtschaftlichen Bereich) wurde bestätigt. Ebenfalls bestätigt wurde die Hypothese, dass Zugang zu Finanzkapital die landwirtschaftliche Produktivität und damit das landwirtschaftliche Einkommen erhöht. Insgesamt ist festzustellen, dass die landwirtschaftliche Produktivität in der untersuchten Region gering war. Die Größe des Landbesitzes spielte eine signifikante Rolle in der landwirtschaftlichen Produktivität, wie auch aus der statistischen Signifikanz des Koeffizienten der Landgröße in der Ordinary-least-squares-(OLS)-Regressionsanalyse ersichtlich ist. Zwischen Haushalten mit männlichen und weiblichen Haushaltsvorständen gab es Unterschiede in der landwirtschaftlichen Produktivität, wobei Haushalte mit männlichem Haushaltsvorstand höhere Erträge auswiesen. Daher kann die Hypothese, dass der beschränkte Zugang von Frauen zu landwirtschaftlicher Nutzfläche zu einer geringeren landwirtschaftlichen Produktivität führt, als bestätigt angesehen werden.

Die OLS-Regressionsanalyse der Determinanten der Nahrungsmittelsicherheit ergab, dass die Ausgaben für Nahrungsmittel, deren Lagerung und die Haushaltgröße die wichtigsten Faktoren bei der Bestimmung der Aufnahme von Kalorien und Proteinen bei Kindern waren (diese Werte werden als Synonym für die Haushalts-Nahrungssicherheit benutzt). Der Anteil des Einkommens, der für Lebensmittel ausgegeben wurde, beeinflusste sowohl die Kalorien- als auch Proteinaufnahme positiv, während ein Anstieg der Haushaltsgröße sich negativ auf die Aufnahme dieser Nährstoffe auswirkte. Der Koeffizient für die Nahrungsmittelausgabe war größer bei der Regressionsanalyse für die Kalorienaufnahme als für die Proteinaufnahme, ein Hinweis darauf, dass das meiste Geld für den Kauf Energie spendender Lebensmittel, z.B. Getreide, in diesem Falle Mais, ausgegeben wurde. Ein größerer Betrag für Lebensmittellagerung zum Eigenverzehr trug zu einer höheren Kalorienaufnahme bei.

Eine stochastische Cobb-Douglas-Produktionsfunktion wurde verwendet um festzustellen, bis zu welchem Grad technische Effizienz, Gesamtarbeitsaufwand und Investitionen die landwirtschaftliche Produktivität beeinflussen. Hierfür wurde eine Analyse von männlich oder weiblich geführten Bauernhöfen durchgeführt, vor dem Hintergrund, dass bei gleichem Technologie-Einsatz, Arbeitsaufwand und Ausbildung die Produktivität in männlich oder weiblich geführten landwirtschaftlichen Betrieben nicht signifikant differieren sollte. Unterschiede in der Produktivität sind auf den unterschiedlichen effektiven Einsatz von Investitionen zurückzuführen als Folge des ungleichen Zugangs zu Ressourcen wie Ausbildung, Einkommen, Kredit und landwirtschaftliche Beratung. Auf Grund der unterschiedlichen Klimata und Bodencharakteristika wurde die Analyse getrennt für die Gebiete Chepareria und Kapenguria durchgeführt. In beiden Fällen erfolgte die Analyse für männlich und weiblich geführte landwirtschaftliche Betriebe getrennt. Die Hauptfaktoren, die offensichtlich signifikant zur technischen Effizienz beitrugen, waren Ausbildung, Zugang zu Kredit, Einsatz von Düngemitteln und die Entfernung des landwirtschaftlichen Betriebes zu Hauptstraßen. Die Ausbildung der Landwirte hatte einen positiven und wesentlichen Einfluss auf die Effizienz der Maisproduktion. Dies deutet darauf hin, dass Landwirte mit längerer Schulbildung einen höheren technischen Effizienzgrad aufwiesen. Ohne Zugang zu Kredit ist keine Verbesserung der technischen Effizienz der Landwirte möglich. Zugang zu Kredit wiederum versetzte Landwirte in die Lage, Investitionen zu tätigen und für den Einsatz landwirtschaftlicher Geräte und moderner Technologie zu zahlen. Für weibliche Landwirte war der Zugang zu Kredit eingeschränkt, was wiederum die technische Effizienz beeinträchtigte. Die Entfernung des landwirtschaftlichen Betriebes von der Hauptstraße war statistisch im 5%-Bereich relevant, was darauf hindeutet, dass die technische Effizienz mit der Nähe des Anwesens zur Hauptstraße zunimmt.

Ergebnisse der zweistufigen Least-squares-Regressionsanalyse der Determinanten des Ernährungszustandes von Kindern zeigten, dass die Schulbildung des Haushaltsvorstandes und die der Mütter eine bedeutende Einflussgröße auf den Ernährungszustand von Kindern war, und dies sowohl in männlich als auch weiblich geführten Haushalten. Für Kinder, deren Mütter keine offizielle Schulbildung hatten, war die Wahrscheinlichkeit einer Unterernährung größer (Resultate der Logit-Regression). Weiterführende und College-Schulbildung trugen signifikant zur Verringerung von Unterentwicklung, Auszehrung und Untergewicht bei. Das Einkommen des Haushaltsvorstands war wesentlicher für den Ernährungszustand der Kinder als das Einkommen der Mütter. Auf Grund ihrer geringen Ausbildung verdienten Frauen im nicht-landwirtschaftlichen Sektor weniger, und daher ist es nicht verwunderlich, dass der Koeffizient für das mütterliche Einkommen nur eine schwache Signifikanz im Vergleich zu dem Koeffizienten für das Einkommen des Haushaltsvorstandes hat. Die Hypothese, dass der begrenzte Zugang von Frauen zu Ausbildung und Finanzkapital zu einem schlechten Ernährungszustand der Haushaltsmitglieder führt, wurde bestätigt.

OLS-Regressionsresultate zeigten, dass die Ausbildung der Frauen für die Verminderung der Kinderkrankheiten und der Fruchtbarkeitsrate wesentlich ist. Frauen mit weiterführender Schulbildung (12 Schuljahre) hatten ein Kind weniger als Frauen, die keine Schule besuchten, während Frauen mit College-

und Universitätsabschluss (mehr als 13 Schuljahre) zwei Kinder weniger hatten als diejenigen ohne Schulbildung. Eine geringere Fruchtbarkeitsrate beruht nicht alleine auf der Ausbildung, sondern auch auf anderen positiven Effekten dieser Ausbildung, wie z.B. Möglichkeiten der Berufstätigkeit und Wissen um Verhütungsmethoden.

Zusammenfassend gilt es als erwiesen, dass Zugang zu Humankapital, Finanzkapital und Land einen Einfluss auf die Ernährungssicherheit und das sozioökonomische Wohl der Haushaltsmitglieder hat. Haushalte, in denen Haushaltsvorstand und Haushaltsmitglieder eine gute Kombination aus Ausbildung, Landbesitz und Einkommen aufwiesen, waren nahrungsmittelsicher hinsichtlich Verfügbarkeit, Zugang und Gebrauch von Nahrungsmitteln. Durch begrenzten Zugang zu Land, Ausbildung, Einkommen, Kredit und Beratungsdiensten waren weiblich geführte Haushalte benachteiligt im Hinblick auf landwirtschaftliche Produktivität; außerdem war ihre Möglichkeit, Lebensmittel auf dem Markt zu kaufen, auf Grund des begrenzten Einkommens beschränkt. Dies führt zu einer schlechten Ernährungssituation der Haushaltsmitglieder, manifestiert am schlechten Ernährungszustand der Kinder. Es besteht auch ein Zusammenhang zwischen Ausbildung und Fruchtbarkeitsrate bei Frauen, ein Hinweis darauf, dass eine bessere Ausbildung von Frauen die Anzahl von Kindern pro Frau in der untersuchten Region verringern wird.

Nahrungsmittelunsicherheit im Distrikt West Pokot kann daher nicht allein auf unberechenbare klimatische Bedingungen der Region zurückgeführt werden. Die bestehende geschlechterspezifische Gewichtung beim Zugang zu den wesentlichen Produktionsgrundlagen spielt eine große Rolle in der Nahrungsmittelsicherheit. Da Frauen mehrere Aufgaben zum Erhalt der Gesellschaft wahrnehmen, ist es schwierig, eine umfassende, nachhaltige Nahrungsmittelsicherheit in dieser Region zu erreichen, ohne die bestehende, traditionell begründete Benachteiligung der Frauen im anzusprechen. Darüber hinaus wird es schwierig sein, ein nachhaltiges wirtschaftliches Wachstum in dieser Region zu erreichen, ohne gleiche Ausbildungschancen für Mädchen und Jungen zu schaffen. Die Ausbildung der Mädchen ist wichtig, um die armutsbedingten Probleme der Region anzugehen, wie hohe Fruchtbarkeitsraten, Kinderkrankheiten, Mangelernährung, schlechte Gesundheit und die daraus resultierende geringe Produktivität.

Politikempfehlungen

Aus den Ergebnissen dieser Untersuchung werden die folgenden Politikempfehlungen abgeleitet:

Investition in Ausbildung und Gesundheitswesen

Die Untersuchung zeigt durchgängig, welche Rolle die Ausbildung bei Ernährung, Agrarproduktion, nicht-landwirtschaftlichen Aktivitäten und dem allgemeinen Wohlergehen der Haushalte spielt. Die Regierung sollte in Schulen und Gesundheitszentren investieren, so dass mehr Frauen in ländlichen Gebieten Zugang zu Schulbildung und Gesundheitsvorsorge haben. Der Besuch von Grund- und weiterführenden Schulen sollte Pflicht für alle Kinder werden. Der Zugang zu Schulbildung, besonders für Frauen, wird mit großer Wahrscheinlichkeit die Fruchtbarkeitsrate, Kinderkrankheiten und Kindersterblichkeit in der untersuchten Region signifikant verringern. Insgesamt scheint klar zu sein, dass Investitionen in Ausbildung das Schlüsselelement sind bei der Bekämpfung der Armut und ihren Begleiterscheinungen, wie Nahrungsmittelunsicherheit, Mangelernährung und hohe Krankheitsraten in West Pokot. Ansätze, die Geschlechtergleichstellung bei der Ausbildung zu fördern, könnten beispielsweise niedrigere Schulgebühren, verbesserte Erreichbarkeit der Schulen, besserer Unterricht und Investitionen in eine zeitsparende Infrastruktur einschließen.

Daten über den Schulbesuch und -abbruch zeigen eine hohe Abbruchrate bei Mädchen. Gründe, die zu der hohen Abbruchrate beitragen, waren hohe Schulkosten (Schuluniform, Schreibmaterialien, Möbel), große Entfernungen zur Schule und Vorurteile. Um die Schulabbruchrate von Mädchen zu verringern, wird empfohlen, die Schulkosten zu senken, Schulstipendien für Mädchen einzuführen, die Lehrer besser auszubilden, die Lehrpläne zu überprüfen und zu revidieren und Eltern dahingehend zu erziehen, dass geschlechterspezifische Vorurteile nicht länger im Klassenzimmer und in der Gemeinde geduldet werden. Investitionen, die die Entfernung zur Schule verringern und Investitionen in Trinkwasser und Energie sowie verringerte Schulkosten könnten den Schulbesuch von Mädchen sprunghaft in die Höhe treiben, wie diese Untersuchung gezeigt hat.

Die Daten zeigen einen schlechten Zugang zu Gesundheitszentren in der untersuchten Region. Ein verbesserter Zugang zu diesen Gesundheitszentren könnte jedoch die Zeit, die Frauen und Mädchen für die Pflege kranker Familienmitglieder aufwenden, wesentlich verringern. Investitionen auf diesem

Sektor bedeuten weniger Arbeitsunterbrechungen bei der bezahlten Arbeit der Frauen und weniger Schulunterbrechung bei den Mädchen.

Abschaffung der Diskriminierung bei Landbesitz

Die Untersuchung zeigt Unterschiede auf beim Zugang zu Land und anderen wirtschaftlichen Produktivwerten, wobei die Frauen eindeutig benachteiligt sind. Eine Gesetzgebung ist nötig, die das Recht der Frauen garantiert, Land zu erben und zu besitzen. Die Regierung von Kenia sollte in ihre Verfassung eindeutige Gesetze bezüglich Landbesitz und Erbschaft aufnehmen, worin die Rechte der Frauen auf Land berücksichtigt sind. Dies wird helfen, den bestehenden Konflikt zwischen Gewohnheits-Landrechten und den Landgesetzen der alten Verfassung von Kenia zu lösen. Die neue Verfassung (noch im Entwurf) sollte einen gesetzlichen Rahmen vorgeben und rechtliche Bestimmungen enthalten, um die berechtigten Ansprüche der Frauen zu stärken. Ein solches gesetzliches Regelwerk würde die Durchführbarkeit von Gesetzen bezüglich Landbesitz erhöhen und gleichzeitig die Ansprüche der Frauen auf natürliche und physische Werte im Falle von Trennung, Scheidung oder Tod des Ehemanns regeln.

Finanzielle Unterstützung für Frauen

Die Untersuchung ergab, dass Frauen nur einen begrenzten Zugang zu Kredit haben. Frauen benötigen beides, festes und Arbeitskapital für die landwirtschaftliche Produktion und ihre nicht-landwirtschaftlichen Tätigkeiten. Es gibt einen Bedarf für ländliche Finanz- und Kreditinstitutionen durch die Regierung und private Investoren. Die Untersuchung hat gezeigt, dass Nahrungsmittelsicherheit, insbesondere in weiblich geführten Haushalten, eng verbunden ist mit der Größe des landwirtschaftlichen Betriebes, dem Einkommen und der Arbeitseffizienz. Daher sollten diese Institutionen Unternehmerinnen und Landwirtinnen als Zielgruppe haben, um ihnen den Start zu ermöglichen oder ihre Unternehmen zu vergrößern. Dadurch würde das Haushaltseinkommen der von Frauen geführten Haushalte zunehmen, was wiederum einen besseren Zugang zu Lebensmitteln für die Haushaltsmitglieder durch Zukauf oder erhöhte Produktion mit sich bringen würde. Als Ergebnis würde sich die Ernährungssituation der Haushaltsmitglieder verbessern. Mit Zugang zu Kredit könnten Frauen auch in kleinerem Rahmen Viehzucht betreiben (eine Tätigkeit, die viele Frauen in der untersuchten Region gerne aufnehmen würden). Dies könnte außerdem auch das Haushaltseinkommen durch den Verkauf von Tierprodukten erhöhen. Der Konsum von tierischen Produkten, wie Milch und Fleisch, könnte zu einer Verbesserung der Ernährungssituation beitragen. Zugang von armen Haushalten zu nachhaltigen und effektiven Finanzmärkten könnte diese Haushalte befähigen, sich nach Stressperioden schneller zu erholen als jene ohne Zugang zu Finanzmärkten. Nicht nur *diese* Untersuchung konnte zeigen, dass unter diesen Umständen die Ernährungssicherung weniger beeinträchtigt ist.

Ernährungs- und landwirtschaftliche Beratungsaktionen

Die Ergebnisse der Untersuchung zeigen einen unzulänglichen Zugang zu Beratungsdiensten für Landwirte, besonders bei Haushalten mit weiblichem Haushaltsvorstand. Es besteht die Notwendigkeit, diese Beratungsdienste auszubauen. Beratungsdienste sollten sowohl auf die Bedürfnisse der weiblichen als auch der männlichen Landwirte abgestimmt sein. Eine Möglichkeit dies durchzuführen, ist das örtliche Radio zu stärken, über das dann Berater Informationen an alle Landwirte weitergeben könnten. Dadurch dass die meisten weiblichen Landwirte in der Untersuchungsregion Analphabeten sind oder nur eine geringe Schulbildung haben, wäre es hilfreich, wenn die Berater die lokale Pokot-Sprache sprechen würden. Dies würde zu keinen zusätzlichen Kosten für die Regierung führen.

Angesichts der unzureichenden Aufnahme von Mikronährstoffen – wie im Rahmen dieser Untersuchung festgestellt wurde – sollten Ernährungsprogramme in dieser Region verstärkt durchgeführt werden. Das örtliche Radio könnte wiederum hierbei hilfreich sein. Solche Programme könnten die Förderung von Haus- bzw. Küchengärten zum Anbau von Gemüse und Früchten beinhalten, was zu einer verbesserten Ernährung führen würde.

Ergänzung durch Mikronährstoffe

Die Analyse des Nahrungsmittelkonsums hat gezeigt, dass die Aufnahme von Mikronährstoffen in der Region unzureichend ist, eine Situation, die zu Mangelerscheinungen führen kann. Die Ergebnisse zeigten, dass das Risiko, unter Mangelerscheinungen zu leiden, für Frauen und Kinder besonders groß ist. Kinder unter 5 Jahren und Frauen sollten von den örtlichen Kliniken mit Eisen- und Multivitaminpräparaten versorgt werden. Für Schulkinder sollte die zurzeit laufende   Schulspeisung   der   kenianischen   Regierung   und   des

Welternährungsprogramms mit den wichtigen Nährstoffen Eisen, Kalzium und Vitamin A angereichert werden.

Arbeit sparende Technologien

Frauen in der untersuchten Region verrichten den größten Anteil an Arbeit. Die Entwicklung von Technologien zur Erleichterung der Arbeit der Landfrauen wäre wünschenswert. Beispiele dieser Technologien schließen Arbeit sparende Öfen, die weniger Feuerholz verbrauchen, und Wasser speichernde Techniken ein. Frauen könnten darin unterrichtet werden, wie diese Öfen von ihnen selbst gebaut werden können, so dass diese Technologie keine finanzielle Belastung darstellen würde. Wasserspeicherung während der Regenzeit kann den Frauen helfen, genügend Wasser in der Trockenzeit zu haben. Diese beiden Technologien können die Arbeitsbelastung der Frauen reduzieren, insbesondere wenn man berücksichtigt, dass die Frauen einen beachtlichen Teil ihrer Zeit dafür aufwenden, Wasser zu holen und Feuerholz zu sammeln, wie diese Untersuchung gezeigt hat. Arbeit sparende Technologien würden mehr Zeit für die Kinderpflege oder für Aktivitäten ermöglichen, die das Einkommen aufbessern und damit die Nahrungsmittelsicherheit verbessern könnten.

Entwicklung der ländlichen Infrastruktur

Auf Grund der schlechten Infrastruktur in West Pokot meiden die meisten privaten Banken und privaten landwirtschaftlichen Unternehmen diese Region. Ohne private Investoren, die landwirtschaftliches Saatgut, Düngemittel, landwirtschaftliche Maschinen oder Kredit bereitstellen, und ohne eine ausreichende Anzahl von Beratern für die Einführung besserer Technologien bei den Landwirten, ist es schwierig, höhere landwirtschaftliche Erträge im Distrikt West Pokot zu erzielen. Deshalb besteht für die Regierung von Kenia die Notwendigkeit, in die Infrastruktur von West Pokot und anderen ländlichen Gebieten zu investieren; dies würde das wirtschaftliche Wachstum erleichtern und wiederum zur Nahrungsmittelsicherheit des Landes beitragen.

Eine auf der Hand liegende Empfehlung, obwohl nicht direkt aus dieser Untersuchung ableitbar, steht im Zusammenhang mit den unberechenbaren Regenfällen in West Pokot und anderen trockenen und halb-trockenen Regionen. Die Regierung sollte auch in Wasserreservoirs für die Bewässerung investieren. Regenwasser könnte aus Flüssen nutzbar gemacht werden, die während der Regenzeit über die Ufer treten. Die Speicherung dieses Wassers würde die Bewohner dieser Regionen in die Lage versetzen, auf künstlich bewässerten Feldern Feldfrüchte anzubauen. Zusätzlich könnte dieses Wasser auch als Trinkwasser, für die Energieerzeugung und für den industriellen Gebrauch verwendet werden. Auf Grund der beträchtlichen finanziellen Investitionen, die nötig wären, um dieses Ziel zu erreichen, sollte die Regierung mit Nichtregierungsorganisationen (NGOs) in dieser Region zusammenarbeiten, um Wege zu finden, neue Bewässerungsprojekte zu finanzieren und existierende auszubauen.

Schulung und Teilnahme am Arbeitsmarkt

Die Untersuchung ergab, dass nur 32% und 13% der Frauen der betrachteten Region eine Grund- oder weiterführende Schulbildung hatten. Mit dieser Ausbildung ist es für solche Frauen schwierig, Beschäftigungen im nicht-landwirtschaftlichen Bereich mit einem hohen Einkommen zu finden. Die Regierung sollte Mechanismen in Kraft setzen, die sicherstellen, dass der Arbeitsmarkt durch berufliches Training auch für diese Frauen zugänglich wird. Arbeitgeber sollten ebenfalls ein solches berufliches Training fördern, um Frauen mit dieser Schulbildung effektiver am Arbeitsmarkt teilnehmen zu lassen.

Frauen-Selbsthilfegruppen betreiben die meisten Projekte in Dörfern und ländlichen Regionen von West Pokot. Diese Projekte sind hauptsächlich auf die Einkommensteigerung ausgerichtet. Solchen Gruppen sollte technischer Beistand und Training gegeben werden, um sicherzustellen, dass ihre Einkommen steigernden Tätigkeiten exportorientiert sind. Dies könnte z.B. die Herstellung von hochwertigen curios oder Handarbeiten sein, die auf den großen Märkten der Großstädte verkauft werden oder für den Export bestimmt sind. Die Regierung sollte solche Projekte unterstützen, die das Haushaltseinkommen ergänzen und schließlich umgesetzt werden in einen höheren Nahrungsmittelkauf und damit den gesundheitlichen, ernährungs- und ausbildungsspezifischen Bedürfnissen der Kinder genügen.

Aktivitäten zur Entwicklung des ländlichen Raumes

Der Ausbildungsgrad in der untersuchten Region ist niedrig; gut bezahlte Arbeit im öffentlichen Dienst zu erhalten ist als Folge davon für einzelne unmöglich. Dies führte zu einer hohen Arbeitslosigkeit in West Pokot. Die Regierung und die NGOs könnten öffentliche Arbeitsprogramme implementieren, um die

Einkommen der armen Arbeitslosen und unterbeschäftigen Menschen zu steigern. Die Regierung könnte davon profitieren, verfügbare Arbeitskraft in dieser Region zu bündeln und den Menschen, die in solchen Programmen eingebunden sind, dies in bar oder Naturalien (z.B. Nahrungsmittel) vergüten. Zusätzlich zur Einkommen- und Kaufkraftsteigerung der Menschen und, letztendlich, zu einem verbesserten Zugang zu Nahrungsmitteln, könnten solche Programme Werte schaffen, wie beispielsweise ländliche Straßen, Dämme und Landerschließung und -pflege. Wenn solche Programme gut geplant sind, nützen sie den Menschen, die keine alternative Einkommensquelle oder Beschäftigung in der Region finden.

Die zurzeit laufenden Hilfsprojekte (z.B. allgemeine Nahrungsmittelverteilung), die Menschen temporär mit Nahrungsmittel versorgen, sollten mehr auf Nahrungsmittel-für-Arbeit- oder Geld-für-Arbeit-Programme setzen, in denen Menschen ermutigt werden, in ihren eigenen landwirtschaftlichen Betrieben zu arbeiten. Solche Programme würden es sowohl Männern als auch Frauen ermöglichen, ihre Nahrungsmittelversorgung und ihr Einkommen wesentlich zu verbessern.

Auswirkungen

Die Untersuchung hat klar ergeben, dass auf Grund ihres niedrigen Ausbildungsstandes die meisten Frauen in der Landwirtschaft arbeiteten, was gleichbedeutend mit niedrigen Einkommen ist. Da die Einkommen im nicht-landwirtschaftlichen Sektor höher sind, besteht die Notwendigkeit, die Einkommen derjenigen zu erhöhen, die weiterhin in der Landwirtschaft tätig sind. Um dies zu erreichen, sollte die landwirtschaftliche Forschung auf solche Technologien gerichtet sein, die die Einkommen der Frauen erhöhen. Dies könnte Technologien einschließen, die die Arbeit der Frauen produktiver machen, z.B. um die Nahrungsmittelherstellung oder Brennstoffgewinnung zu erleichtern, oder der Anbau neuartiger Feldfrüchte, die rentabler sind und einen höheren Gewinn versprechen.

Durch die niedrige Nährstoffaufnahme in der untersuchten Region besteht ein Bedarf, Untersuchungen über den Mangel an Mikronährstoffen durchzuführen, der ungünstige Auswirkungen auf die Gesundheit und Entwicklung der Menschen in der Regionen hat, und Wege zu finden, dies auszuschließen. Durch unzureichende Aufnahme von Mikronährstoffen besteht eine hohe Wahrscheinlichkeit, dass sowohl Kinder als auch Erwachsene an Mangelerscheinungen leiden, die zu einer kognitiven Verzögerung in der

Entwicklung bei Kindern, Erblindung oder sogar Tod führen können. Sich für Programme einzusetzen, wie ein Programm zur Verbesserung des Zugangs zu Ausbildung, ohne das Problem des Mikronährstoffmangels anzusprechen, ist kontraproduktiv. Kinder mit kognitiver Verzögerung erbringen schwache Leistungen, die schließlich zu schlechten Ausbildungsergebnissen führen.

Die Analyse hat einen geringen Viehbestand in Haushalten mit weiblichem Haushaltsvorstand ergeben. Die Resultate zeigen weiter eine geringe Nährstoffaufnahme in der untersuchten Region. Viehhaltung kann zum Verbrauch von tierischen Produkten wie Milch und Fleisch führen und dadurch die Nahrungs- und Nährstoffaufnahme der Haushalte verbessern. Es sollte untersucht werden, ob Zugang zu offiziellen Finanzinstitutionen weibliche Landwirte ermutigen kann, ihren Viehbestand zu erhöhen, um die Nahrungsmittelsicherheit des Haushaltes zu verbessern

REFERENCES

Abagi J, and Otieno W. 2000. Counting the Social Impact of Schooling: What Kenyans Say about their School System and Gender Relations. Institute of Policy Analysis and Research (IPAR).

Alderman H, Hoddinott J, Haddad L, and Udry C.R. 2003. Gender Differentials in Farm Productivity: Implications for Household Efficiency and Agricultural Policy. In *Household Decisions, Gender, and Development: A Synthesis of Recent Research.* Quisumbing A.R (ed.): 61-66. Washington D.C, USA: IFPRI.

Alderman H., Hoddinott J, Haddad L, and Udry C. 1995. Gender Differentials in Farm Productivity: Implications for Household Efficiency and Agricultural Policy. Washington D.C: IFPRI.

Andersen P, and Pandya-Lorch R. 1998. Achieving the 2020 Vision, with Special Reference to Gender Issues. Switzerland: ACC/SCN.

Andersen P, Pandya-Lorch R, and Rosegrant M.W. 2001. Global Food Security: A Review of the Challenges. In *The Unfinished Agenda: Perspectives on Overcoming Hunger, Poverty, 205 and Environmental Degradation.* Andersen P et al. (ed.): 7-17. Washington D.C: IFPRI.

Annan K. 2000. Global Nutrition Challenges: A life cycle. *Food and Nutrition Bulletin* 21 (3): 18-34.

Appleton S, Hoddinnot J, Knight J. 1996. Primary Education as an Input into Post Primary Education: A Neglected Benefit, *Oxford Bulletin of Economics and Statistics* 58:1, pp. 211-19.

Appleton S, Bigstein A, and Manda K.D. 1999. *Educational Expansion and Economic Decline in Kenya: Returns to Education in Kenya, 1978 - 1995.* Oxford: Centre for the Study of African Economies, University of Oxford.

Basiotis P.P. 1992. Validity of the Self-reported Food Sufficiency Status Item in the US department of Agriculture's Food Surveys. In American Council on Consumer Interests 38th Annual Conference: The proceedings. Columbia: MO

Battese G.E, and Coelli T.J. 1988. Prediction of Firm-level Technical Efficiencies with a Generalised Frontier Production Function and Panel Data. *Journal of Econometrics* 38 (387-399).

Battese G.E. 1992. Frontier Production Functions and Technical Efficiency : A Survey of Empirical Applications in Agricultural Economics. *Agricultural Economics* 7 (185-208).

Battese G.E, and Coelli T.J. 1995. A Model for Technical Inefficiency Effects in Stochastic Frontier Function for Panel Data. *Empirical Economics* 20 (325-332).

Batzlen C. 2000. Migration and Economic Development: Remittances and Investment in South Asia. A case Study of Pakistan. Frankfurt: Peter lang Europäischer Verlag der Wissenschaften.

Bedi S.A, Kimalu P.K, Manda K.D, and Nafula N.N. 2002. The Decline of Primary School Enrolment in Kenya. Nairobi: Kenya Institute for Public Policy Research and Analysis (KIPPRA).

Benson T. 2004. Africa's Food and Nutrition Security Situation: Where are We and How Did We Get Here. Washington D.C: International Food Policy Research Institute (IFPRI).

Bouis H.E, Costello P.M, Solomon , Westbrook B, and Limbo A. 1998. Gender Equality and Investments in Adolescents in the Rural Phillipines. Washington D.C: IFPRI.

Borooah, Vani Kant. 2002. *Logit and probit*. Thousand Oaks, CA: Sage Publications.

Briere B, Hallman K, and Quisumbing A.R. 2003. Resource Allocation and Empowerment of Women in Rural Bangladesh. In *Household Decisions, Gender, and Development: A Synthesis of Recent Research*. Quisumbing A.R (ed.): 89-93. Washington D.C: IFPRI.

Brown, L R., and L. Haddad. 1995. Time Allocation Patterns and Time Burdens: A Gendered Analysis of Seven Countries. Washington D.C: International Food Policy Research Institute, Washington, D.C.

Brown R.B, Feldstein H, Haddad L, Pena C, and Quisumbing A. 2001. Generating Food Security in the Year 2020:Women as Producers, Gate keepers, and Shock Absorbers. In *The Unfinished Agenda: Perspectives on Overcoming Hunger, Poverty, 205 and Environmental Degradation*. Andersen P et al. (ed.): 205-209. Washington D.C: IFPRI.

Buchenrieder G. 2004. Non Farm Rural Employment - Review of Issues, Evidence and Policies. *Quarterly Journal of International Agriculture* 44 (1): 5-8.

Buchenrieder G, Kirk M, and Knerr B. 2005. Poverty Impacts and Policy Options of Non-farm Rural Employment. In *Poverty Impacts and Policy Options of Non-farm rural Employment*. Buchenrieder G et al. (ed.): 1-11. Weikersheim, Germany: Margraf Verlag.

Central Bureau of Statistics. 1998. *First Report on Poverty in Kenya. Volume II: Poverty and Social Indicators*. Nairobi: Government Printers.

Central Bureau of Statistics. 2000a. *Second Report on Poverty in Kenya. Volume I. Incidence and Depth of Poverty*. Nairobi: Government Printers.

Central Bureau of Statistics. 2000b. *Second Report on Poverty in Kenya Volume II: Poverty and Social Indicators*. Nairobi: Government Printers.

Central Bureau of Statistics. 2001. *Population and Housing Census. Volume II: Social and Economic Profile of the Population*. Nairobi: Government Printers.

Central Bureau of Statistics 2002. *Kenya Participatory Impact Monitoring. Perspectives of the Poor on Anti-Poverty Policies in Selected Districts*, Nairobi: Government Printers

Central Bureau of Statistics. 2003a. Kenya Demographic Health Survey: A Preliminary Report. Nairobi: Government Printers.

Central Bureau of Statistics. 2003b. Geographic Dimensions of Well-being in Kenya. Where are the poor? From Districts to Locations. Volume 1. Nairobi: Regal Press Kenya Ltd.

Central Bureau of Statistics. 2005. Geographic Dimensions of Wellbeing in Kenya: Who and Where are the poor? Volume 2. Nairobi: The Regal Press Limited

Central Intelligence Agency (CIA). 2004. World Fact Book 2004. www.cia.gov/cia/publications/factbook/geos/ke.htm. Accessed on 20.01.2004

Coates J, Webb P, and Houser R. 2003. *Measuring Food Insecurity: Going Beyond Indicators of Income and Anthropometry*. Food and Nutrition Technical Assistance Project, Academy for Educational Development.

Coelli, T.J., Rao, D.S and Batesse, G.E. 1998. *An Introduction to Efficiency and Productivity Analysis*. Kluwert Academic Publishers

Coelli T.J. 1995. Recent Developments in Frontier Modelling and Efficiency Measurement. *Australian Journal of Agricultural Economics* 3 (3).

Cogill B. 2003. Anthropometric Indicators Measurement Guide. Food and Nutrition Technical Assistance Project, Academy for Educational Development, Washington D.C., http://www.fantaproject.org/downloads/pdfs/anthro_1.pdf (Accessed in October, 2003).

Doppler W. 1994. The Role of Quantitative Methods in Integrating Farm, Village and Regional Approaches, in Systems Oriented Research in Agriculture and Rural Development, Publication of Papers, international Symposium 21 – 25.11.1994. Montpellier

Dowler E. 1997. Inequalities in Diet and Health. In *Diet, Nutrition and Chronic Disease: Lessons from Contrasting Worlds*. Shetty P et al. (ed.): 77-97. West Sussex, England: John Willey and Sons Ltd.

Du Guerny J. and Topouzius D.1996. Gender, Land and Fertility - Women's Access to Land and Security of Tenure. In: *Modules on gender, population and rural development with a focus on land tenure and farming systems*, Rome: FAO

Ezzati M., Lopez AD, Rodgers A, Vander H.S., Murray CJL and the Collaborating Risk Assessment Group. 2002. Selected Risk Factors and the Global and Regional Burden of Disease. Lancet, 360 (1347 -1360).

Ezzati M., Lopez A.D., Rodgers A., Murray CJL (eds). 2004. *Comparative Quantification of Health Risks: The global and Regional Burden of Disease Attributable to Selected Major Risk Factors (Volume 1 and 2)*. Geneva: World Health Organisation

Fadani, A. 1999. *Agricultural Price Policy and Export and Food Production in Cameroon: a Farming System Analysis of Pricing Policies. The Case of Coffee- Based Farming Systems*. Frankfurt am Main; Germany: Peter lang Europäischer Verlag der Wissenschaften.

Fafchamps M, and Quisumbing A.R. 2003. Control and Ownership of Assets in Rural Ethiopia. In *Household Decisions, Gender, and Development: A Synthesis of Recent Research.* Quisumbing A.R (ed.): 159-168. Washington D.C: IFPRI.

FAO. 2002. Food and Agriculture in Kenya. http://www.fao.org/giews/english/basedocs/ken/kentoc1e.htm (Accessed in February, 2003)

FAO. 2002. *The State of Food Insecurity in the World 2002.* Rome: FAO.

FAO. 2003. *The State of Food Insecurity in the World 2003: Monitoring Progress Towards the World Food Summit and Millenium Development Goals.* Rome: FAO.

FAO. 2004. *The State of Food Insecurity in the World 2004: Monitoring Progress Towards the World Food Summit and Millenium Development Goals.* Rome: FAO.

FAO. 2004. Food Outlook. Global Information and Early Warning System on Food and Agriculture. ftp://ftp.fao.org/docrep/fao/006/J2518E/J2518E00.PDF Accessed on 12.06.2004

Frankenberger T.R, and Maxwell S. 1992. Household Food Security: Concepts, Indicators, Measurements: A Technical Review. New York: UNICEF.

Faulu Kenya. 2003. Enabling People to Succeed through Small Business Loans. http://www.faulukenya.com/amfi.htm

Fritschel H, and Mohan U. 2001. The Fruits of Girls Education. In *The Unfinished Agenda: Perspecitves on overcoming Hunger, Poverty and Environmental Degradation.* Andersen P et al. (ed.): 215-222. Washington D.C: IFPRI.

Geda a, De Jog N, Mwabu G, and Kimenyi M. 2001. Determinants of Poverty in Kenya: Household-Level Analysis. Nairobi: Kenya Institute for Policy Research and Analysis (KIPPRA).

Ghaida A.D, and Klasen S. 2004. The Cost of Missing the Millenium Development Goal on Gender Equity. *World Development* 32 (7): 1075-1107.

Girma W, and Genebo T. 2002. Determinants of Nutritional Status of Women and Children in Ethiopia. http://www.measuredhs.com/pubs/pdf/FA39/02-nutrition.pdf Accessed on 14.01.2004.

Gobotswang K. 1998. Determinants of the Nutritional Status of Children in ARural African Setting: The Case of Chobe District, Botswana. *Food and Nutrition Bulletin* 19 (1): 42-45.

GoK. 1985. *West Pokot District Atlas.* Nairobi: Government Printer.

GoK. 1986. Republic of Kenya, Sessional Paper No 1 of 1986: Economic Management for Renewed Growth. Nairobi: Government Printers.

GoK. 1994. National Food Policy. Nairobi: Government Printers.

GoK. 1996. *West Pokot District Development Plan 1997 - 2001.* Nairobi: Government Printers.

GoK. 2000. Interim Poverty Reduction Strategy Paper 2000 – 2003. Nairobi: Government Printers.

GoK. 2001. Poverty Reduction Strategy Paper for the Period 2001-2004. Nairobi: Government Printers.

GoK. 2002. *West Pokot District Development Plan 2002-2008.* Nairobi: Government Printer.

GoK. 2003. Economic Recovery Strategy for Wealth and Employment Creation 2003 - 2007. Nairobi: Government Printers.

GoK. 2004. Millenium Development Goals for Kenya. Progress Report for Kenya 2003. Nairobi: Government of Kenya.

GoK. 2004. Interim Poverty Reduction Strategy Paper 2002 - 2003/2004. Nairobi: Government Printers.

GoK and GTZ. 2001. Second Report on Poverty in Kenya. Volume II: Poverty and Social Indicators. Nairobi, Kenya: Government Printers.

GoK and UN. 2002. Millennium Development Goals Progress Report for Kenya. Nairobi: Government Printer.

Grantham-McGregor, S and Ani, C. 2001. A Review of Studies on the Effect of Iron Deficiency on Cognitive Development in Children. *Journal of Nutrition* 131 (649-668).

Greene, W. 1993. *Econometric Analysis.* New York, USA: Macmillan Publishing Company.

Groenewold W.G, and Tilahun M. 1990. Anthropometric Indicators of Nutritional Status, Socio-economic Factors and Mortality in Hospitalized Children in Addis Ababa. *Journal of Bio- sociological Sciences* 22:373-379.

Gujarati D. 1992. Essentials of Econometrics. Singapore: McGraw-Hill, Inc

Haddad L, Hoddinott J, and Alderman H. 1997. *Intrahousehold Resource Allocation in Developing Countries.* Washington D.C: IFPRI.

Handa S, Simler K, and Harrower S. 2004. Human Capital, Household Welfare, and Children's Schooling in Mozambique. Washington D.C: IFPRI.

Harrero I., and Pascoe S. 2002. Estimation of Technical Efficiency: A Review of Some of the Stochastic Frontier and DEA Software. *Computers in Higher Education Economics Review* 15 (1)

Harris-White, B. and Saith, R. 2000. "The Gender Sensitivity of Well-being Indicators", in Razavi, S. ed. Gendered Poverty and Well-being. Oxford/Massachusetts: Blackwell Publishers.

Hassan R.M. and Karanja D. 1997. Increasing Maize Productivity in Kenya: Technology Institutions and Policy. In Byerlee D and Eicher C.K, *Africa's Emerging Maize Revolution*. London, UK: Lynne Rienner Publishers

Heidhues F. 1989. Introduction: The Farming Systems Concept in Agricultural Research. *Quarterly Journal of International Agriculture* 28 (3/4): DLG-Verlag Frankfurt.

Heidhues F, and Schrieder G. 1994. Impact of Financial markets in on the Food Security of the Poor. In *Short and Long Time Food Security. AIEA*. 2nd International Conference of the Association Internationale di Economie Alimentaire et Agro-industrielle (AIEA2) /1994. Cordoba, Spain.

Heidhues F. 1994. *Food and Agricultural Policies under Structural Adjustment*. Frankfurt: Peter Lang.

Heidhues F. 1995. Rural Financial Markets - An Important Tool to Fight Poverty. *Quarterly Journal of Agricultural Economics* 34 (2): 105-108.

Heidhues, F. 2000. The Future of World, National and Household Security. Universität Hohenheim, The Future of World, National and Household Security, Discussion Paper No. 7. Frankfurt: Peter Lang Verlag

Heidhues F, Atsain A, Nyangito H, Padilla M, Ghersi G, and Vallee C. 2004. Development Strategies and Food and Nutrition Security in Africa. Washington D.C: IFPRI.

Heidhues F, and Buchenrieder G. 2004. Rural Financial Market for Food Security. In *Food and Nutrition Security in the Process of Globalization*. Schulz M et al. (ed.): Münster, Germany: Lit-Verlag.

Heidhues F. 2004. Africa's Food and Nutrition Security: Where We Do We Stand? Successes, Failures, Lessons Learned. Paper Presented at the CTA Seminar on The Role of Information Tools in Food and Nutrition Security, Maputo, Mozambique, 8-12 November. http://www.cta.int/ctaseminar2004/HeidhuesDraft151004.pdf

Hoddinott J. 1999. *Choosing Outcome Indicators of Household Food Security. Technical Guide number 7*. Washington D.C: IFPRI.

Hoddinott J, and Johannes Y. 2002. *Dietary Diversity as a Household Food Security Indicator*. Washington D.C: Food and Nutrition Technical Assistance Project. Academy for Educational Development.

IFAD. 2004. Household Food Security and Women's Work Burden. Potential Tradeoffs. http://www.ifad.org/gender/thematic/rural/rural_6.htm Accessed on 14.05.2005.

Institute of Economic Affairs (IEA). 2002. *The Little Fact Book. The Socio-economic and Political Profiles of Kenya's Districts*. Nairobi, Kenya: Institute of Economic Affairs.

Jayne T.S., Kelly V. and Crawford E. 2003 Fertilizer Consumption Trends in SSA: USAID Policy Synthesis http://www.aec.msu.edu/AGECON/fs2/polsyn/number69.pdf Accessed on 20.05.2004

Jiggins J, Samanta R.K, and Olawoye J.E. 1997. Improving women Farmers' Access to Extension Services. In *Improving Agricultural Extension: A Reference Manual.* Rome: FAO.

Jones G., Steketee R.W, Black, R.E. 2003. How many Child Deaths can we prevent this Year. *The Lancet* 362 (65-71).

Kenya Agricultural Research Institute (KARI). 2005. Strengthening Kenya's Food Security and Income. http://www.kari.org/food_crops/default.htm Accessed on 12.10.2005

Kennedy E. 2004. Qualitative Measures of Food insecurity and Hunger.

    http://www.fao.org/documents/show_cdr.asp?url_file=/DOCREP/005/Y4249E/y4249e0c.htm Accessed on 18.11.2004

Keino S. 2004. Nutrition and the Millennium Development Goals: A Kenyan Perspective on the Eradication of Extreme Poverty and Hunger. In *Standing Committee on Nutrition News. Nutrition and the Millennium Development Goals.* UK: Lavenham Press

Kimenyi S.M. 2002. Agricultural, Economic Growth and Poverty Reduction. Nairobi: KIPPRA.

Kameri-Mbote, P 2002. Property Rights and Biodiversity Management in Kenya. Nairobi: ACTS Press.

Kinyua J. 2004. Towards Achieving Food Security. /2004. Washington D.C:

Kiplang'at J. 2003. Does Agricultural Extension have a new beginning because of ICTs? Reflections on experience in sub Saharan Africa. A Keynote Paper Presented at the ICT Observatory 2003: ICT'S-Transforming Agriculture Extension. Wageningen, 23 – 25 September, 2003.

Kiriti T, and Tisdell C. 2002. Gender, Marital Status, Farm Size and Other Factors Influencing the Extent of Cash Cropping in Kenya: A Case Study. Discussion Paper. Brisbane : School of Economics

Kiriti T, and Tisdell C. 2003. Gender Inequality, Poverty and Human Development in Kenya: Main Indicators, Trends and Limitations. Brisbane: School of Economics.

Klasen S. 1999. *Does Gender Inequality Reduce Growth and Development: Evidence from Cross Country Regressions.* Washington D.C: The World Bank.

Klasen S. 2000. Malnourished and Surviving in South Asia, Better Nourished and Dying Young in Africa: What Can Explain This Puzzle? University of München: SFB Discussion Paper.

Klasen S. 2002. Low Schooling for Girls, Slower Growth for All? Cross Country Evidence on Effect of Gender Inequality in Education on Economic Development. *World Bank Economic Review* 16 (3): 345-373.

Klasen S, and Wink C. 2002. A Turning Point in Gender Bias in Mortality? An Update on the Number of Missing Women. *Population and Development Review* 28 (2): 285-312.

Klasen S, and Lahanna F. 2003. The Impact of Gender Inequality in Education and Employment on Economic Growth in the Middle and North Africa. http://www.iai.wiwi.uni-goettingen.de/klasen/klasenlamanna.pdf   Accessed   on 12.04.2004

Kramer, M. S. 1987. Determinants of Low Birth Weight. Methodology and Meta Analysis. *Bulletin of the World Health Organisation* 65 (663-737).

Kramer, M. S., and R. Kakuma. 2002. *The Optimal Duration of Exclusive Breast Feeding: A systematic review*. Geneva: World Health Organisation.

Kumbhaker, S., and C. A. K. Lovell. 2000. *Stochastic Frontier Analysis*. Cambridge: Cambridge University Press.

Lenaola I. 1996. Land Tenure in Pastoral Lands. In *In Land we Trust: Environment, Private Property and Constitutional Changes*. Juma C et al. (ed.): Nairobi: Initiative Publishers.

Liao, T.F. 1994. *Interpreting probability models: Logit, Probit, and other Generalized Linear Models*. Thousand Oaks, CA: Sage Publications.

Luibrand, A. 2002. Transition in Vietnam: Impact of the Rural Reform Process on an Ethnic Minority. PhD Dissertation. Frankfurt am main, Germany: Peter Lang Europäischer Verlag Der Wissenschaften

Manda K.D, Kimenyi M.S, and Mwabu G. 2000. A Review of Poverty and Antipoverty Initiatives in Kenya. KIPPRA Working paper No. 3. Nairobi: KIPPRA

Manda K.D, Mwabu G, and Kimenyi M. 2002. Human Capital Externalities and Returns to Education in Kenya. Nairobi: KIPPRA

Morris S.S. 1999. Measuring Nutritional Dimensions of Food and Household Food Security. Washington D.C: IFPRI.

Morrison, D. 2000. Resource Use Efficiency in An Economy in Transition: An Investigation into the Persistence of the Co-operative in Slovakian Agriculture. PhD Thesis. WYE College: University of London

Möllers J, and Buchenrieder G. 2003. A Theoretical Framework for the Analysis of Diversification Decisions in the Rural Economy. In Conference Proceedings: Poverty Impacts and Policy Options of Non farm Employment. 25th International Conference of Agricultural Economists (IAAE) Durban, South Africa 16 -22 August, 2003. http://www.uni-hohenheim.de/~shrieder/pdfs/IAAE-2003-MS.PDF

Munyua, H. 2002. Information and Communication Technologies for Rural development and Food Security: Lessons from Field Experiences in Developing Countries. Food and Agricultural Organization (FAO), http:// www.fao.org/sd/Cdre0055b.htm (Accessed: 20.01.2005).

Munzir, A. 2001. Technical Efficiency Performance of Small Fish Farmers' Production in West Sumatra, Indonesia. PhD Dissertation, University of Hohenheim-Stuttgart, Germany

Murthi, M., A. C.Guio and J. Dreze. 1995. "Mortality, Fertility and Gender Bias in India: A District Level Analysis." *Population and Development Review*, 21 (745-782).

Mutoro B. 1997. *Small-scale Farming and the Role of Women in Vihiga District, Kenya. A Case Study of North Maragoli.* Utrecht: Rozenberg Publishers.

Njehia. 1994. The Impact of Market Access on Agricultural Productivity: A Case Study of Nakuru District, Kenya. Dissertation, University of Hohenheim- Stuttgart, Germany.

Nyangito H, and Nzuma J. 2004. Impact of Agricultural Trade and Related Policy reforms on Food security in Kenya. Nairobi: KIPPRA.

Nyangito H.O. 2003. Agricultural Trade Reforms in Kenya under the World Trade Organisation Framework. Nairobi: KIPPRA.

Nyangito H. 1998. Towards Maize Security in Kenya. An Evaluation of the Self Sufficiency Strategy. Nairobi: Institute of Policy Analysis and Research (IPAR).

Nyariki D.M, Wiggins S.L, and Imungi J.K. 2002. Levels and Causes of Household Food and Nutrition Insecurity in Dryland Kenya. *Ecology of Food and Nutrition* 41 (155-176).

Odhiambo W, and Nyangito H. 2002. Land Laws and Land Use in Kenya: Implications for Agricultural Development. Nairobi: KIPPRA.

Odhiambo W, Nyangito H, and Nzuma J. 2004. Sources and Determinants of Agricultural Growth and Producitvity in Kenya. Nairobi: KIPPRA.

Olson R.E, Schmidt P and Waldman D.M. 1980. A monte Carlo Study of Estimators of Stochastic Frontier Production Functions. *Journal of Econometrics* 13 (67 – 82).

Oniang'o R, and Kimokoti A. 1999. Trends in Women's Contributions to Agricultural Productivity: Lessons from Africa. Paper Presented at the Conference on the Roles, Constraints and Potentials of Women in Agricultural Development, Held at the Centre for Social Development, Bonn, Germany, August 26 and 27, 1999. http://www.uneca.org/popia/gateways/Women_Back_doc6.htm

Oniang'o, R. and Mukudi, E. 2002 Nutrition and Gender. In: ACC/SCN News 2002. *Nutrition : A Foundation of Development.* Geneva: ACC/SCN

Otieno G.A. 2001. Gender and Agricultural Supply Response to Structural Adjustment Programmes: A Case Study of Smallholder Tea Producers in Kericho Kenya. Electronic Publication from Kenyatta University, Nairobi, Kenya. www.fiuc.org/iaup/sap/ Accessed on 2.02.2005.

Panin, P., and B. Brümmer. 2000. Gender Differentials in Resource Ownership and Crop Productivity of Smallholder Farmers in Africa. *Quarterly Journal of International Agriculture* 39(2000), No.1 (93-107).

Psacharopoulos, G 1994. Returns to Investment in Education: A Global Update. *World Development* 22:9, 1325-1343.

Pingali P.L. 2001. CIMMYT 1999 – 2000 World Maize Facts and the Trends. Meeting World Maize Needs: Technological Opportunities and Priorities for the Public Sector. Mexico D.F: CIMMYT

Quisumbing A. 2003. Health and Nutrition. In *Household Decisions, Gender, and Development: A synthesis of Recent Research.* Quisumbing, A (ed.). Washington D.C: IFPRI

Quisumbing A.R. 1995. Gender Differences in Agricultural Productivity: A Survey of Empirical Evidence. Washington D.C: IFPRI.

Quisumbing A.R. 2003. Power and Resources within the Household: Overview. In *Household Decisions, Gender, and Development: A Synthesis of Recent Research.* Quisumbing A.R (ed.): 19-22. Washington D.C: IFPRI.

Quisumbing A.R, Estudillo J.P, and Otsuka K. 2003. Investment in Women and its Implications for Lifetime Incomes. In *Household Decisions, Gender, and Development: A Synthesis of Recent Research.* Quisumbing A.R (ed.): 231-237. Washington D.C: IFPRI.

Quisumbing A.R. 2003. Health and Nutrition: Overview. In *Household Decisions, Gender, and Development: A Synthesis of Recent Research.* Quisumbing A.R (ed.): 109-113. Washington D.C: IFPRI.

Quisumbing A.R, Estudillo J.P, and Otsuka K. 2004. *Land and Schooling: Transferring Wealth across Generations.* Washington D.C: IFPRI.

Radimer K. L., Olson C. M., Greene J. C., Campbell C. C., Habicht J.-P.1992. Understanding hunger and developing indicators to assess it in women and children. *Journal of Nutrition Education* 24(suppl), 36-44.

Radimer, K.L., Olson, C.M. & Campbell, C.C. 1990. Development of indicators to assess hunger. Journal of Nutrition., 120 (Suppl. 11): 1544 -1548.

Republic of Kenya. 1965. *Sessional Paper No. 10 of 1965 on African Socialism and its Application to Planning.* Nairobi: Government Printer.

Republic of Kenya. 1981. *Sessional Paper No. 4 of 1981 on National Food Policy.* Nairobi. Government Printer.

Republic of Kenya. 2000. *Interim Poverty Reduction Strategy Paper for the Period 2000-2003.* Nairobi: Government Printer.

Republic of Kenya. 2001. *Poverty Reduction Strategy Paper for the Period 2001-2004, Volume. 1.* Nairobi: Government Printer.

Republic of Kenya. 2005. Kenya Gazette Supplement, 2005: The Proposed New Constitution of Kenya. Nairobi: Government Printers.

Rice. R.C. 1994. Logistic Regression: An Introduction. In *Advances in Social Science Methodology.* Thompson, B (ed.): 191-245. Greenwich: CT: JAI Press.

Ruthenberg H. 1980. *Farming Systems in the Tropics*. Oxford: Clarendon Press.

Schrieder G. 1997. Rural Financial Institution Building and Gender Sensitive Demand Analysis in a Food Insecure Environment. In *Food Security, Diversification and Resource Management: Refocusing the role of agriculture*. IAAE. 22nd International Conference of Agricultural Economists (IAAE) Proceedings, 10.-16. August, 1997. Sacramento, USA

Schrieder, G. 1994. *The Role of Rural Finance for Food Security of the Poor in Cameroon*. Frankfurt: Peter lang Europäischer Verlag der Wissenschaften.

Schrieder, G. 1996. The role of rural finance for food security of the poor in Cameroon. PhD Dissertation Universität Hohenheim –Stuttgart, Germany.

Schutz T. 1990. Women's Changing Participation in the Labour Force. *Economic Development and Cultural Change* 38 (3): 457-488).

Schutz T.P. 2002. Why Governments Should Invest More in Girls. *World Development* 30 (2): 207-225.

SCN, 1996. Summary of Results for the Third Report on the World Nutrition Situation. Geneva, Switzerland: ACC/SCN

SCN, 2000. 4th Report on the World Nutrition Situation, Geneva, Switzerland: ACC/SCN

SCN. 2004. Nutrition and the Millennium Development Goals. UK: Lavenham

Sen A., 1999. Comprising Poverty and Famines; Hunger and Public Action India: Economic Development and Social Opportunity. New Delhi: Oxford University Press

Sharma S. 2001. Microfinance: Reaching the Poor Rural Women. In *The Finished Agenda: Perspectives on Overcoming Hunger, Poverty, 205 and Environmental Degradation.* Andersen P et al. (ed.): 197-201. Washington D.C, USA: IFPRI.

Smith L.C, and Haddad L. 2000. Explaining Child Malnutrition in Developing Countries: A Cross Country Analysis. Washington D.C: IFPRI.

Smith L.C, and Haddad L. 2001. Overcoming Child Malnutrition in Developing Countries: Past Achievements and Future Choices. In *The Unfinished Agenda: Perspectives on Overcoming Hunger, Poverty, 205 and Environmental Degradation.* Andersen P et al. (ed.): 21-25. Washington D.C USA: IFPRI.

Smith L.C, Ramakrishnan L, Haddad L, Martorell R, and Ndiaye A. 2003. The Importance of Women's Status for Child Nutrition in developing Countries. Washington D.C: IFPRI.

Smits, J. 2001. Estimating the Heckman Two-step Procedure to Control for Selection Bias with SPSS. http://home.planet.nl/~smits.jeroen/selbias/selbias.html Accessed on 12.02.2004

SPSS Inc. 2001. SPSS Regression Models 11.0. Chicago, USA: SPSS Inc.

Tadesse F.B. 2004. Impact of Policy Reform and Institutional Transformation on Agricultural Performance: An Economic Study of Ethiopian Agriculture. PhD Dissertation. Frankfurt am Main: Peter Lang Europäischer Verlag der Wissenschaften

Thomas D. 1997. Incomes, Expenditures, and Health Outcomes: Evidence on Intra-household Resource Allocation. In *Intra-household Resource Allocation In Developing Countries: Models, Methods and Policy.* Haddad L et al. (ed.): 142-164. Washington D.C: IFPRI.

UN.1999. World Survey on the Role of Women in Development: Globalization, Gender and Work. http://www.un.org/womenwatch/daw/cedaw/ (Accessed on 12.12.2004)

UNDP. 1995. Human Development Report 1995. Gender and Human Development. http://hdr.undp.org/reports/global/1995/en/

UNDP. 2001. Kenya Human Development Report 2001. Nairobi: UNDP

UNDP. 2002a. Human Development Report 2002. http://www.undp.org/hdr2002/indicator/cty_f_KEN.html Accessed on 12.02. 2004.

UNDP 2002b. Kenya Human Development Report 2001. Addressing Social and Economic Disparities for Human Development. Nairobi: UNDP

UNDP. 2003. Human Development Reports. http://www.undp.org/hdr2003/indicator/pdf/hdr03_table_22.pdf. Accessed on 12.02. 2004

UNDP. 2004. Human Development Report 2003. http://hdr.undp.org/reports/global/2003/ Accessed on 12.02. 2004

UNESCO. 2005. Education for All (EFA) Global Monitoring Report 2003/2004. www.portal.unesco.org/education/efa-report.pdf accessed on 14.05.2005

UNICEF. 1998. Child Nutrition in Botswana. *Food and Nutrition* 19 (1): 42-45.

UNICEF. 1998. *The State of World's Children 1998- Focus on Nutrition.* New York: UNICEF.

UNICEF. 2000. *The State of World's Children 2000: Focus on Leadership.* New York: UNICEF.

UNICEF. 2003. The State of World's Children 2003: Child Participation. New York: UNICEF.

UNICEF. 2004. *The State of World's Children 2004: Focus on Girls' Education.* New York: UNICEF.

UNICEF. 2005. *The State of World's Children 2005: Childhood under Threat.* New York: UNICEF.

Von Braun J. 2004. *Assuring Food and Nutrition Security in Africa by 2020.* Washington: IFPRI.

Wanjala S. 1990. Land Law and Disputes in Kenya. Nairobi: Oxford University Press

Wanjala S. 2000. Land Ownership in Kenya: Past Present and Future. In *Essays on Land law: The Reform Debate in Kenya*. Nairobi: Faculty of Law, University of Nairobi.

Webb P, and Weinberger K. 2001. *Women Farmers: Enhancing Rights, Recognition and Productivity*. Frankfurt: Peter Lang Verlag.

Wehler, C.A., Scott, R.I. and Anderson, J.J. 1992. The Community Childhood Hunger Identification Project: a Model of Domestic Hunger - Demonstration Project in Seattle, Washington. *Journal of Nutrition Education*, 24(1): 29 -35.

Weinberger K. 2001. What Determines Micronutrient Demand of the Poor? A Case Study from Rural India. *Quarterly Journal of International Agriculture* 40 (4): 343-359.

WHO. 1995. Severity Index for Malnutrition in Emergency Situations based on Prevalence of Wasting and Mean Weight for height Z score for Children Under 5 years. In *Physical Status*. Geneva: WHO.

WHO. 1999. *Management of Severe Malnutrition: A Manual for Physicians and Other Senior Health Workers*. Geneva: World Health Organisation.

Wright, R. E. 1995. Logistic Regression. In *Reading and Understanding Multivariate Statistics*. Grimm, L. M et al. (ed.): Washington, DC: American psychological Association.

World Bank. 1996. Assessing Poverty in Kenya. World Bank Report on Africa Region. Number 15 January, 1996. http://www.worldbank.org/afr/findings/english/find55.htm Accessed on 12. 12.2004.

World Bank. 2000. *Women in Development*. http://genderstats.worldbank.org/wdevelopment.pdf Accessed on 02.02. 2004.

World Bank. 2001. Engendering Development. New York: Oxford University Press.

Wooldridge, J.M. 2002a. Unobserved Heterogeneity and Estimation of Average Partial Effects, mimeo. East Lansing, MI: Michigan State University

Wooldridge J.M. 2002. Econometrics of Cross-Sectional and Panel Data. London, England, Cambridge Massachusetts: The MIT Press.

Yoon P.W, Black R.E, Moulton L.H, and Becker S. 1997. The Effect of Malnutrition on the Risk of Diarrhoeal and Respiratory Mortality in Children < 2years of age. *American Journal of Clinical Nutrition* 65 (1070-1077).

Zeller M, Schrieder G, Braun J von, and Heidhues F. 1997. Rural Finance for Food Security of the Poor: Implications for Research and Policy, Food Policy Review 4. Washington D.C: IFPRI

Zeller M, and Sharma S. 2001. Rural Financial Services for Poverty Alleviation: The Role of Public Policy. In *The Unfinished Agenda: Perspectives on Overcoming Hunger, Poverty, 205 and Environmental Degradation*. Andersen P et al. (ed.): 191-196. Washington D.C: IFPRI.

Development Economics and Policy

Series edited by Franz Heidhues and Joachim von Braun

Band 42   Roukayatou Zimmermann: Biotechnology and Value-added Traits in Food Crops: Relevance for Developing Countries and Economic Analyses. 2004.

Band 43   F. Markus Kaiser: Incentives in Community-based Health Insurance Schemes. 2004.

Band 44   Thomas Herzfeld: *Corruption begets Corruption*. Zur Dynamik und Persistenz der Korruption. 2004.

Band 45   Edilegnaw Wale Zegeye: The Economics of On-Farm Conservation of Crop Diversity in Ethiopia: Incentives, Attribute Preferences and Opportunity Costs of Maintaining Local Varieties of Crops. 2004.

Band 46   Adama Konseiga: Regional Integration Beyond the Traditional Trade Benefits: Labor Mobility contribution. The Case of Burkina Faso and Côte d'Ivoire. 2005.

Band 47   Beyene Tadesse Ferenji: The Impact of Policy Reform and Institutional Transformation on Agricultural Performance. An Economic Study of Ethiopian Agriculture. 2005.

Band 48   Sabine Daude: Agricultural Trade Liberalization in the WTO and Its Poverty Implications. A Study of Rural Households in Northern Vietnam. 2005.

Band 49   Kadir Osman Gyasi: Determinants of Success of Collective Action on Local Commons. An Empirical Analysis of Community-Based Irrigation Management in Northern Ghana. 2005.

Band 50   Borbala E. Balint: Determinants of Commercial Orientation and Sustainability of Agricultural Production of the Individual Farms in Romania. 2006.

Band 51   Pamela Marinda: Effects of Gender Inequality in Resource Ownership and Access on Household Welfare and Food Security in Kenya. A Case Study of West Pokot District. 2006.

Band 52   Charles Palmer: The Outcomes and their Determinants from Community-Company Contracting over Forest Use in Post-Decentralization Indonesia. 2006.

Band 53   Hardwick Tchale: Agricultural Policy and Soil Fertility Management in the Maize-based Smallholder Farming System in Malawi. 2006.

Band 54   John Kedi Mduma: Rural Off-Farm Employment and its Effects on Adoption of Labor Intensive Soil Conserving Measures in Tanzania. 2006.

Band 55   Mareike Meyn: The Impact of EU Free Trade Agreements on Economic Development and Regional Integration in Southern Africa. The Example of EU-SACU Trade Relations. 2006.

Band 56   Clemens Breisinger: Modelling Infrastructure Investments, Growth and Poverty. A Two-Region Computable General Equilibrium Perspective on Vietnam. 2006.

www.peterlang.de